FUTURE JOURNALISM

Future Journalism investigates where journalism has come from, where it is now and where it might be going, through a range of case studies on organisations pushing the traditional boundaries of journalism, including Vice, BuzzFeed, Bellingcat, The Washington Post, the Guardian, Circa and Narrative Science. Sue Greenwood presents an analysis of the significant trends and practices shaping contemporary journalism and investigates what they can tell us about possible new directions for the news industry in the future.

Chapters explore:
- the rise of new business models for digital news production and their future;
- debates around the potential for non-human "journalists";
- the fluctuating figures around news consumption by audiences and what they can mean;
- the growing importance of ethical journalism in the digital age;
- practical exercises and recommended further reading.

In a constantly evolving media environment, this book guides readers through some of the most vital contemporary debates and important technological developments. It is essential reading for students and young professionals preparing for a future in the journalism industry.

Sue Greenwood is a senior lecturer in the School of Journalism at Staffordshire University, UK. She teaches and specialises in digital and future journalism. Before joining academia, Sue spent over 25 years working in the media, from newspapers, news websites and community television, to radio. As an entrepreneur, she has launched two publishing start-ups.

FUTURE JOURNALISM

Where We Are and Where
We're Going

Sue Greenwood

LONDON AND NEW YORK

First published 2018
by Routledge
2 Park Square, Milton Park, Abingdon, Oxon OX14 4RN

and by Routledge
711 Third Avenue, New York, NY 10017

Routledge is an imprint of the Taylor & Francis Group, an informa business

© 2018 Sue Greenwood

The right of Sue Greenwood to be identified as author of this work has been asserted by her in accordance with sections 77 and 78 of the Copyright, Designs and Patents Act 1988.

All rights reserved. No part of this book may be reprinted or reproduced or utilised in any form or by any electronic, mechanical, or other means, now known or hereafter invented, including photocopying and recording, or in any information storage or retrieval system, without permission in writing from the publishers.

Trademark notice: Product or corporate names may be trademarks or registered trademarks, and are used only for identification and explanation without intent to infringe.

British Library Cataloguing-in-Publication Data
A catalogue record for this book is available from the British Library

Library of Congress Cataloging-in-Publication Data
A catalog record for this book has been requested

ISBN: 978-1-138-67871-2 (hbk)
ISBN: 978-1-138-67872-9 (pbk)
ISBN: 978-1-315-55877-6 (ebk)

Typeset in Bembo
by Apex CoVantage, LLC

Printed and bound by CPI Group (UK) Ltd, Croydon, CR0 4YY

CONTENTS

List of figures   *vi*

1   Where we came from and where we are now   1

2   Change and why it happens   19

3   New ideas and how they got here   38

4   Audience chasing   55

5   New news generations   78

6   The new (human) journalists   95

7   The new (non-human) journalists   113

8   New narratives in news   129

9   Your turn   143

10   My turn   157

Appendix: suggested essay assignments with related chapters   *171*
Index   *175*

FIGURES

1.1	Don Sapatkin, Deputy Science and Medicine Editor, 6:44pm, 2009	2
1.2	Don Sapatkin, 3:10pm, 2011	3
1.3	Afrobarometer Data report 'AD69: Building on progress: Infrastructure development still a major challenge in Africa', 2016	7
1.4	Part of The Washington Post newsroom	14
1.5	Photo of Jeremy Gilbert, Director of Strategic Initiatives at The Washington Post	15
2.1	Screenshot of Yahoo's 1997 homepage	21
2.2	Screenshot of Google's 1998 homepage	22
3.1	Jim Waterson, BuzzFeed UK Politics Editor	50
4.1	1960s' advert from RCA (Radio Corporation of America)	56
4.2	Googling "New York Yankees" delivers this helpful – or directed – grouping of results	59
4.3	Screenshot taken October 8, 2016, of results of Google search for "Syria"	60
4.4	Reuters Digital News Report, 2015	66
5.1	Photo of Jenny Stevens, then Managing Editor at Vice UK	91
6.1	WITNESS supports people in using video and technology to protect and defend human rights	99
6.2	Eliot Higgins speaking at the SKUP festival of investigative journalism in Norway	105
7.1	Kris Hammond of Narrative Science	120
7.2	Screenshot of News at Seven	121
8.1	Telegram detailing the assassination of Abraham Lincoln	130
8.2	David Cohn pictured at work at Circa	138

1
WHERE WE CAME FROM AND WHERE WE ARE NOW

In Will Steacy's striking photo-essay 'Deadline', the slow decline of the Philadelphia Inquirer is captured over five years. Beginning in 2009, Steacy photographed the newsroom through shrinking sales, bankruptcy, and round after round of staffing culls.

His father was among those to lose their job as the newspaper, founded in 1829, shed staff like a second skin: from around 700 employees in the 1990s, to just over 200 by the time Steacy began his project. In his online introduction, Steacy (2016) writes about newspapers as the "fastest shrinking industry in America" and laments the human cost of technological changes:

> When we lose reporters, editors, newsbeats and sections of papers, we lose coverage, information, and a connection to our cities and our society. . . . The newspaper is much more than a business, it is a civic trust.

Steacy's photographs of the decline of the Pulitzer-winning Inquirer could be seen as a visual metaphor for the wider decline of the newspaper industry in the US and elsewhere.

Perhaps.

While it is true that newspapers in the US and the UK have shed hundreds of thousands of jobs since 1990,[1] and indeed that the industry has shed hundreds of newspapers,[2] what we have also seen is a news business that has shifted and changed and evolved in directions unimaginable in 2009.

Take the picture in Figure 1.1 of Deputy Science and Medicine Editor Don Sapatkin in 2009. The desk is piled high with papers and books and notes, spilling out of boxes, wrapping around that bulky computer, drifting onto neighbouring desks. Almost a caricature of the working journalist.

2 Where we came from and where we are now

FIGURE 1.1 Don Sapatkin, Deputy Science and Medicine Editor, 6:44pm, 2009. Photo by Will Steacy.

But this was not a photograph of a disappearing world, this was a photograph of a world that had already arrived.

In 2009, the World Wide Web had been public for 18 years, Google for 11 years, and Facebook for five. Twitter had been going for three years (Sapatkin himself joined Twitter in 2009), but Snapchat wouldn't arrive for another two. Despite those piles of print, the Inquirer was already part of a world in which information and content was largely digital, public and shared.

By 2011, Sapatkin's desk (Figure 1.2) had not only lost its paper mountain but Sapatkin had lost his place as primary source of public health news for his public, who now had access to acres of information online – much of it from the same sources he might use – and at the time they wanted to access it.

Sapatkin's role was no longer just digging up health news stories and writing about them, but about finding those stories in new places and sources, and delivering the information in new ways. By 2015, he was marrying the fashionably new data journalism with old-style contact-chasing to deliver *Clean Plates* – an online project enabling instant access for the Inquirer's readers to official restaurant inspection reports.[3]

Creating a restaurant report look-up tool may not sound like high-end, President-toppling journalism (although a mistake in reporting a restaurant inspection

FIGURE 1.2 Don Sapatkin, 3:10pm, 2011. Photo by Will Steacy.

report provided a valuable lesson in journalistic technique for the pre-Watergate Bob Woodward[4]). But journalism delivers information stories as well as news stories, and knowing whether that restaurant where you plan to take your family has a clean kitchen is an information story that matters.

It's that issue of how and why journalism matters that is worth hanging on to here.

Steacy's photographs may have captured the slow death of newspapers, but that does not mean that journalism is also dying. Changing certainly, shrinking perhaps, but not dying. This book is called 'Future Journalism' because journalism has a future as well as a past.

While there may have been fewer job openings at the Inquirer in 2016, its summer internships programme included ads for "Digital Interns", and an "Audience Development Intern" tasked with identifying social media influencers and spotting viral stories. The job of the traditional newspaper journalist has changed, but so too has the range and types of jobs in journalism. Today's journalism graduate is just as likely to find her or himself monitoring a website's comment threads as taking shorthand notes in a court case.

It is not just that the job of a journalist has changed, but that the nature of what it means to be a journalist – when we are "doing" journalism and when we might not be – is rapidly changing.

Coupon-clipping, coffee and money

While the future for the business models which fund the practice of journalism continue to shift and change, and for many individual examples have collapsed (goodbye Independent newspaper,[5] hello and goodbye the New Day,[6] goodbye crowdfunding pioneer Spot.Us[7] and goodbye mobile news innovator Circa[8]), news still happens and journalism still matters.

There's a video on YouTube from 1981 about the San Francisco Chronicle's early foray into digital news.[9] I love that video. Not only as an illustration of how much the technology of delivering the news has changed (taking two hours to deliver something not "spiffy looking" enough) but of that early arrogance of news workers in seeing the web as a quirky sidebar to their world, rather than the four horsemen and plagues of locust apocalypse it was to deliver.

In 1981, we were still ten years off the World Wide Web going public. However, the changes have not only been in the technology we use to deliver the news, it is the social change in the way we consume, share and interact with news that has had the biggest impact on the business of news.

Those Chronicle readers clipped out a coupon, posted it back to the newspaper, spent two hours downloading the basic text, then perhaps printing sections they wanted to save and read later, choosing to do all that rather than just have the newspaper delivered to their door.

They were not only e-newspaper reading pioneers[10] but an early taste of our willingness to make a personal effort to seek out and gather information if it means we can control what we read and how and when we access it. That switch from largely passive receivers of news to largely active seekers and sharers of it has driven the change from traditional to digital media.

The process of journalism has changed alongside our behaviour as consumers of news. We expect news that we are interested in to be available to us whenever we want it and wherever we are. And the business of making money from journalism has had to fit into an open-all-hours shop-of-news model. And that can be expensive.

In the village next to the one I live in is a large Nestle factory. Nestle makes Nescafe, those Dolce Gusto coffee pods, KitKat, Crunch, Maggi seasonings, Carnation canned milk – and so on. The branding is in each product, rather than in the company. You know what to expect from an Aero or a Baby Ruth chocolate bar. You know which Nescafe coffee you prefer.

The business model is that you buy the Nestle products you like and, 130 years ago, that was pretty much the business model for newspapers. You bought the newspaper you found most interesting or entertaining or reflective of your thoughts, or a mixture of those. We do not pay a monthly subscription to drink Nescafe. Shopkeepers do not give us free chocolate bars in the hope that we will read the advert for insurance on the wrapper. We do not donate to Nestle because we want to support them in continuing to make the products we like.

But those models are all currently used in the news business: free newspapers making their money from adverts; paid subscriptions to access content beyond paywalls; donation and crowdfunding schemes to support individual journalists, stories, or news organisations. The picture is similar in broadcast news, with the majority paid for directly or indirectly through advertising.

As Nathan Rosenberg observed, technological change is "path dependent" (shaped by things that happen along the way) and industries bear the cost of that change, not just in R&D costs but in whether individual businesses, or sectors, survive the change:

> The starting point for serious thinking about technological knowledge is the recognition that one cannot move costlessly to new points on the production isoquant, especially points that are a great distance.
>
> *(1994: 12)*

But the biggest threat to journalism has come not from the changes in the technology or the readers' expectations, but in changes within the business that journalism depends on – advertising. The traditional business model for journalism has not been to sell journalism but to sell the attention the journalism attracts.

News publishers have to do a lot of different things to get the attention they can sell to advertisers. They have to find or gather stories people want to know about; they have to present – tell – stories in ways that will make people want to read/watch/listen to them; they have to deliver those stories so people can easily find them. Finding and telling those news stories is generally what we think of when we talk about journalism.

But there is no direct profit for news publishers in producing journalism; it is a cost absorbed by that business in order to deliver the content that will attract the audience that advertisers will pay to reach. And, in a world in which advertising has become part of the problem – whether because of cut-price digital ads or the rise of ad-blocking software – both news publishers and freelance journalists are struggling to find models that might fill the gap left by shrinking ad revenue.

In 2012, US newspapers earned the same amount from advertising that they had earned in 1950.[11] The income was the same but the cost of producing a newspaper was not the same as in 1950.

In 1837, it cost £690 ($860) to launch the Northern Star newspaper in the UK. Two years later, the national daily was delivering an annual profit equivalent to around £892,000 ($1.1 million) today, almost entirely from print sales. Contrast that with Lord Northcliffe's estimate of the £500,000 needed to launch the Daily Mail in the UK in 1896; or the £2 million poured into Lord Beaverbrook's Sunday Express after its launch in 1918 to get it to break-even profitability (Curran and Seaton, 2010). Or the £18 million investors sank into launching Eddy Shah's technologically ambitious but doomed Today newspaper in 1986.

New printing technologies introduced in the 1880s onwards advanced mass circulation, but producing more newspapers required bigger operations, and bigger operations meant higher costs. News was an industry, and journalism, as a product of that industry, needed to be "sold" to a larger and larger consumer base to cover costs and return a profit. The Northern Star had to sell just 6,200 copies to break even, while Beaverbrook's Sunday Express needed to sell 250,000 copies. The New York Times, with a print circulation of just under 1.4 million and 1.2 million digital subscribers in 2016, was still posting losses and cutting jobs.[12]

The issue is that the cost of producing a newspaper has outstripped earnings from newspaper sales since the 1880s. Since then, the business model has become almost entirely dependent on the delivery of an audience to advertisers – and the valuing of that audience according to both demographic and size. The assumption that equated size of audience to share of advertising revenue has been disintermediated by the audience shift to digital, and the value of an advert has been worn away with each technological iteration.

It should have been a neat equation – money from ads offline in newspapers, magazines, on TV and radio goes down, but online ad income goes up to fill the gaps. But while the online media of web and mobile have rapidly grown the audience for news, they have also devalued audience size as a metric. As media analyst Michael Wolff wrote:

> The news business has been plunged into a crisis because web advertising dollars are a fraction of old media money. And mobile is now a fraction of web: the approximate conversion rate is $100 offline = $10 on the web = $1 in mobile.
>
> *(Wolff, 2012)*

He was responding to a 2012 report by Pew Research Center[13] showing that over a quarter of Americans were using mobile devices as their primary news source. Pew predicted that figure would have grown to half of American news consumers by 2015. They were right – Pew's 2015 report[14] showed 55 percent of smartphone users regularly accessing the news through their phone and 68 percent using phones to follow breaking news stories that interested them.

The rise of mobile use is extraordinary. According to UNICEF, in 2013 more people had a mobile phone than access to a toilet. Cisco predicts that by 2020, more of the world will have a mobile phone than access to electricity.[15] Across the continent of Africa, you're currently three times more likely to get a mobile signal than sewerage services (see Figure 1.3).[16]

Mobile phone use has been driven by development of smartphones which, in 2015, delivered 76 percent of all global mobile phone traffic. The smartphone's computing power (providing an affordable alternative to a laptop or home computer), its transportability (we can access it wherever we are, and particularly whenever we are bored[17]) and its usefulness as a connected social device have made it indispensable (indeed there are a number of studies looking at smartphone dependency and "addiction").

Where we came from and where we are now 7

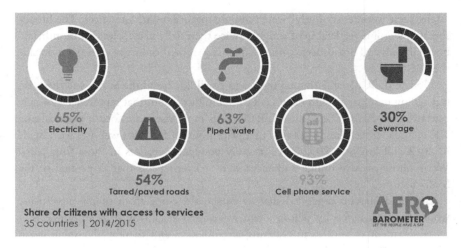

FIGURE 1.3 Afrobarometer Data report 'AD69: Building on progress: Infrastructure development still a major challenge in Africa', 2016, available at http://afrobarometer.org.

News is not what the news media is selling

However, it is not the traditional media companies making money from the rise of smartphones; it is the newer kids on the block – Google, eBay, Amazon, Facebook and so forth. If you have Facebook's business model, where it costs comparative peanuts to generate the content your users want (because it's mostly the users producing that content), then you don't need to earn as much from advertising to still turn a healthy profit. Facebook made almost $18 billion in 2015, mostly from advertising, with $3.69 billion of that net profit.[18] Contrast that with the New York Times, which earned a little over $1.5 million and just $63,246 profit.[19] And won three more Pulitzers.

A future business model for web-delivered journalism may not be any of the ones we have right now. However, while Jeff Jarvis was right to pose the question: "What would Google do?" (2009) and challenge news businesses to think radically, Google is not the model to replicate because its business is based on advertising attached to content search, not to content production.[20]

The profession of journalism has been based on how to deliver news that most people would want to know. However, 'most' on the web is most products, most choices, most information, most of our friends, most people like us, or most like the thing we're searching for. Apply that to news and you get most of the news that interests me, and some of my friends, and some people with the same interests as me, without me having to look for it. That level of personalisation doesn't sit easily with the traditional 'most people we can reach' news model.[21]

Cole and Harcup (2010) drew on ABC circulation figures from November 2008 to show how even national UK newspapers such as the Sun that "came late to taking their websites seriously" were winning massive online audiences. The broadsheets saw online readership of roughly twice their daily print sales that month, and both tabloids and broadsheets gained a majority of their online readers from outside the UK.

Update the Cole and Harcup figures to April 2012, and the Sun is still the UK's top-selling newspaper with daily sales of 2.3 million – but that represents a 24 percent drop on 2008. The Daily Mail, for all its rapid rise from fourth place among UK newspaper websites in 2008 to first place position for news websites worldwide in 2012, still lost over 200,000 of its daily newspaper readers in those four years. Worse, those massive online audiences were delivering less than 3 percent of the Mail's income.

Cole and Harcup suggested that newspapers' income from online advertising would be determined by whom a site was aimed at and by page impressions as a measurement of success in reaching an audience, and thereby the value to an advertiser (2010: 188). Their assertion that journalism matters to the news industry because "somebody still has to go out there and find things out" ignores the reality of a news industry dependent on selling attention.

In fact, the disproportionate pricing of new media advertising against traditional media, means that doubling, or in the Mail's case quadrupling, online readership figures is not enough to plug the holes in the balance sheet caused by the shift to digital advertising.

I argued that news is not the product that news publishers sell; the attention attracted by news is what is being sold. The business model of newspapers, radio, TV and websites is still overwhelmingly rooted in providing an effective channel for advertisers. For advertisers that had meant one of two things – either lots of people seeing your advert, or the right type of people (your target buyer) seeing your ad.

Google's launch of AdWords in 2000 punched another hole in news publishers' advertising balloon. In the past, it had been enough to simply tell an advertiser how many people bought your newspaper or watched or listened to your news programme as justification for buying that ad space. But with AdWords, advertisers were being told not only how many people had visited the web page that carried their ad (and therefore potentially had noticed it), but how many people had been interested enough to click on the ad.

AdWords disintermediated advertising metrics and changed the power dynamic between news publishers and advertisers. The focus was no longer only about volume – how many had seen the ad – but actions – how many people showed interest by doing something with it.

Advertising got forensic: this many people who are interested in these things saw your ad and liked it so much they shared it with this many other people, and this many of them went on to buy the product, and then this many of them told other people they had bought it, and all these people who clicked on the ad but didn't buy anything bought something else from you later.

Some newer journalism business models are engaging with data gathering to deliver interactive or native advertising models, but what we have yet to see is the

Where we came from and where we are now 9

emergence of a sustainable and grow-able business model in which journalism – not advertising – is the product being sold.

Back to journalism and (some) definitions

All this talk about money and advertising metrics may seem a prosaic assessment of the effect of new technology on journalism, but it's unavoidable: journalism has always been more a business than a calling. And, as the rest of the book explores, it isn't all doom and gloom; the future of news is brighter in many ways. Pavlik said that the digitisation of news means the "rules and constraints of the analog world no longer apply" (2001: xii), while Deuze argued that online journalism is redefining journalism and its culture "as a whole" (2003: 216). It's a wilder world out there, but also a more interesting one.

If we believe in journalism as a commodity that has a value in its own right, or if we believe journalism is essential to delivering public knowledge (Schudson, 1995) and perhaps therefore worth supporting from public money, then journalism needs scalable models that do not start from the news industry as it is now, with that same dependency on advertising. As Chapter 10 suggests, we have to ask, what would it take to make journalism the asset sold, rather than the attention journalism attracts?

In this chapter and throughout this book, I refer to news and to journalism. While "news" is comparatively easy to define,[22] "journalism" is much more subjective. I frequently do an exercise with students where I ask them to define "journalism" and "journalist". The words that come up most often are attributes such as "honest", "truth-seeking", "observant", "tenacious". Occasionally, students will suggest skills (i.e. "good at shorthand", "good listener") but mostly they – we – define the practice of journalism by a set of ideal attributes – even as we recognise that those ideals may be ones we aspire to as journalists, rather than ones we are individually able to deliver.

Deuze showed that our understanding of what journalism is is largely based on what journalists themselves think it is. He drew on previous thinkers (referencing Schlesinger, 1978; Golding and Elliott, 1979; Hallin, 1996; Kovach and Rosensteil, 2001; Zelizer, 2004) in highlighting the occupational ideology that defines "real" journalists and "real" journalism, as a set of ideals shared among journalists to self-legitimise their position in society (2005: 446–447).

That ideology has changed little in the last 50 years and is summarised as five broadly identified values of the good journalist of: public service, objectivity (more usually referred to as "balance" in the UK), autonomy, immediacy and ethics, rather than by the medium the journalist works in or the publication they work for. That is, the definition of a good journalist is not someone who works in TV rather than for a website, or who writes for the New York Times rather than for the National Enquirer, but as someone objectively and ethically engaged in a public service.

Schudson (1995: 153) describes this ideology as a shared cultural knowledge constituting "news judgement". He shows how journalism evolved as a profession, from the early 19th century of note taking and observation of what was happening, to produce descriptive sketches of events, to one in which interviewing skills "took like wildfire" in 1870s American newsrooms to become central to the occupation and craft of journalism (2001: 157).

The 20th century saw the further professionalisation of journalism, with the development of industry codes of ethics, unionisation setting workplace standards, industry-regulated training and qualifications, and universities delivering higher qualifications.[23] In the UK, the National Union of Journalists shared with other journalism-related bodies a commitment to elevating the role of journalism beyond that of a regulated trade. In its submission to the 1947 Royal Commission on the Press, the NUJ said:

> We seek above all else, as a body of professional men and women, that the industry in which we serve the community should be directed and managed primarily in the public interest.
>
> *(cited in Elliott, 1978: 176)*

Two recent surveys – Reuters in 2015 and Poynter in 2014 – show that the profession of journalism continues to be self-defined by journalists, and against similar ideals. Reuters found UK journalists believe their job is to provide accurate information, to hold power to account and to entertain – in that order. Poynter's thousands of recent journalism and media graduates put "ethics" equal first with "writing" as the most important skills needed in their work now, while "accuracy" and "curiosity" were the two most important skills needed to be a good journalist in the future.

As journalists, we continue to define our profession based on fairly nebulous personal traits; "curiosity" alongside equally nebulous aims: "hold power to account". Not knowing what we mean by those phrases, or more importantly not being able to explain why and exactly how those traits enable journalism to make the world a better-informed and more progressive place, limits and undermines what we do. As Chapter 10 argues, we are not only observers, we are interpreters.

Radio, then TV and then the internet began to challenge newspapers for the public's attention in delivering the news and, moving into the 21st century, journalism began to coalesce around skills and practices based on maximising attraction and attention – from the tabloid's "splash" front page, to "clickbait" headlines online, to interactive storytelling, to docudramas, and event re-enactments. We learned SEO, we got Social.

Changes in the job of journalists have mirrored changes in the business – producing more content for less money while battling to be credible and shifting from print to online.

The Reuters survey of 700 of the UK's 64,000 professional journalists[24] found 98 percent were university graduates, with 36 percent holding a Master's degree. However, 20 percent were on salaries at or below the living wage, while 83 percent of journalists in their twenties were earning under £30k a year. Almost a third of journalists did other work to boost their salary. In 2012, 56 percent worked in newspapers, but by the time of the 2015 survey, that had fallen to 44 percent. Steacy's photographs of a shrinking newspaper newsroom continued to play out.

Conversely, the number of journalists working exclusively online had risen from 26 percent to 52 percent – and those online journalists were typically producing double the number of stories of their offline colleagues.

The American Press Institute[25] looked at over 10,000 communications and media graduates. It found three-quarters had undergraduate degrees in journalism and 18 percent had Master's degrees in journalism. Of those now working in journalism jobs, most say they are doing more work for no more money and 46 percent said they hadn't had a pay rise in five years.

Regardless of whether an individual publisher is profiting from news, the producers of the bulk of that news, the journalists, are certainly not profiting. This is and always has been a comparatively low-paid profession and that is a reflection not just of the surplus of would-be journalists to jobs but also the undervaluing of journalism both as profession and purpose.

Why should media profits and the price of a mobile ad matter to a journalist? In part because as journalists we should know the challenges our industry is facing. But also because it's important to recognise that the news industry and the journalism may not be going in the same direction.

Good journalism matters and good journalists matter. There are stories that need to be told and there is news that is not reported, is under-reported, or not reported truthfully. Misreporting and "truthiness" may attract attention from an audience comfortable with confirmation bias, but that is not journalism and we have to start being very clear about what journalism is and what purpose it serves. Until we can show how and why journalism matters beyond attracting an audience for advertisers, it will continue to be secondary to the business of news.

CASE STUDY: THE WASHINGTON POST

Founded in 1887 and winner of 62 (at time of writing) Pulitzer Prizes for journalism, The Washington Post is a great example of how traditional print media has engaged with digital over time. Current Deputy Editor Tracy Grant was The Post's first web editor, back in 1999.

"Steve Coll was Managing Editor at the time," she said. "What Steve and I started was an online print edition that went up at 1pm. The idea was that if the President had a 10am press conference, people should know about it before the next day's paper dropped on their doorstep. So, we created a 1pm digital edition. That was in response to the bell curve of traffic.

"At the time, people had high-speed access only in the office and we saw a peak in traffic in the lunch hour. We wanted to take advantage of that. We all sort of assumed that the bell curve would flatten out when people got high-speed access at home. But that hasn't really happened. It was one of the many things we got wrong."

The introduction of a web edition of The Post, and Coll's early commitment to real-time updating, wasn't straightforward – Grant remembers a newsroom revolt against the idea and union action. However, the web had arrived in newsrooms at a key moment with the Iraq war, Bush vs Gore, and 9/11 all fast-moving and historically important stories that suited the immediacy of the web and its increasing use as a personal research tool by the public.

As with many other newspapers at the time (including ones I worked for back in the UK), The Post kept its web operations separate from its print operation. Not just a separate production team, but a separate company (until 2009). That separation of print and web journalism teams became a concern for The Post.

Grant recalls that the web team would read the stories produced by The Post's own journalists, check them against the Associated Press (AP) version of the story and then use the one they liked better:

"The website ran a story about terrorist hits on Jakarta, even though our own journalist said it wasn't terrorist but a local mafia attack. We told them but the website went with the AP version of the story, which was wrong, rather than The Washington Post story.

"There was a lot of tension between the two newsrooms, and the web team didn't want to be told by 'Mother Post' what to do. In their minds, we didn't get the web; in our minds, they didn't necessarily get the journalism. It led to some decisions being made for not the best journalistic reasons."

Marcus Brauchli took over as editor in 2009. The website closed down and staff were brought into one unified newsroom before relaunching the site. But in a newsroom of 500, people created their own silos and, while the management saw things were changing, Grant noted they "were still clinging to the print edition like Linus clinging to his blanket."

In 2013, Marty Baron took over as editor and appointed a new editorial team, including a new managing editor digital, Emilio Garcia-Ruiz, and emphasised the web as The Washington Post's route to building an audience beyond Washington.

Along with most other newspapers, The Post was struggling financially, but rather than see the web as part of the threat, Baron and his team saw it as part of the solution.

Grant tells me the story of an early meeting with her new editor: "We knew we were presiding over decline, but we knew were going to preside over it in a Washington Post fashion. In May 2013, Marty said to me: 'Tracy, it's the f***ing Washington Post, it's time we got our swagger back.'"

She said Baron wanted The Post to focus on getting its stories "out there", adding: "He wanted stories that had impact. He wanted us to look at our journalism and see how to connect with more readers. In the past, we might have done a schoolboard story that directly connects with a few readers, but can we create context and make this story matter to more people?"

In August 2013, Amazon founder and owner Jeff Bezos bought The Post. In many ways, that investment closed a circle in the link between web and news.

When Rupert Murdoch bought MySpace in 2005 for $580 million, it signalled to other media owners that the web – and particularly the social web – was much more important than they had perhaps realised: if Murdoch was ready to spend half a billion dollars buying one website, perhaps they needed to get on board the digital train too?[26] However, MySpace didn't survive becoming part of News Corporation. Six years later, Murdoch sold it for $35 million, admitting later: "We just messed it up."[27]

But if traditional media buying digital media didn't always work out, how would a digital revolutionary fare taking on a traditional print product? Grant again: "What became very clear was that Bezos wanted us to be national and international. When I need to buy something, personally, Amazon is where I go to, it's the default proposition. If five years from now, The Washington Post, which had been a niche publication, a niche player in the news business, were that kind of default proposition for news content and analysis, that would be pretty cool."

Bezos' investment added over 150 new jobs to The Post's roster, with an additional 70 positions slated to be added in 2017.

Throughout the editorial team there is a focus on user metrics – who is reading what and when and which headlines grabbed their attention. My visit to morning conference saw editors' discussion focused on what stories are attracting attention online and why, and predicting which stories would attract interest as the day moves on. The editorial team, led by Baron, pored over live streams of page and story traffic analytics.

This scrutiny of analytics is something that is played out – to a greater or lesser degree – in most newsrooms as the metrics measuring attention, part of advertising for decades, translate to measuring the effectiveness of news stories. It isn't enough to measure the success of your journalism by the total number of papers sold or viewers or listeners saying they tuned in; we now measure attention by minutes spent reading a story and attraction by who read it and what else they read. In that sense, the middle managers of journalism – the section heads and verticals editors – are the closest they've ever been to seeing journalism as a measurable product.

Eric Rich is The Post's universal news editor, running the web display pages – the two desktop web homepages, mobile, tablet and app homepages. Analytics – in particular which headlines and pictures work for each digital audience – are embedded into his job.

"We have a lot of real-time analytics and we get immediate feedback on what people are reading, so we can tell if a presentation [of a story] is effective," he told me. "A part of that is literally trying to improve how to make our presentation engaging and be sure that we are explaining to readers correctly why they should read this incredible story.

"So we change headlines, change the display pictures, watch what happens to the traffic and then revise them. On any story, you could write a dozen journalistically legitimate headlines so part of the question is which one is going to be the most effective in drawing readers?"

FIGURE 1.4 Part of The Washington Post newsroom; ground floor centre is the area occupied by Eric Rich and his team – Rich is pictured in the foreground.
Credit: Author's own photo, taken on visit to The Washington Post, April 2016.

Rich and his team will – either manually or using a tool built in-house – change and test headlines and pictures over percentages of site visitors attracted to the story to find a winner. He attributed part of the success of The Post in growing its digital audience[28] to this upfront focus on headlines, rather than an afterthought to story creation: "Some stories you know are stories that are going to work in the social world and we want to make sure that those have headlines that are going to work in the social world. And not just headlines but images – you share a story and you want the right image to pop up. And that has required newsroom focus and development in our systems to be able to do that effectively."

That development has included changing the structure of teams to create a decentralised newsroom, with sections (e.g. national, finance news) responsible for their own story gathering, for pitching and delivering stories and for writing "one great headline that accomplished the social, that accomplished the search. . . . [It's] got to be readable, it's got to have enough keywords in it that search engines will spot it, and it's got to be sharable."

It also includes changing the lead and display stories on the homepages frequently to keep things fresh – the aim is to make sure that readers see something new – either a new story or a story that has moved on – when they log in to The Post's digital platforms when they wake in the morning, at lunchtime, on the journey home, in the evening (Grant's traffic "bell curve").

Jeremy Gilbert, The Post's director of strategic initiatives, told me they focused on two kinds of metrics – lag and lead. Lag metrics are: "things like time spent, page views, and unique visitors; those are really tricky to do much about.

"We know how we fared yesterday, and it's important to be able to compare yesterday to other days or to compare ourselves to other publishers. But a lead metric like scroll speed allows us to actually change a story in the moment, before it's too late to improve the experience, to make it more engaging, to capture the attention of more readers."

He said they were trying to move the newsroom to focus on lead metrics and boosting reader engagement with a story: "Engagement is incredibly important; we talk a lot about recirculation, we talk a lot about time spent, we talk a lot about scroll speed."

FIGURE 1.5 Photo of Jeremy Gilbert, Director of Strategic Initiatives at The Washington Post.

Gilbert leads much of the experimentation at The Post, an area of activity that has grown since Bezos bought it. Experimental projects in AR, VR and 360 video,[29] plus new tools to help newsroom workflow have been delivered by Gilbert and his colleagues. Bezos's investment in new journalists and technologists had helped deliver a "pervading sense of optimism" in the newsroom and a willingness to experiment, said Gilbert.

"We had a great foundation with Don Graham who grew up in the newsroom and knew how to do great day-to-day journalism. Under the helm of Jeff Bezos, we see his knowledge of operational speed and his understanding of how the right kinds of algorithms and the right speed of the user experience can lead to a massive digital audience.

"I think the combination of a newsroom that already had a pretty good sense of how to tell stories with a person who really knew how to build a big digital audience, it helped, that definitely helped."

Those new projects are not just about playing with emerging technologies but about getting people to engage with Post stories for longer or at a deeper level – even if the way the reader has arrived at that story is through Facebook or Apple News, when the question becomes: "How do you know when you experience our content on other people's platforms that it's ours?"

Part of the answer has been to put more focus on the brand of The Washington Post – tests in making The Post branding bigger on stories showed positive responses from readers.

Nonetheless The Post is grappling with the same issues faced by other newspapers – how to increase the identifiable share of digital audience, and make money from that, while print circulation falls or stagnates ("our goal, our hope, is . . . to hold on to the print audience that we have", said Gilbert).

But Bezos's investment has delivered a cushion for Baron's journalism and The Post in 2016 was a positive place to be a journalist. Said Gilbert: "I don't think by any means The Post has figured it out, we're just more committed than we were a few years ago to figuring it out. There's less fear of change, there's less fear of loss of control."

Notes

1 US Labor Department statistics show a decline of almost 60 percent in jobs in newspapers and 27 percent in radio broadcasting between 1990 and 2016: Bureau of Labor Statistics, US Department of Labor. *The Economics Daily*, 'Employment trends in newspaper publishing and other media, 1990–2016'.
2 There is no global list, or even pan-Atlantic list, of closed newspapers but useful information sources are: Newspaper Death Watch, Wikipedia's list of defunct newspapers of the United States, The Guardian (Peter Greenslade, February 19, 2009) and the Press Gazette; 'Some 48 regional newspapers have closed since 2012 – but 39 have launched', January 16, 2015.
3 See www.philly.com/philly/health/special_reports/clean-plates.
4 In this video, Bob Woodward talks about how he almost wrote a front page story about the wrong restaurant after being sent an inspection report from his source in the local

health department: 'Tips from Bob Woodward on Investigative Journalism': www.youtube.com/watch?v=VVKGUctuoXE.
5 The UK national Independent newspaper switched to online-only in 2016.
6 Trinity Mirror closed the national title in 2016, just ten weeks after launch.
7 Public Insight Network closed the journalism crowdfunding platform in 2015, citing, among other reasons, the 63 percent failure rate for journalism projects, compared to other projects.
8 The mobile app pioneered the concept of "following" a breaking or ongoing news story, but closed in 2015 after failing to find further investment. My interview with founding editor David Cohn is part of chapter eight's case study.
9 '1981 primitive internet report on KRON', Video: www.youtube.com/watch?v=5WCTn4FljUQ.
10 The newspaper has recently recovered that "pioneer" status in another way. After years of losing money and cutting editorial jobs, like other daily newspapers, the San Francisco Chronicle turned around its fortunes and has been profitable since 2014. In 2016, it reinvested in quality journalism, building a new I-team for investigative reporting.
11 Business Insider 'Chart of the day: And now let us gasp in astonishment at what just happened to the newspaper business', Henry Blodget, September 12, 2012, BusinessInsider.
12 May, 2016 Q1 financial report: www.nytimes.com/2016/05/04/business/media/new-york-times-co-q1-earnings.html.
13 'State of the News Media 2012', Pew Research Center, March 19, 2012.
14 'U.S. Smartphone Use in 2015', Pew Research Center, April 1, 2015.
15 '10th Annual Cisco Visual Networking Index (VNI) Mobile Forecast Projects 70 Percent of Global Population Will Be Mobile Users', February 3, 2016, Cisco newsroom release.
16 Afrobarometer Data report: 'Building on progress: Infrastructure development still a major challenge in Africa', based on field-team observations in 35 African countries in 2014/15. Available at www.afrobarometer.org.
17 'U.S. Smartphone Use in 2015', Pew Research Center, April 1, 2015.
18 'Facebook Reports Fourth Quarter and Full Year 2015 Results', January 27, 2016, Facebook Investor Relations newswire.
19 Source: downloaded annual report, 2015 financials, from press room.
20 Google earned $74.5 billion in 2015 – more than four times Facebook's tally. Source abc.xyz investor news.
21 However, chapter seven explores how newspapers from Le Monde to the Sun are delivering some of that level of news personalisation via algorithms and software.
22 Whether you lean towards UK media baron Lord Northcliffe: "News is what somebody somewhere wants to suppress; all the rest is advertising" or US media baron Phillip Graham that news is "a first rough draft of history", news is essentially new information – reporting on recent or current events. However, as Harcup and O'Neill recently explored, news today is just as much about events that may have happened to a celebrity, or entertaining pictures of animals (2016).
23 Joseph Pulitzer's proposal for a School of Journalism in which journalists, as teachers and critics of society, would acquire the necessary moral and intellectual properties, resulted in the establishment in 1912 of the College of Journalism, at Columbia University. The earliest school of journalism is thought to be the Ecole Superieure de Journalism in Paris, France, established in 1899.
24 Reuters Institute for the Study of Journalism: Journalists in the UK 2016.
25 American Press Institute 2015 survey of communication graduates: www.americanpressinstitute.org/publications/reports/survey-research/api-journalists-survey/.
26 That same year, ITV television group in the UK bought social connection site Friends Reunited for £175 million, but lost millions when they sold it in 2009 for just £25 million.
27 Speaking at the Wall Street Journal's WSJ.D conference in October 2014 (source: Gigaom), ITV also lost out on their deal – selling Friends Reunited in 2009 for £25 million.

28 By October 2015, The Post was breaking online visitor records and beating arch rival the New York Times: 'Here's the Washington Post's Memo on Its Record-Breaking Traffic Month', Andrew Beaujon, November 13, 2015, Washingtonian.
29 During my interview with Gilbert (April 11, 2016) he demonstrated some of his projects including the Mars VR project, the Freddie Gray AR story, the Waypoint interactive story, and the Galapagos 360-video project.

References and further study

Cole, P. and Harcup, T. (2010) *Newspaper journalism*, Sage, London.
Curran, J. and Seaton, J. (2010) *Power without responsibility: Press, broadcasting and the internet in Britain*, seventh edition, Routledge, London.
Deuze, M. (2003) 'The web and its journalisms: Considering the consequences of different types of newsmedia online', *New Media & Society* 5(2), 203–230.
Deuze, M. (2005) 'What is journalism? Professional identity and ideology of journalists reconsidered', *Journalism* 6(4), 442–464.
Elliott, P. (1978) 'Professional ideology and organizational change: the journalist since 1800', in G. Boyce, J. Curran and P. Wingate (eds.) *Newspaper history from the seventeenth century to the present day*, Constable, London.
Harcup, T. and O'Neill, D. (2016) 'What is news? News values revisited (again)', *Journalism Studies*. DOI: 10.1080/1461670X.2016.1150193
Holcomb, J. and Mitchell, A. (2014) 'The revenue picture for American journalism and how it is changing', *Pew Research Center*, 24 March 2014. http://www.journalism.org/2014/03/26/the-revenue-picture-for-american-journalism-and-how-it-is-changing/
Jarvis, J. (2009) *What would Google do?* Harper Collins, New York.
Pavlik, J. (2001) *Journalism and new media*, Columbia University Press, New York.
Rosenberg, N. (1994) *Exploring the black box*, Cambridge University Press, Cambridge.
Schudson, M. (1995) *The power of news*, Harvard University Press, Cambridge, MA.
Schudson, M. (2001) 'The objectivity norm in American journalism', *Journalism* 2(2), 149–170.
Steacy, W. (2016) *Deadline* (Vol. 2), B. Frank Books, Zurich.
Thurman, N., Cornia, A., and Kunert, J. (2016) 'Journalists in the UK', *Reuters Institute for the Study of Journalism*. Available at: https://reutersinstitute.politics.ox.ac.uk/sites/default/files/Journalists%20in%20the%20UK.pdf
Wolff, M. (2012) 'Mobile and the news media's imploding business model', *Guardian Opinion*, 27 March 2012.

Author interviews

Tracy Grant, Deputy Editor, The Washington Post, April 2016
Jeremy Gilbert, Director of Strategic Initiatives, The Washington Post, April 2016
Eric Rich, Universal News Editor, The Washington Post, April 2016

2
CHANGE AND WHY IT HAPPENS

The previous chapter looked at the effect of change on the news industry and, to a lesser extent, on the profession of journalism. This chapter takes a step back to look at why change happens – what drives change.

There are four wheels on the big truck of change. They are: technology, behaviour, markets and regulation.

Like truck wheels, they're both linked and interdependent; you can just about drive with three of the wheels but you need all four to get maximum progress. And, to stay with the truck analogy for just a little bit longer, two of them do most of the driving. Think of it as a front-wheel-driven truck, with technology and behaviour pushing the speed, and markets and regulation chugging along behind, sort of stabilising the load.

For example, Google. Pretty much a great big giant truck of change in itself; however, if we look at the changes that have affected Google as a business, we can see the impact of each of those four drivers.

Technology first. Google only in part invented itself. Larry Page and Sergey Brin didn't invent the internet (that was Vint Cerf, Bob Kahn, Yogan Dalal, Richard Karp, Carl Sunshine, Robert Metcalfe, Peter Kirstein and a bunch of others [Abbate, 1999]). Nor did they invent the World Wide Web (Sir Tim Berners-Lee[1]), nor even the computer servers at Stanford University that provided Google's first "home". But all those things needed to be in place before Page and Brin could get anywhere near designing the most-used website in the world.[2]

But then, round about 1996, Backrub was born.

Backrub was basically Google Part One and, like Berners-Lee's invention of the World Wide Web, it grew out of looking at how academics share and reference academic papers.

Page and Brin used the concept of citations, whereby academics cite (reference) other academic works in order to prove the validity of their argument. Page reasoned that citations were basically back links, and as such provided a list of the most relevant papers and information sources – i.e. if lots of academics cite your paper in their work, then your paper must not only be relevant to the subject, but an example of the best research in that field.

The search engines that were around at the time were struggling both to crawl the rapidly expanding web and to deliver the most relevant search results. As Page notes in the research paper he wrote with Brin: "Only one of the top four commercial search engines finds itself (returns its own search page in response to its name in the top ten results)" (1997).

Those competing search engines largely focused on a keywords-type approach to search – assessing the relevance of a page to a search term based on whether those words appeared in the text on the web page. What Page began playing with – and Brin soon joined him in the task – was how to use the links (hyperlinks) going to that page as a measure of its relevance to the search term. Thus, taking the concept of academic citations as a measure of relevance and importance to a subject and translating it to use hyperlinks as the measure.

The duo created an algorithm called PageRank which looked for search terms in the title of a page (e.g. "Future Journalism research project"), then looked for other web pages that linked to it, and then looked at whether those pages used some or all of the same words (e.g. "What is the future for journalism?"), in order to rank the importance of the web page to the search term (e.g. "future journalism").

Thus, they produced a search engine that was massively more successful in delivering relevant results than its rivals and which, because it focused on finding and following links, could scale (grow) with the web. In fact, the bigger the web got, the better their search engine – now renamed Google – became. It blew its search rivals out of the water, and has done so pretty much since the company launched in 1998.

Google was built on the back of existing technology (the web itself and computers with the capacity to handle increasing amounts of web traffic; processors able to deliver the speed needed to follow and rank all those hyperlinks). Page and Brin had looked at the existing search engines and worked out where they were failing – what was the problem that needed solving? The best new ideas, as the next chapter explores further, begin with identifying a problem for users and then coming up with a way to solve that problem.

But creating a better search engine would have been pretty pointless if no-one had wanted a better search engine. Which is where the behaviour wheel on the truck of change comes in.

It isn't enough to just invent something that's a bit better, even a lot better, than something that already exists if it isn't also solving a problem for the users of that thing. If Alta Vista, Excite or Yahoo had already been delivering really relevant search results, even if they were a bit slow, most users would have stuck with it. The theories of change (or loss) aversion and status-quo bias evolved from acres of research proving that as consumers we tend to stick with what we know. We don't make the effort to switch unless the alternative delivers enough of a benefit (and often unless people we trust are also using that alternative).

But the problem for the 1997 users of Yahoo, Excite et al. was not only that they were being served too many irrelevant results, but that relevant results were being wrongly filtered out, and sometimes even replaced by adverts.

What Brin and Page had also spotted was that users were being served too many results in general. The problem was that while the number of documents available to search had increased massively, the user's ability to look at documents had not. People, they noted, were only willing to look at the "first few tens of results".

> Because of this, as the collection size grows, we need tools that have very high precision (number of relevant documents returned, say in the top tens of results). Indeed, we want our notion of "relevant" to only include the very best documents since there may be tens of thousands of slightly relevant documents.
>
> *(Brin and Page, 1997)*

What they had identified is user behaviour that combined our hunger for knowledge with an inherent laziness. Even in 1997, we weren't willing to look beyond page one results.[3]

A search via Yahoo starts with Yahoo's human-edited 1997 homepage (Figure 2.1) of the things its editors think we might want to search for:

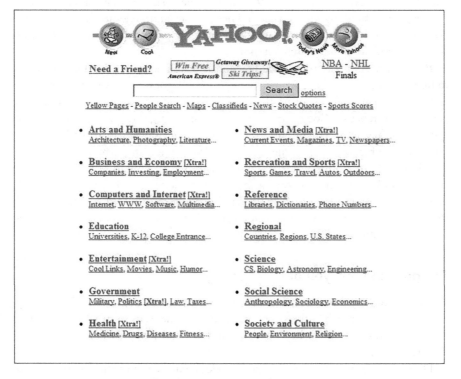

FIGURE 2.1 Screenshot of Yahoo's 1997 homepage from Yahoo (on Flickr) album '15 years of Yahoo.com'.

22 Change and why it happens

FIGURE 2.2 Screenshot of Google's 1998 homepage, via Wikipedia and the Wayback Machine internet archive (https://en.wikipedia.org/wiki/Google).

Yet Google's homepage is this calm and simple page (Figure 2.2) – an almost blank screen inviting us to just leap right in and search for something, anything we might imagine:
And when we searched, Google in 1998 gave us a neat page of really relevant results.[4]

Google was fulfilling our behavioural need for a simple, relevant, fast search that doesn't overload us with choices, and that does a big part of the filtering job for us without taking away our search autonomy.

Putting the emphasis on us – we type in the search terms for the thing we want to find, rather than Yahoo or Excite trying to second-guess what we might be interested in – began a process of us, the users, getting better at searching. Around 80 percent of searches on Google are now "long tail", using three or more words in a search. Basically, we've taught ourselves to search, and Google has adapted to match our changing behaviour: machine learning following human learning.

We want to search for a video – Google had to learn how to search video titles and back links. We want to find a picture of something – the web can't "see" images, it only sees text, specifically the text in code such as HTML – so Google had to find a way to search text information about that picture to work out what it is a picture of. Until recently.[5]

The push-me pull-you beast of change

The technology arrives, the behaviour arrives, sometimes one arrives first, mostly they arrive pretty much at the same time, and each one leads to tweaks and further changes in the other: the technology-push and demand-pull pillars of technological change.

Dosi (1982) argued that technological development is driven both by demand-pull from users choosing to do one thing rather than another, and the technology-push of what is possible at that stage. Users in choosing a particular technology, or in using it in a particular way, shape how it then progresses (Rosenberg and Mowery, 1979; Rosenberg, 1994). A sort of push-me, pull-you process of incremental, back and forth change.

McLuhan (1964) said that it is the technology – specifically media technology – that shapes societies. This theory of technological determinism argues that, rather than having free will to interact with technology, each new media technology determines how we will act and think as individuals and as a society (McLuhan, 1964; Postman, 1993). Others (Silverstone, 2005; Miller, 2016) have suggested a sort of cross pollination with media technology transforming society, and that technology then being shaped in return to mirror society.

For example, technological change arrives in the form of personal computing (PCs) and suddenly we can access masses more information, massively faster, and do more with it. But we don't just want our PC to deliver information; we want it to help us talk to each other – we are social animals after all. So, we prioritise communication and social tools on our PC, which means developers build more of that stuff – email, SMS, forums, the internet, social networking, co-op gaming and so forth.

Abbate (1999) said the arrival of the internet placed computers at the center of a new communications medium. Two things happened – the internet pushed the trajectory of computing to shape the use of the PC as a new communications media, while user demand-pull dragged the internet towards a new *social*, communicative use:

> The Internet's identity as a communication medium was not inherent in the technology; it was constructed through a series of social choices.
>
> *(1999: 6)*

Papacharissi (2002: 21) said that people's real-world social relations drove society to repurpose the internet to create spaces for private and public expression. The rise of "social" in our online world is the inevitable result of taking our offline interactions onto the web.

That technical design is shaped by social values is a generally accepted concept (Abbate, 1999; Bowker et al., 1997; Friedman, 1997; Feenberg, 1995; MacKenzie and Wajcman, 1985). This development of a social constructivist theory of technological design is neatly summarised by Flanagin et al. (2009: 180) who extend social constructivism to the internet and further argue that the internet was built and designed in ways that encourage new forms of collective action. The internet created a shift towards networked activity and interconnectivity that undermines the power of the traditional mass media in favour of the individual: "an enhanced sense of empowerment, in as much as internet users feel their collective efforts result in desired outcomes" (p. 186).

Each new online outpouring of anger; of public will; of campaigning for change, encourages us to believe that what we say and do collectively carries more weight than opinions reflected in the traditional media. That enhanced sense of personal power becomes something traditional media has to deal with too – no more readers' letters pages: instead space for hundreds of comments on any news story posted online and a symbiotic relationship where readers add to and may even collaborate on delivering the news story.

Our technology becomes more social to reflect our behaviour; social technology development speeds up and develops in new unexpected ways that impact on society, transform it even (think Facebook). But because we behave in particular ways, there are social norms we tend to stick to in order to be accepted by our peers and we take those behaviours with us into the shiny new social tech communication – we watch what we say (mostly); we filter online "friends". The technology mirrors society again, albeit a shifted, tweaked version.

The genesis of Google and birth of AdSense

As the technology and behaviour mature and become embedded in our culture, those other two wheels – markets and regulation – take a bigger role in driving our truck of change.

Google started as a better way to search. Brin and Page had no commercial model in mind when they launched Google; its early years were funded by investors. It was two years, in October 2000, before Google was to launch AdWords and, as the previous chapter outlined, AdWords radically changed advertising models not only on the web but in newspapers, magazines and other media business.

In 2004, Page and Brin gave a TED talk on the genesis of Google. It was not so much about how Google was created, more about what it was up to in 2004 and the new ideas that were then floating the founders' boat.

Page spoke about the development of AdSense, using an example of AdSense adverts running on the 2004 version of The Washington Post's news website. He explained how the ads were generated automatically from the content on the site, so that only the most relevant ads, from the millions available to Google, would be served to the site's readers: "The idea is that we can make advertising useful, not just annoying."

He also spoke about the importance of AdSense in providing a new income stream for the content producer (both for producers like The Washington Post and the lone blogger): "It makes the internet work better, it makes content get better, it makes searching work better, when people can really make their livelihood from producing great content."

Page was effectively suggesting that Google, via AdSense, could help solve the conundrum of shrinking advertising revenue for content producers. Setting aside that Google may be competing with The Washington Post for those advertiser dollars (and winning), here was a way The Post and other content producers could claw revenue back, after Google had taken its share.[6]

Google's user may be us – we're the ones using the system to search for stuff – but Google's market (and our third truck wheel) is the advertisers paying to have their advert returned alongside keyword search results (AdWords), or added to the homepages of relevant blogs and websites (AdSense) or running on videos uploaded to YouTube (YouTube Partner Programme).

As that market becomes more sophisticated, Google is able to adjust the prices it charges for each of those adverts, according to both the popularity of particular keywords (AdWords) or the popularity of a blog or website (AdSense) or of a YouTube channel and the desirability of that search term to competing businesses.

Research by Search Engine Watch, which analysed the most expensive AdWords keywords in early 2016, showed that in the UK most of the 20 most expensive keywords related to gambling.[7] While in the US, the most expensive keywords related to personal injury legal services. These words shift as markets change – there's no reason to assume that gambling or personal injury lawyers will still be the biggest buyers of search ads in five years' time.

Finally, that last wheel on the truck of change – regulation. As Google has grown to dominate search, it has attracted the attention of regulators. Among the legal battles Google faced in 2016 were a copyright case brought by Oracle on using Java code in the Android operating system, plus three antitrust complaints brought by the European Commission[8] over potentially restrictive trading practices, plus a class action lawsuit over AdWords which has rumbled through the US court system since 2008, plus an investigation by French prosecutors into a potential $1.8 billion of unpaid taxes. The bigger a company gets, the more attention it attracts from regulators and lawyers – something Facebook is also now dealing with.

Google and the nearly-Facebook

In that 2004 TED talk, co-founder Sergey Brin highlighted another project that they were really excited about at Google – Orkut. At its height (around 2012) Orkut was used by 30 million people predominantly in Brazil and India.

Orkut was a social networking site and, in February 2004, had been running in live beta for about a month and already had 100,000 members, 59 percent of them in the US.

It was built by Google staffer Orkut Büyükköktenon, who persuaded his bosses to let him work on what would be his second social networking project.

You need to take a moment here to picture this. Brin and Page were showcasing Orkut in the same month – February 2004 – that Zuckerberg, Moskowitz, Saverin, McCollum and Hughes launched Facebook. Each would have known something about the other's project.

Orkut Büyükköktenon had built his first social network in 2001 as a doctoral student at Stanford University. That project – Club Nexus – was built for Stanford students in the same way that Zuckerberg built his social network for his fellow Harvard students three years later, and Zuckerberg would almost certainly have known about Club Nexus.

There are core similarities between Club Nexus and Thefacebook (as it was), such as using real-world identities to register, and creating "buddies" on Club Nexus similar to Friends on Facebook. (Kirkpatrick, 2010: 77). But Club Nexus was over-complicated for users and failed. Orkut, built by Büyükköktenon for Google, was much better and, at the time of that TED talk, poised to run away with the social networking crown.

But it didn't. Within a few months it was struggling with performance problems and, as Kirkpatrick notes in his book *The Facebook Effect*: "Even the great Google couldn't help a social network grow smoothly" (2010: 87).

Orkut didn't take off. Facebook did. Facebook has been snapping at Google's heels ever since people decided it was easier to ask a friend than ask a search engine. But it's got to hurt when you're Google and the most popular, richest web business on the planet, and you almost delivered Facebook too.

So why, in a book about the future of journalism, have I taken pretty much a whole chapter to talk about Google?

In large part because everything is linked – the internet, the technology that underpins and drives it, the companies, particularly the behemoths like Google and Facebook that are making a commercial success out of digital. But more importantly because what Google and Facebook do directly impacts on news companies.

Google News, Google Trends, Google AMP, Facebook News Feed, Facebook Instant Articles, Facebook Live – and whatever follows over the next few years. Each engagement with news by Google and Facebook involves news publishers and, for better or worse, the revenue they earn. In 2015, Google earned over $67 billion from advertising, with around $10 billion of that paid back to the content producers via AdSense, DoubleClick, etc.[9]

Alongside Orkut, Brin showcased the work of another of Google's maverick engineers in that 2004 talk. Krishna Bharat "got really interested in the news"[10] because of what he saw as US-centric dominance of reporting around 9/11, and went on to develop Google News.

The service set out from the start to do much more than deliver a bunch of links. It grouped stories in real time and ranked them by editorial reliability to aim for a diversity of views:

> Linking to a diverse set of sources for any given story enabled readers to easily access different perspectives and genres of content. By featuring opposing viewpoints in the same display block, people were encouraged to hear arguments on both sides of an issue and gain a more balanced perspective.[11]

How different does that sound now, that desire to educate people by deliberately exposing them to opposing viewpoints, to recent concerns of filter bubbles, confirmation bias and fake news that has undermined Facebook's "trusted referral" approach to news?

Google is interested in news, as it is in all content that travels across the web as krill for Google's search whale. Here's former Google executive Marissa Mayer way back in 2009:

> Journalism at its core remains the same, but the way it's delivered changes and evolves. We [Google] think like this: if you reinvented news and the business model in the industry, how would you go about it? And we have to conclude a lot needs to change.[12]

A year later, then Google CEO Eric Schmidt told the American Society of Editors[13] they had "a business model problem", not a news problem. The solution to their business model problem, he said, was to follow where Google planned to lead – onto mobile and devices and particularly into personalised news delivery: a news site should "know" its visitors.

> [I want that news site] to know about me and what I care about. I don't want to be treated as a stranger. . . . So, remember [me], show me what I like but I also want you to challenge me – I want you to say here's something new; here's something you didn't know; here's an opposing view, in case you want to read it.

Google and Facebook have become the dominant delivery mechanisms for news and journalism. Just as once the delivery mechanism was newsprint, and then it became radio and newsprint, and then radio and TV and newsprint, and then the internet (through websites) and radio and TV and newsprint, now it is search and social and internet and radio and TV and newsprint. As Chapter 1 explored, the challenge for news producers is to be able to deliver their content across all the places users might find it – and at least cover the cost of doing so.

In 2016, current CEO Sundar Pichai spoke of Google's over-arching mission to make "great content", information and knowledge available for everyone and that, for that content to be available, it needed investment via Google:

> [A]dvertising helps fund content for millions and millions of people. So we work hard to build great ad products that people find useful – and that give revenue back to creators and publishers.[14]

But what about the not-so-great content? I'll return to the issue of so-called "fake news" in Chapters 4 and 10, but in a world where more than one-in-ten people and 28 percent of 18- to 24-year-olds use social media as their primary source of news,[15] distribution systems which reward content based on popularity rather than veracity are dangerous. Pichai himself acknowledged that fake news could have been an issue in Donald Trump winning the 2016 US presidential election, but "there should just be no situation where fake news gets distributed, so we [Google] are all for doing better".[16]

Google has been criticised for paying out on AdSense ads running on sites promoting fake news, and for delivering a top search result for the final election count that gave Clinton's popular vote win to Trump.[17] Google has also been accused of manipulating search algorithms to omit negative terms in relation to particular political candidates, and of not doing enough to stop extremist and conspiracy theory groups using SEO techniques to "game" search (Cadwalladr, 2016).

The issue is not "what would Google do" in relation to journalism, but what must Google and Facebook *not do* as they become the primary source of news for billions of people.

It matters to news publishers whether consumers will find their content on Google or Facebook. Those top search results, trending stories and viral shares lead to hard cash from Facebook's and Google's advertisers. But for journalists, it's the quality and source of the content that consumers find that matters most. We are journalism's guardians.

If what Google does today matters to journalism and the business of news, what it does tomorrow is also important. A final quote from Pichai on where Google is going:

> [T]he next big step will be for the very concept of the "device" to fade away. Over time, the computer itself – whatever its form factor – will be an intelligent assistant helping you through your day. We will move from mobile first to an AI first world.

But for Google, he said, the end-goal isn't the devices or the products the company builds, but technology itself as "a democratizing force, empowering people through information. Google is an information company. It was when it was founded, and it is today."

CASE STUDY: GUARDIAN NEWS AND MEDIA

Guardian News and Media – producers of multi-award-winning newspapers and websites – is one of the legacy news publishers having to react to the reality of a market dominated by Google and Facebook.

In 2016, the company had been losing money for some time and, even with its cushion of support from the Scott Trust, Guardian Media Group (GMG) losses meant the company had already announced plans to shed over 300 jobs.[18] In the week that I arrived, in July 2016, to conduct interviews for this book, managers were grappling with the additional news that the loss on the year to March 2016 was £10 million higher than expected at £69 million.

GMG, like other media companies, has several parts to the company but its news publishing is delivered through Guardian News and Media (GNM), responsible for both the Guardian and the Observer newspapers and digital output across its websites, app and social media.

A few years earlier, GNM developed a sort-of 'all-pile-in' policy on digital – throwing everything they had at expanding reach across digital global markets. The strategy was working in user terms – April 2016 unique users of 155 million for theguardian.com were almost 30 million more than a year before, and there had been over 5 million downloads of the Guardian's news app. But the business was failing in financial terms, with digital revenues down on the previous year and still under 40 percent of total income.[19]

The turning point had been 2011, when then-editor Alan Rusbridger led a radical overhaul of journalism output and thinking – pushing into digital media and developing the concept of "open journalism", with readers in a "two-way relationship" with journalists in newsgathering and production. GNM wasn't the only news publisher in 2012 to decide that it made business sense to have readers contributing content.[20] If the drive was to produce more content across more platforms but with fewer staff, then involving readers may also be a financial necessity.

While Guardian Media Group as a whole was still turning a profit in 2011 (thanks to Auto Trader and other outside interests) GNM was not. The core business of delivering news has been failing financially for almost a decade. And that investment in a digital future contributed to losses – £75 million down in 2012[21] – despite massive growth in audience. In 2016, digital audiences were three times higher than in 2012 and digital income had risen to £81.9 million, but the business was still failing.

David Teather joined the Guardian in 1999 from the Express. He moved from being a business specialist to the national news desk in 2010, ahead of the changes introduced by Rusbridger, and now, under current editor Katharine Viner, is editor of the print edition – that is of the Guardian newspaper itself.

He told me the challenge for GNM is to keep producing quality journalism in a climate of expanded need and reduced income: "The horrible truth is we're going to be asked to do more for less. The money is shrinking, but [not] the tasks that you have to do.

"Ten years ago, all we were doing was producing one paper a day. Now, we're producing a paper, we're making films, podcasts, we're updating stories ten times a day, we're trying to be a proper seven-day-a-week operation. . . . Fewer people are going to have to do more stuff. Unless you do start making choices, then that's when you start worrying about quality in journalism. A bit depressing."

Since my visit, the Guardian had begun on a programme of content reduction. A lot of content online had been getting less than 5,000 hits and the exercise aimed to produce less but better journalism: one attempt, Teather told me, to tackle that problem of fewer people doing more and more.

Teather has seen a lot of changes, including physically moving the print editors' news desk from the centre of the newsroom in order to reduce the emphasis on the Guardian newspaper and to reinforce the idea that what matters is the journalism, not the delivery mechanism. When we talked, that centre space was occupied by the section news desks – sections for international news, national news and business.

"That structural separation has changed the way I'm working quite a lot," he said. "Because I would say the print used to be the key driver of commissioning. The need to print is still important, and we do still commission, but the need to print is in a way sort of secondary. We just have to put digital first because that's where the future is." It's a difficult balance, he added, because print is still generating 60 percent of GNM's revenue.

I reminded him that a few years ago, there had been discussions about getting rid of the print edition of the Guardian, or printing just a few days a week, but he said that conversation isn't happening nowadays.

"It certainly would come around again to the idea that print is valuable," he added. "It's important not just from a revenue standpoint, which is very important, particularly because digital revenues haven't evolved in a way that it was expected, but also just in terms of the brand."

In recent weeks, he said he'd seen a change with increasing year-on-year print sales "for the first time in as long as I can remember".

"I think what's happening is we've had all of these slightly seismic events going on for the past month, people turn to print because print has some authority and it's curated."

Teather's role is to decide which stories go into the print edition and where they go. The decision about which stories go into the various digital editions are taken by those editors. During the period that paring down the print edition was under discussion, Teather said there had been an idea that print would simply scrape stories from the web, but that didn't happen. Instead, journalists produce stories intended for both print and digital output and the editors control what they use, and where and how they use it.

"Stuff that's done for the web is often not appropriate for print because things will often be done as a [live] blog, or tweets will be embedded into it," he said. "Also, you might have a story that's been updated ten times that day. It might be a little bit scrappy, it might be that because of the needs of the web, you've lost the natural core of the story because they've updated it all the time. Sometimes you have to take it back a step and say: 'Actually, what is the story here?' Is it that incremental thing which you've added to the top at five o'clock, or do we need to take it back a bit? Sometimes you think: 'How can we take it forwards?' because it's a paper that's coming out the day after something has happened."

Teather will talk with section heads, journalists and sub-editors in developing and shaping stories ("Good communication is the absolute key to making this thing work") and the process will to-and-fro across the day, which for Teather starts with listening to the Today programme on Radio 4 on his walk into work, and his office day finishes when the last pages are sent to print, round about 9.30pm.

When he gets home, he also has to deal with the night team to discuss the later edition, which goes at 1am, taking account of any stories that have broken and whether they need to look at stories on the front pages of the Guardian's rivals.

Copy comes to Teather through the desks but he'll often rewrite intros for print ("you have to write for a different audience, for a different time zone if they're getting it the next day"), tweak headlines, and manage the look and feel of the paper – particularly the front page and allowing for the fold (what you see in a stack of folded newspapers on a shelf). Thinking about how the newspaper looks on the stand is a key part of his role.

"I think it's actually vital. Above the fold, you're always thinking if it's a picture of a person for example, am I getting the whole head above the fold? You need it to be recognisable. You need the image to work above the fold, it can't just be a blank space. You want [full] headlines above the fold."

But it's about balance – "bread and roses" – the idea that you have to sell the newspapers to get people to see the journalism. The "sweet spot" he said, is having a story like the Panama Papers that achieves both – strong, public service journalism that also sells newspapers.

A couple of years ago, commissioning (of stories, of staff to work on stories, of freelancers) operated through parallel structures, with print and web each doing their own commissioning. Unsurprisingly that caused confusion and "stuff fell through the gaps", but the more streamlined system now operating, with commissioning done via the section editors is, Teather said, more effective.

"We have a lot of very good relationships actually here, because a lot of us have been here for a long time. We like each other and we get on. I think that makes it work. I think that there probably isn't an ideal way of doing these things really, because web and print have two very, very different demands. I think we probably have got to a point which is the best way of servicing both."

Lizzy Davies is one of those specialist editors that Teather works with. As Deputy Head of International News, she corrals staff and freelance foreign correspondents around the world to deliver international stories for both print and digital output, working through the Guardian's foreign desk of a "core nucleus" of London editors like Davies, plus an editor in New York and one in Sydney.

She explained how that works, with the London desk focusing broadly by time zone on Europe, Africa, the Middle East; her colleague in Sydney focused on correspondents in Tokyo, Beijing, Southeast Asia; and the New York editor working with correspondents in Latin America and Canada.

"Obviously there's overlap," she added. "The guy in Delhi wakes up with Sydney, goes to bed with London. There is lots of overlap sometimes. The guys in those offices also, we will speak to the man in Rio. But that's broadly how it's meant to divvy up. We find it actually works really, really well."

She shows me a map of correspondents and editors across the globe, at any time around 50–60 staff and freelancers, with around four international desk editors based in London.

Like Teather, Davies arrived at the news desk from a fairly traditional journalism background, serving time as both a home news and foreign news reporter, and living and working in Italy as the Guardian's Rome correspondent.

The job she does is also 'traditional' news editing at its core, but the process has evolved with the foreign desks passing stories from one to another across time zones to deliver a global 24-hour cycle, particularly on big breaking stories. The Guardian's digital output focuses coverage of ongoing, breaking stories around its Live Blog ("the traffic is huge") and their newer, "what we know so far" round-ups. Managing that coverage over a 24-hour news cycle can be a challenge, said Davies.

"The notion that you can hand over between the offices is amazing. I'm pretty sure that, for the [Europe] terrorist attacks for instance, we did a round-the-world live blog handover. Not just of the blog but of the story in general of course. They've [the readers] gone from reporters here, to reporters in the US office, to reporters in the Sydney office, and they've come back to us."

"The other day we were talking about how we started doing these 'what we know so far' pieces for terror attacks or big stories. They work really well online and I guess three months ago no one was talking about it, and now we're doing them and now everyone else is as well. I'm not claiming that we started them, but certainly they were a novelty for us.

"The way that we do journalism is changing every month. Things are changing at a pace which never ceases to amaze me really."

The further challenge – particularly for the international desk – is that of managing fast-moving stories from multiple sources. It's been a long time since the foreign correspondent was the only person reporting on the ground; now sources and information will range across social media, blogs, and rival news websites creating a verification headache.

"We try never to be quick at the expense of being right," said Davies. "In that sense, it hasn't changed in a journalistic approach at all. We won't publish anything unless we are sure that it's true. It does feel like sometimes, there is a kind of huge chamber of conflicting information. Especially when big stories happen; terror attacks.

"I wasn't actually here, but my colleagues told me that the aftermath of the Munich shooting was extremely confusing and difficult to navigate. In the hours after it broke, there were reports all over social media that there were multiple shooters and [the shooter's] profile was really unclear. We were very cautious about using too much that was coming out on social media."

Ethics is an issue that engages the Guardian editorial team. Davies gave an example of a picture that other media had used in the aftermath of the Brussels attack of two women, one partly dressed and covered in blood, that the Guardian initially chose not to use.

"We didn't know who the women were; they hadn't been named," she said. "We didn't know what had happened to them; how badly they'd been hurt. We didn't know where the story was going at that point so we put them on ice basically, the pictures. We came back to them later in the day. By then the woman had been named, we knew that she was okay, we knew that she had got out safely. Her family had spoken. We felt that enough time had passed and the situation had clarified enough that we decided to use the pictures in the paper."

For Davies and her colleagues, there's a "Guardian way" of covering the news, particularly on breaking stories such as the Brussels attack, that can involve "really tricky conversations" about ethics in the newsroom.

"We try not to give in to pressure when we see the others in the British media publishing things that we feel uncomfortable with. We don't necessarily feel under pressure to do the same. I think we pride ourselves on making sure that we take decisions collegiately and we have conversations about whether we use certain images, whether we feel that it's the right time to publish certain information.

"We try to cultivate a much more kind of international approach to stories and we find that sometimes some of the other British papers have a more parochial view of international news stories which we try to avoid."

But Davies, like Teather, was concerned about what the future held: "I can't say where the international desk will be in five years' time. At the moment it feels like we're in a decent place. You never know. You never know."

If the core of Guardian News and Media's output is traditional, responsible journalism, the delivery of that across multiple media, and how to make money doing so, is its biggest challenge. I began this section with an outline of the scale of the financial problem GNM faces and how much of the focus for balancing the books has been on cutting staff costs.

The group has also introduced new revenue streams, in particular putting an emphasis on the Guardian Members scheme, supporters and sponsors (two of those, Rockefeller and the Gates Foundation, sponsor international news websites), and work on branded content and native advertising through Guardian Labs.

Aron Pilhofer was part of that membership drive ("on the tech side, the development side, membership is a huge priority for us"), but he's also a good example of Teather's point that the GNM's financial problems lead to fewer people doing more.

Pilhofer was the interim chief digital officer and also executive editor of digital at GNM, but the week we met, he'd just announced that he was leaving to return to the US to take up a professorship at Temple University's School of Media and Communication, in Philadelphia.

He joined GNM in June 2014 and put together the teams and processes that have created some of GNM's most interesting future journalism products – a multimedia piece on global warming following the Mekong river;[22] the 6x9 solitary confinement VR package;[23] data and multimedia-led elections packages; an "amazing piece" for the Manchester Arts Festival.[24]

But Pilhofer's time has also been about juggling very different jobs, having been asked to step in as first Tanya Cordrey, GNM chief digital officer, left, followed by deputy editor (and web editor-in-chief) Janine Gibson. Pilhofer took on parts of their teams to find himself suddenly carrying responsibility for around 200 staff.

He said his various teams work in different ways: "The technology team is more about our enterprise technologies, so they are building the content management system, the apps, the website, things like that. They operate I would say . . . in a pretty modern way, classic, sort of Agile[25] . . . continuous deployment.

"In the newsroom [team], it operates pretty much like my teams did at the Times.[26] It's a lot like a news desk. It's a news desk that has borrowed somewhat from Agile's software development technologies, but very, very loosely."

Building membership, ad revenue ("trying to figure out what to do there"), dealing with ad blocking ("a very big deal for us") and expanding video output ("a huge deal for us right now") are on his teams' priority lists. Despite the challenges of his combined jobs, Pilhofer sees working across both commercial and editorial as important – something he's used to doing and believes more journalists should do, including the Guardian's journalists:

"[This] newsroom is by far the most digital newsroom I've ever worked in, and we're nowhere near where we need to be. There is almost no understanding in the newsroom of how the organisation makes money. How we have to change, evolve and adapt to a world in which the future of journalism might be launching on Facebook.

"It's going to take years, years sadly that I don't know that we have, to get to that point. What I hope to do [in his future job in teaching] is to help foster that transformation, because when the shit really hits the fan, as it did at the New York Times right around the mortgage meltdown, and here where it's very serious right now, if the newsroom isn't intimately involved in whatever the solution is, it won't work."

Suggested assignments

Practical exercise

All journalists need to know how to read and interpret a company's annual report – whether a company you're writing a story about or the one you work for. Pick a national news publisher; work out which company it belongs to (for example both the New York Post in the US and the Sun in the UK are part of News Corp). Dig around the company information, including annual and quarterly reports/returns and reports to investors, to create a picture of how well the news publishing part of that company is doing, and then write about it. You may decide to write a news story (if there's a clear and current news angle); a news feature (for example, using the news publisher as an example of changes in the news business); or write as an investigation into how the fortunes of that particular news publisher have changed over time.

Group analysis

The early part of this chapter focused on Google – the technological changes which enabled Google to exist and flourish, and the behavioural changes that influenced how search developed. It contrasted the simplicity of Google's 1998 homepage for users with the curated complexity of rivals Yahoo and Excite. Your group has been given one of the pairs of products below to compare and discuss. Focus on which product is most effective in terms of the service they deliver to users. What is good and bad about each of them? What could they do better? What annoys you about them as users? Finally, which one do you think you'll still be using in five years' time, and in what ways do you think that product might have changed or evolved by then?

> BuzzFeed vs Wall Street Journal (or the Financial Times)
> CNN vs Twitter
> BBC vs Facebook
> Instagram vs Pinterest
> Snapchat vs WhatsApp
> YouTube vs Facebook Live
> Twitter vs Facebook
> Netflix vs Amazon Prime

Notes

1 Source: http://home.cern/topics/birth-web.
2 According to analysts at Alexa: www.alexa.com/topsites.
3 Researchers have shown that around 90 percent of searches on Google don't progress beyond the page one results.
4 In 2013, Google released a web "Easter Egg" to transport users to the 1998 version of Google. It links with the Wayback Machine to produce live links to other 1998 archived web pages.
5 This is changing as I write this book. Google's ongoing work in developing AI (artificial intelligence) applications (currently feeding from our human image recognition skills via photo captchas) has seen radical work on the task of recognising images, using AI working on massive computing systems. Google Photos, released in 2015, can recognise and search images to automatically organise them. For example, searching for "dog" would show you photos of dogs, regardless of the picture name or caption. If you're within the Google universe (for instance using an Android phone with a Google Photos account) the system would show you pictures of dogs, or photos with dogs in them, in all the images accessible via your phone, including photos sent to you by people in your WhatsApp groups, etc., as well as images you've taken yourself with your phone.
6 Google says it pays 68 percent of recognised revenue earned by each AdSense advert to the publisher displaying the ad on their website or blog.
7 Including misspellings of roulette as "rolete" (£144.76 per click) and "rullet" (£111.62 per click). Perhaps online casinos felt there was an advantage in signing up gamblers with poor literacy? Source: SearchEngineWatch April 14, 2016 and May 31, 2016.

8 'European commission files third antitrust charge against Google', Samuel Gibbs and agencies, July 14, 2016, the Guardian and European Commission competition cases search '39740 Google Search'.
9 According to the 2015 Annual Report submitted by Alphabet/Google.
10 'Google News founder Krishna Bharat: For news consumers, "the whole experience is what counts"', Megan Garber, April 8, 2011 for NiemanLab.
11 'Google News turns 10', Krishna Bharat, September 22, 2012, on the Google blog.
12 Marissa Mayer interviewed on stage at LeWeb conference December 9, 2009 (video).
13 Eric Schmidt, April 11, 2010, Keynote speech, American Society of News Editors (video).
14 Google CEO Sundar Pichai in the company's annual Founders' Letter to investors and staff, 2016.
15 Reuters' 2016 survey of digital news consumption.
16 In a video interview for BBC News on November 15: www.bbc.co.uk/news/business-37992016.
17 A few days after the election, the top Google search result for "final election count" displayed a tally from a Wordpress blog called '70 News' that said Trump had won the popular vote by a margin of almost 700,000 votes. In fact, it was Clinton who was winning by that amount. 'Google looking into grossly inaccurate top news search result displayed as final popular-vote tally', November 14, 2016, BusinessInsider.
18 'Guardian Media Group to cut 250 jobs in bid to break even within three years', Jane Martinson, March 17, 2016, Guardian.
19 GMG annual report, year results to April 3, 2016, GMG press office.
20 WAN-IFRA Open Journalism Report, 2012.
21 GMG annual report, year results to April 2012, GMG press office.
22 'Mekong: A river rising', 2015, Guardian website.
23 '6x9: A virtual experience of solitary confinement', 2016, Guardian website.
24 'Manchester International Festival's Mayfield depot – 360-degree interactive', 2013, Guardian website.
25 An iterative, incremental method of managing the design and build activities of engineering, information technology and other business areas that aims to create new, highly flexible products or services.
26 Pilhofer was Associate Managing Editor for Digital Strategy and Editor of Interactive News at the New York Times before joining GNM.

References and further study

Abbate, J. (1999) *Inventing the internet*, MIT Press, Cambridge, MA.

Bowker, G.C., Turner, W., Star, S.L., and Gasser, L. (1997) *Social science, technical systems, and cooperative work: Beyond the great divide*, Erlbaum, Mahwah, NJ.

Brin, S. and Page, L. (1997) *The anatomy of a large-scale hypertextual web search engine*, Stanford University, Redwood City, CA. Accessed at http://infolab.stanford.edu/~backrub/google.html

Cadwalladr, C. (2016) 'Google, democracy and the truth about internet search', *Observer*, 14 December 2016.

Dosi, G. (1982) 'Technological paradigms and technological trajectories', *Research Policy* 11, 147–162.

Feenberg, A. (1995) 'Subversive rationalization: Technology, power, and democracy', in A. Feenberg and A. Hannay (eds.) *Technology and the politics of knowledge*, pp. 3–22, Indiana University Press, Bloomington.

Flanagin, A.J., Flanagin, C., and Flanagin, J. (2010) 'Technical code and the social construction of the internet', *New Media & Society* 12(2), 179–196.

Friedman, B. (ed.) (1997) *Human values and the design of computer technology*, Cambridge University Press, Cambridge.

Kirkpatrick, D. (2010) *The Facebook effect*, Simon & Schuster, Pymble, NSW.
MacKenzie, D. and Wajcman, J. (1985) *The social shaping of technology: How the refrigerator got its hum*, Open University Press, Philadelphia.
McLuhan, M. (1964) *Understanding media: The extensions of man*, McGraw-Hill, New York.
Miller, D. et al. (2016) *How the world changed social media*, UCL Press, London.
Papacharissi, Z. (2002) 'The virtual sphere: The internet as a public sphere', *New Media & Society* 4(1): 9–27.
Postman, N. (1993) *Technopoly: The surrender of culture to technology*, Vintage Books, New York.
Rosenberg, N. (1994) *Exploring the black box: technology, economics, and history*, Cambridge University Press, Cambridge.
Rosenberg, N. and Mowery, D. (1979) 'The influence of market demand upon innovation: A critical review of some recent empirical studies', *Research Policy* 8(2): 102–153.
Silverstone, R. (2005) 'Mediation and communication', in C. Calhoun, C. Rojek, and B. Turner (eds.) *Handbook of sociology*, pp. 188–207, Sage, London.
Watch Alan Rusbridger (2012) Talking about Open Journalism, and watch the advert for the Guardian that epitomised the concept, at: www.theguardian.com/media/series/on-open-journalism

Author interviews

Lizzy Davies, Deputy Head of International News, Guardian News and Media, July 2016
David Teather, editor of the print edition, Guardian News and Media, July 2016
Aron Pilhofer, Interim Chief Digital Officer and Executive Editor of Digital, Guardian News and Media, July 2016

3

NEW IDEAS AND HOW THEY GOT HERE

While the first two chapters looked at the problems the media industries face, this chapter considers the role of the individual entrepreneur, for whom the issue isn't usually a business problem but a customer problem.

New ideas start with a problem that needs solving. Often a personal irritant to the idea's "inventor" – Netflix co-founder Reed Hastings says he came up with the idea for his service after he was hit with a $40 fine for returning a film late to Blockbuster.[1]

The new idea may be based on pre-existing technology or products. Netflix began as a DVD subscription and postal service. The new tech at the time was DVDs, but the new idea was to use the funding model used for gym membership and (until internet streaming became possible) a delivery mechanism of posting DVDs to customers, rather than expect them to trek out to your store to choose and return movies. A successful idea introduces radical change for customers or users and with it market disintermediation – that is, it disrupts the way the market had been operating.

Let's timeshift back to 2010 and another video viewing model. YouTube had its fifth birthday that February, and in May 2010 hit a record 2 billion daily video views. In just five years, YouTube had radically changed what we watched, when and where we watched videos, and who produced what we watched. It was already a great big ball of disruption in the media landscape.

And then YouTube did something even more radical – they allowed us to watch videos without having to sit through an advert first. On December 1, 2010, YouTube launched TrueView ads.[2] For the first time, viewers could skip an ad after five seconds – and the advertiser only paid if we watched the whole ad or at least 30 seconds of it.

The viewer had been put in control of which ads they chose to watch. From the advertiser's point of view, it changed the relationship with the viewer – they might assume that if someone did not skip their ad, that signalled interest in the product or in the advert, while the need to hook us in those first five seconds created a new challenge for ad makers.

Google, YouTube's owner since 2006, had brought the concept of AdWords to video and in doing so disintermediated the way advertisers engaged with consumers of advertising. TrueView delivered, said YouTube, "an end to passive advertising". Giving the YouTube audience choice over what ads they watched tackled two problems. For the audience it reduced the annoyance factor of advertising; for advertisers they now knew who had actually watched their ad.

Think about how the introduction of TrueView ads has continued to change your own behaviour; how often are you annoyed when the ad at the start of a YouTube video doesn't offer a "skip" option? How likely are you to use ad-blocking software, or to pay to upgrade your Spotify or similar account in order to get an ad-free service? We've become used to seeing advertising as optional to content.

Recognising that advertising is both a problem (i.e. annoying) and a solution (i.e. it pays the bills) for content providers is part of understanding the enormous challenge that the news industry faces as disruptive technology – whether skip ad or block ad – makes advertising increasingly optional for news consumers.

New ideas, such as TrueView and skip ad, emerge from the need to solve a *compelling* problem for the user/audience/customer. As marketing guru Seth Godin acknowledged: "No one cares about the 'I'd like a slightly better version of something that is already just fine' problem." Successful entrepreneurs need the ability to identify that compelling problem, and the ability to identify who will benefit from solving that problem (i.e. the potential market) and the ability to identify the solution, or part of the solution, to that problem.

We tend to think of entrepreneurs and innovators as only being about that last bit – the solution, perhaps as the inventor of some whizzy new gadget or service. But it doesn't matter how great the new thing is; if no-one really wants it then the new idea will die. If all it does is introduce a "slightly better version", it will fade. Equally, if nobody wants it just yet, then it will die – being too early to market has killed plenty of great new ideas and, as this chapter highlights, many of them in the hyper-local and user-generated news zones.

When we're talking about the "market" for an idea, we're also talking about market as audience or reader. Your content, your journalism, fails if it doesn't have an audience, a market for the story you're trying to tell. Market is who you're selling (or distributing) your product to; marketing is how you bring your product to the attention of that market.

The exercises at the end of this chapter encourage you to think radically about news delivery and how to identify problems – and then devise innovative ideas for solving those problems – that would change and expand the market for news. But the starting point is developing your own creative thinking abilities. While some people are naturally gifted writers whose storytelling ability is improved by journalism training, most of us become good news writers through journalism training and by learning from better journalists.

Similarly, few people are naturally creative thinkers but everyone can learn techniques to encourage creative thought processes. There are a great many tools, techniques and even courses out there – from brainstorming to Six Hats techniques; lateral thinking to daydreaming; SWOT analysis to Morphological analysis; mind mapping to reframing.

On a personal level, as someone who has come up with and launched a bunch of new business ideas,[3] my own technique is closest to the process outlined by James Webb Young in his 1940 book, *A Technique for Producing Ideas*. He came up with a five step sequence:

1. *Gathering raw material* (the building knowledge and research phase)
2. *Digesting the material.* Better described as focused, hard thinking about the problem
3. *Incubation and unconscious processing.* Taking a physical and mental break from the problem and letting your unconscious mind work in the background
4. *The "a-ha!"* or Eureka moment when the core idea lights up your brain
5. Developing the *idea to reality* ("the cold, gray dawn of the morning after")

In my own experience, it isn't quite so linear. Often, I'll start with half an idea (a partial Eureka moment) and follow that up with the gathering knowledge phase or the hard-thinking stage. I never live or work anywhere without a whiteboard on a wall; I never sleep without a notepad next to the bed. Being ready to jot down every idea, every partial Eureka moment, no matter how mad it sounds a week later, is about giving your brain permission to think creatively. It's saying to the creative half of your brain: "Yep, go wild, I'll back you up."

"Because of the journalism"

I keep using that word "entrepreneur". It's a clunky word, I don't like using it myself, but we should make sure we're on the same page in terms of what we understand by it.

The Oxford Dictionary describes an entrepreneur as someone who sets up a business or businesses, taking on financial risks in the hope of profit. The Cambridge Dictionary similarly defines the entrepreneur as someone who starts their own business, especially when this involves seeing a new opportunity. My battered 1996 Oxford Compact that's travelled with me to jobs in three newspaper newsrooms describes an entrepreneur simply as someone who undertakes a commercial venture (entrepreneur comes from the French word *entreprendre* to "undertake").

We might reasonably ask what the word "entrepreneur" has to do with journalism – where's the "hope of profit" in reporting on Syrian refugees or the "commercial venture" in releasing thousands of MPs' expense claims? The idea of entrepreneurial journalism or the journalist entrepreneur has attracted a lot of attention in recent years; I spent several years teaching a course in entrepreneurial journalism myself and I blog about the entrepreneurs, geeks and mavericks shaking up journalism and the digital world.

But still, I think the word and its definitions are clunky. Base-level, it describes the freelance journalist, the self-employed news producer that's always been around. And if we want to extend that concept to the freelancer trying to build a business from their journalism, they've always been around too. Is the difference between the freelancer and the entrepreneur one of the level of financial risk or the scale of commercial intent? A more useful term perhaps might be the journalist as "social entrepreneur", defined by the Oxford as "a person who establishes an enterprise with the aim of solving social problems or effecting social change".

Personally, I prefer the word "innovator" to "entrepreneur" because what we're trying to deal with here is the idea of the journalist innovator experimenting with new models for news – models that may or may not hold promise for the future of journalism, but which introduce change into the way journalism is practiced: the innovators, mavericks and experimentalists delivering journalism in new ways, or finding new ways to fund journalism.

When mavericks Norman Mailer, Daniel Wolf and Edwin Fancher launched the Village Voice in New York's Greenwich Village in 1955, they planned an alternative weekly newspaper – one which would deliver a new style of writing and of journalism: "free-form, high-spirited, and passionate" contrary to the staid reporting style of other US newspapers. This was a community newspaper in the most enduring sense of the word, reflecting not only what the community did in local news stories and personal ads, but reflecting that community's soul, its individualism, its creativity.

And it was successful. As Louis Menand writes in his 2009 New Yorker article, by 1967 the Voice was the US's best-selling weekly newspaper:

> with a single-day circulation higher than the circulations of ninety-five per cent of American big-city dailies. It survived the deaths of four other New York City newspapers and most of its imitators . . . . But, in books about the modern press, it is given a smaller role than it deserves.

Under Wolf's freewheeling editorship, the Voice became a repository for new writing and new writers – a place that accepted work other newspapers didn't want or know how to use.

Wolf wrote in 1962 that the weekly was "a living, breathing attempt to demolish the notion that one needs to be a professional to accomplish something in a field as purportedly technical as journalism". It was a statement that anyone could be a journalist and that great journalism was defined by great writing and a great story, not by the education and career path of the writer. It was the precursor to Vice, the antecedent of YouTube's vloggers.

Chapter 6 looks at some of the bloggers who have built profitable businesses from their approach to journalism, but what about the innovators developing not-for-profit journalism projects?

Paul Steiger was able to start up investigative journalism non-profit ProPublica in 2008 on the back of philanthropy from the Sandler Foundation. Today, alongside

42 New ideas and how they got here

continuing support from Sandler, around 3,000 individuals, foundations and charitable trusts support the 45-strong news team. ProPublica follows a model pioneered by the Center for Investigative Report, founded in 1977 by journalists Lowell Bergman, Dan Noyes and David Weir, and still going strong (recently re-branded as Reveal).

The Voice of San Diego (VoSD), launched by journalist Neil Morgan and entrepreneur Buzz Woolley in 2005, was the first local, online-only, non-profit news publisher in the US, mixing investigative journalism with participative reporting.

In 2009, venture capitalist John Thornton, Evan Smith (then editor of the Texas Monthly) and Ross Ramsey (Texas Weekly editor/owner) launched the digital-first, member-supported Texas Tribune, a model the Guardian in the UK would later pursue.

But VoSD and the Tribune are virtual babies next to New Internationalist magazine, launched way back in 1973 in the UK, and the Chicago Reporter founded by civil rights activist John McDermott in 1972.

The Correspondent (decorrespondent.nl) is one of several recent journalism start-ups to make use of crowdfunding. Launched in September 2013 by Rob Wijnberg, the Dutch start-up raised over a million euros from 19,000 donors in three weeks[4] to kick start the analytical and investigative journalism project. It continues to operate via a business model depending on member-supporters – at the time of writing, 40,000 of them paying 60 euros a year.

Aron Pilhofer is a fan; during our interview at the Guardian he said he talked about the Correspondent so much "people think I'm on their payroll!"

"What I think is amazing about what they did and are doing is the exemplar," he told me. "I think of how a journalist like Rob Wijnberg and a technologist like Ernst-Jan Pfauth can get together and say: 'All right, how can we make a go of very serious, in-depth journalism – the journalism we love and we know is essential. Journalism we know people will find essential. How can we create a model that works, commercially and editorially?' From launch through now, they had a plan."

CORRECT!V, a German non-profit working with data and investigative journalism, is using a similar model. Started by journalist/publisher David Schraven in 2014, it gives away much of its work for free in order to reach a bigger audience. From its website:

> We are one of the many answers to the media crisis. The old models of business are losing effectiveness. At the same time, journalists need to find better ways of explaining an increasingly complex world. Publishers are shutting down newspapers or cutting their budgets. Digital media has not been able to make up for this loss. The media has trouble fulfilling its watchdog role. CORRECT!V aims to change this.

Current plans include fundraising for a Haus des Gemeinnutzigen Journalismus, to combine bricks and mortar with journalism ideals in a building for non-profit journalism with editorial spaces, training, living space, hostels for international reporters and apartments.

Like the Correspondent, CORRECT!V's funding comes from donors, charities and foundations, principally (currently) the Brost Foundation of philanthropist publishers Erich and Anneliese Brost.

The non-profit journalism model has another recent addition kick started by philanthropy. In April 2016, the owner of the Philadelphia Inquirer Gerry Lenfest donated his media group and a $20 million endowment to a new, non-profit Institute for Journalism in New Media, part of the Philadelphia Foundation,[5] saying: "Of all the things I've done, this is the most important. Because of the journalism."

On and off the citizen journalism bus

Lenfest is not the only philanthropic entrepreneur to come up with new news models "because of the journalism". In May 2005, Arianna Huffington and ex-AOL executive Ken Lerer launched the Huffington Post (along with Jonah Peretti who went on to found BuzzFeed a year later) in order to deliver a politically left-leaning alternative to Matt Drudge's powerful and right-wing Drudge Report website.

In the event, HuffPost built its model less "because of the journalism" than through creating sticky news and viral stories, with early blog posts written by celebrities and not-so-famous contacts of Huffington, and a demonstrably different attitude to building traction (Shapiro, 2012).

Huffington, despite never having previously been an editor, became editor-in-chief, introducing a range of new journalistic ideas such as focusing on news aggregation with reporters summarising stories reported elsewhere, and using bloggers and community reporters to produce masses of content. An early web-only news baby, HuffPost pioneered search-engine-optimised headlines and the kind of A-B headline testing that The Washington Post now does with algorithms (as Eric Rich outlines in Chapter 1's case study).

I mentioned the Huffington Post's use of bloggers and community correspondents to provide large chunks of content. That idea – of using unpaid bloggers and volunteer reporters to fill space and expand geographical coverage – one that many news entrepreneurs have tried but always with limited success.

Sometimes referred to as "distributed reporting" or "citizen-assisted reporting" or "pro-am reporting", or Rusbridger's "open journalism" (see previous chapter), or "crowd-sourcing" (albeit each of those can mean slightly different versions of the public and journalists co-working on stories), the HuffPost's use of an army of on-the-ground volunteer correspondents enabled it to deliver masses of hyper-local content with its Off the Bus projects during the 2008 and 2012 US presidential elections.

Amanda Michel ran the 2008 Off the Bus project and wrote about the project[6] and the work of key contributor Mayhill Fowler. Fowler had scooped the "official" press pack during Obama's 2008 campaign by reporting from a private (i.e. off-record) event. She captured Obama's off-the-cuff criticism of "bitter" working-class voters in rural Pennsylvania. Inevitably the story became Bittergate. Michel praised Fowler as an example of what pro-am reporting could achieve:

> Collectively, we could do what a single reporter or traditional news organization could not. We dispatched people to report on dozens of events happening simultaneously around the country. We distributed research tasks among hundreds of volunteers, instead of a handful of paid reporters working full-time for weeks. Ground-level access, networked intelligence, and distributed labor became our editorial mainstays.

With more than 12,000 people and 1,700 writers participating in some way, Michel wrote, Fowler's Bittergate story "or something like it – was almost inevitable".

But by 2010, Fowler had stopped working for the Huffington Post, specifically because of lack of pay and support[7] and a year later, a group of bloggers brought (although ultimately lost) a class action lawsuit against the company arguing for payment for their work. Michel herself moved from Huffington Post to ProPublica (in 2009) and to the Guardian in 2011.

The Huffington Post wasn't AOL's first venture into community journalism, having previously bought Patch – a network of hyper-local online news sites – in 2009.

Patch was founded in 2007 by serial entrepreneurs Tim Armstrong, Warren Webster and Jon Brod. Armstrong had a track record in local newspapers and media sales, spotting the potential of online media and shifting to focus on it in the mid-1990s. Webster had been Director of Magazine Publishing at Gannett for three years, and Brod had been an early player at Ask Jeeves.

As with Netflix, Patch came about after a founder identified a problem that needed solving – the lack of community-level news and information, initially the lack of information about Armstrong's hometown of Riverside, Connecticut.[8] Armstrong became CEO of AOL and Patch came with him as part of the deal, along with co-founders Webster and Brod.

Patch stuttered – almost to a stop – within AOL, before being sold off to another company, Hale Global, in 2014, which promptly cut the workforce by four-fifths.[9] For the second time, Patch, and the hyper-local journalism model generally, was being written off by analysts who saw a system that just could not seem to scale from the single local project to a financially viable network.

Patch is in a bit of a fightback as I write. Its network of over 900 community-specific websites is reportedly in profit and traffic is healthy; boosted by email notifications to subscribers, traffic from Facebook and traffic – 70 percent of it – now coming from mobile devices. Changing technology has helped Patch's business model, keeping costs down and making it easier for readers to also be contributors of content. Armstrong told the Wall Street Journal: "The first version of Patch was very much local journalism, whereas the new version is more of a social, mobile and alerts platform."

And other entrepreneurs have entered the hyper-local network market – Mike and Lauryn Shapiro grew their single hyper-local site into a network of 50-plus franchises within the TAPinto network, while several journalists who lost their jobs in Patch's earlier culls are now successfully running their own hyper-local news products.[10]

By hanging on as other hyper-local news sites fell by the wayside (BackFence, for example[11]) and as the technology developed in ways that suited the hyper-local model, Patch and others may have been able to find space in a market that community journalism can profit from.

The lesson is that for new news models to work, or at least to work for longer than a couple of years, they need three things: an identity shared with their users; unique (or hard to find) content; an investor who's backing the journalism.

There are some interesting experiments out there already hitting those three buttons – Quartz (qz.com) for example. Its target users are businesspeople, particularly high-flyers who see themselves as part of the "new global economy" and spend a lot of time on portable devices – smartphones, tablets. That's the shared identity bit. The unique content comes from a journalism team focused on what would interest that user group ("core topics and knotty questions of seismic importance to business professionals", according to the About page). The investors backing that journalism are parent company Atlantic Media group keystone advertisers Chevron, Boeing, Credit Suisse and Cadillac (who also benefit from Quartz's native advertising expertise).

The danger for journalism however is that by trying to hit those three buttons, what can get lost is that commitment to public service, to go beyond informing an audience to speak truth to power. Any one of those three buttons could trigger the inclusion of bias, or the exclusion of large groups of the public.

CASE STUDY: BUZZFEED

The year after Jonah Peretti co-founded the Huffington Post, he launched another start-up – BuzzFeed. Its content was markedly different to HuffPost – more irreverent, generally lighter, aimed at a much younger audience – but the real significance was that BuzzFeed would ditch the idea that success is measured by visitors to your own site, in favour of measuring success by the impact of individual news stories.

BuzzFeed took the concept of cross-platform publishing but, instead of building lots of platforms or content "verticals" to carry their content, as traditional news companies were doing, the BuzzFeed model concentrates on pushing its stories out across social platforms built by others – Facebook, Twitter, YouTube, Snapchat, and so on. Visitors to BuzzFeed.com are irrelevant, what matters are visitors to a story.

And the ambition has grown from tracking and reflecting what makes a story viral to having a positive impact on the world through those stories, as Peretti told staff:

> Over the past decade, we have been witnessing an exciting evolution in the metrics that matter, from "impressions" to "clicks" to "shares" to "time spent" and now to "impact". We aren't building BuzzFeed

to get as many impressions or clicks or shares or time spent as we can. We are building BuzzFeed to have a positive impact on people's actual lives. Put another way, we measure our success by our scale multiplied by our impact.[12]

BuzzFeed UK's office, just off Oxford Circus in London, is a splicing together of buzzy new tech and busy newsroom. The techy side is in the cutesy naming of conference rooms after types of biscuit (cookies); the scattered toys and gizmos on desks and the visually flat hierarchy of a vast open-plan office. The newsroom side comes out in the piles of review books; the TVs set to news channels; the bashing of keys; the lack of chatter.

It's very cramped on my visit in the summer of 2016 – row on row of journalists and salespeople and editors and techs all squished together: no screen hidden.

Stuart Millar is Head of News. He walks me to our meeting room (Bourbon – the biscuit) telling me they currently employ around 100 people[13] – 40 or so on the news side and about 20 reporters in the London office, and desperately need to expand: "we'll probably knock through some walls."

Millar came from the Guardian, as did others at BuzzFeed UK including editor-in-chief Janine Gibson who left her job as the Guardian's deputy editor after losing out to Katharine Viner for the editorship. I asked him what was different about running the news operation at BuzzFeed.

"In a way, there's much less of a difference than I think I expected," he said. "Because fundamentally, it's about doing stories that are going to cut through the noise. That will engage the audience and make them react to it, and share it. You don't do that just by reproducing whatever's at the top of Google News or on PA – you have to actually break stories, or have really smart ideas.

"I think it's much more like when I launched Guardian US, where you're a small uncertaincy trying to cut through against big, established players. That's where you establish those principles that get to journalism, where you can't just do the same as everybody else. It's all about the second idea, or the third idea, or the better idea, or the bigger scoop. The Guardian is sort of ahead of the pack, of the traditional organisations, in having that approach."

The audience Millar is dealing with is younger than the Guardian's, around 75 percent Millennials, he says, and is mostly on social and mobile. The audience for BuzzFeed's mobile app is a bit older but "still in the mid-30s, rather than high 40s, which is where the Guardian was at".

That younger audience has shifted the news agenda too, with BuzzFeed chasing stories and types of stories that will engage them but are barely covered by the traditional media.

"Mental health is a huge issue. That's been bubbling up, even before I came here, that had been bubbling up as an issue. It's something that the vast Millennial audience is incredibly aware of and interested in and has a lot of personal experience of."

The ASOS investigation[14] too: "That was a perfect example of a story that hit two things that the audience cared about, which was a big brand and worker rights and working practices and conditions.

"I'm most proud of the fact that there were these two young reporters who'd never embarked on anything like this before, but they did an absolutely brilliant job over months and months and months of tracking people down. Really proper shoe-leather reporting. Winning their trust. Getting their stories. Persuading them to go on record. Putting it all together. Then a really difficult legal dance with ASOS and managing to get a story out there that just completely blew up and is still blowing up.

"Consumer brands, worker rights, mental health. The housing crisis, but not as in lots of stats or: 'Here's what's going to happen to mortgage rates.' Much more about the condition of rent accommodation and intergenerational stuff, where people might be able get on the housing ladder."

Delivering that more personalised, less "top-down, Whitehall-y" version of the news is a BuzzFeed thing, said Millar.

"We tend to bring a lot of empathy into how we cover things. What's our understanding of the experience, and try and reflect the experience.

"All the data shows that people will engage with stories and share them if they have that emotional reaction to them. That applies whether it's in news, or entertainment, or whatever. . . . I think what we're trying to do, and I think it's still is a work in progress, I don't think we've nailed it at all, is trying to make [the news] more human and real."

Different but also the same. When Millar and Gibson arrived, there wasn't a recognisable news desk system and the news team was inexperienced – young reporters at the start of their careers and lots of people from non-conventional journalistic backgrounds. Millar, Gibson and other new colleagues such as investigations head Heidi Blake, ex-Sunday Times, brought experience that has had an immediate impact on the quality of content produced by the UK team.

"One of the most important things we've been able to bring has just been us, really," said Millar. "Also, we know our way around the trickiest of stories and, therefore it means we can be more ambitious as to what we go after. Heidi had started already and was just starting the investigation team and Janine and I arrived and that's when we started to really dial up the more investigative, difficult end of the news market."

Millar's role includes involvement in the legal strategy for some of those "difficult" stories, along with Gibson, Blake and others, and leading the news strategy: reporting priorities, themes, key stories and newsroom operation.

"There's a rigorous desk side to it now," he added. "That was one of the things that I was, not surprised by, but most comforted by when I moved here from the Guardian, is that all this rigour and importance of reporting and source handling and trust; those issues are just as important as they were at the Guardian. It's got that sort of US robustness to the reporting, which I think's really important. People say: 'It's just a cat gif website' but actually the reporting's pretty bulletproof."

If Millar and his colleagues are trying to set a new news agenda for content, they are doing so based on a pretty radical distribution agenda. BuzzFeed distribution is about impact – sharing stories; discussing stories, rather than about clicks and page views.

"The thing at BuzzFeed is it's born out of sharing and it's never been about getting people to click on your site next to the display ad. Probably 18 months, two years ago, they recognised the way wind was blowing in terms of off-site, new platforms becoming way more important. So, they already made a whole bunch of changes in terms of Facebook and Snapchat and all those other channels.

"They have a whole data operation now that is about how to track content through those and understand why something that was published as a video on the site will blow up on Twitter, then Facebook, then it'll be shared as something else on Snapchat. They can track all that.

"The knowledge they have and the understanding of the way BuzzFeed content travels round the internet is a gazillion miles ahead of anything else I've seen. The Guardian had amazing data, but not anything like this."

Millar says this deep understanding of the content journey means not just following a story as it's blown around the internet, but knowing how you create content to give it the life you want it to have online: "Is it a 600-word post? Or is it a video for Facebook? Or what is the thing that will make this fly on Facebook as opposed to on Twitter, say? Those are editorial decisions as to the best way of doing a story."

That thinking goes further – not just what will people want to read or watch, but what will they want to share with their friends? BuzzFeed uses a success measure of its own called "social lift" to show how effective a piece has been in engaging people enough that they share it. It's the key measure for BuzzFeed, said Millar: "What people's reaction to the story is and their willingness to share it is much more important for us.

"Those stories that people share a lot is a level of engagement beyond they just clicked a link on Twitter. We're less interested in people clicking a link and then another link and then another link. It's much more about share and engage that way."

But why should that matter? What's the business case for BuzzFeed in monitoring shares rather than clicks on a story? Millar believes it's twofold: breaking strong stories builds a premium journalism reputation that brands want to be identified with, and those skills in knowing what works on social, what content people share and engage with, the "data smarts", cross over to the commercial team and the branded content they produce.

"That's been the BuzzFeed model," he said. "BuzzFeed sort of invented that internal ad agency sort of model. That's why we've been more immune to the collapse in digital ad sales because we do an entirely different thing." With a big wall between commercial and editorial: "on news we don't know what they're up to, and they're not allowed to know what we're up to."

The expansion of the UK office – that knocking through of walls – isn't only to create more desk space for the growing team, but to build two video studios. BuzzFeed had just announced a restructure to bring more video into the mix. Previously, there had been little relationship between BuzzFeed's editorial side, the New York "mothership", and its entertainment film studio in an old Fox Films studio in Los Angeles, said Millar. "If you needed news video, there was nobody to talk to."

But the changes were designed to embed video into both news and the entertainment material. "Now we're at the start of figuring out what news video works best for BuzzFeed," he said. "Many news organisations have been grappling with this question for years and haven't cracked it, so it'll be interesting."

News operations have jumped into video – the Guardian and the New York Times have produced some "amazing" work, said Millar, but video hadn't yet found a life online. However, short videos added to news stories were taking on a similar role to pictures.

"I think little bits of video are almost becoming like whether or not you have a picture in the story. Nobody'll think about reading a story now without a picture on it. Video's like that as well. There's a sort of expectation that it'll be there. The way Channel 4 has used clips with text rather than too much voice, and things that you can quickly skim through when you're sitting on the bus. They're very mobile-friendly, little mini-packages."

Jim Waterson joined BuzzFeed before Millar. As the politics editor he is, in many ways, a traditional "beat" reporter – culturing contacts, developing stories – but BuzzFeed's 16- to 36-year-old Millennial audience presents a particular challenge.

He told me: "I think if there's one thing that people get wrong with BuzzFeed is that they think there's a secret sauce where you could just take any old story, put a sort of nippy headline on it, and suddenly people are reading your court report. I think in reality it's much more about choosing a story that will go viral, and if the goods aren't there, then you can't make people read it."

Waterson came to BuzzFeed from City AM – a print-only publication – and had to learn how to deliver a story online. But BuzzFeed also gave him the journalistic freedom he wanted: "There's not the political party line to follow. There's not the feeling that you have to write up every select committee report, every speech, and every pronouncement."

FIGURE 3.1 Jim Waterson, BuzzFeed UK Politics Editor. Image supplied

A good political story for him is "exclusive, different or funny" – hit two of those and you're basically going viral, he said.

"I filed a piece at 2am this Saturday morning which did really well, which was on the US election and how the guy that Donald Trump had put up to defend him from allegations of groping was a British man who used to run an antique shop in York. That's an odd story. In a newspaper, that would probably be a box-out, like a hundred words: 'Doubts have been raised over him following this' because it would just be seen as like a side story, but instead I wrote probably eight hundred words on it, and it went really viral."

Just covering the allegations, rewriting stories that everyone already knows about, doesn't make sense in BuzzFeed-land: "avoiding rewrites is one of the main things". The aim is to go deeper on a story or find a different line; to fill the gaps that the traditional media are creating on big stories.

"You can still be tempted to fall into the trap of writing today's news," he said. "And sometimes you can also fall into the trap of forgetting that something is so big that our readers care about it regardless. We still need to write a story for BuzzFeed when the Prime Minister has resigned; you can't just ignore that. That is what our editor-in-chief Ben Smith would term 'commodity news' in the sense that everyone has got it and it's got almost no value as setting us apart.

"But there are certain things you just can't ignore because they're so big. The risk online, though, is that you end up writing too much commodity news and try to have a story on everything. Our rule is that you can still do the same stories everyone will have but you need to have an extra quote or new material."

The range of work Waterson and his colleagues produce ranges from long-form features (his behind-the-scenes feature on the failed Labour coup[15] was particularly well received) to short, newsy stories, to quizzes, to games, to the infamous "listicles".

When he joined BuzzFeed, there were no clear editorial directions – everyone was still working out what a BuzzFeed UK way of covering the news would mean. Waterson's early work was mainly lists: "'Twenty pictures of politicians when they were younger'; '21 pictures of politicians in wellies staring at floods': an early viral hit, and something I probably wouldn't do now but, if you look it up, it was great!"

BuzzFeed's "light piss-taking" style was so different and did really well because there was no competition, said Waterson. "The bar was quite low on being funny because you had all the political reporters, but they were still mainly doing the 'Story of the Day', while maybe being funny on their Twitter personal account. One thing I've noticed is essentially that's tipped to the point where the trivia story is now often better read and goes more viral than 'The Real Story'."

He worries that as a journalist he may be partly complicit in a shift to focusing on gossipy, identity politics online where a "This Tory MP was caught not tipping the waitress" story is read by more people than "This Tory MP is deeply concerned about the level of funding for homelessness".

But the "new political journalism" if such a thing exists he says, isn't politicians in wellies, or even lengthy backgrounders on the Labour coup, but perhaps a blurring of the lines between what Waterson calls the battle between Westminster bubble news cycle and the general news cycle, with political gossip and emotive statements by politicians becoming more well read, while interest in some aspects of traditional political coverage declines.

"There is the argument that 'horse race' journalism in Westminster is really unhealthy," he said. "However, we tend to find that people still really love reading it. As much as they say they wish it wasn't all about constantly trying to stir up internal battles; constantly trying to get people to brief against each other, I'm slightly defensive of that because people do seem to actually want it. The classic: 'I just want positive news.' No, you don't! 'I just want to read explainers and policy analysis.' No, you don't! You want to know what the thinking coming out of Jeremy Corbyn's office is."

Waterson also worries about the influence of Facebook on journalism, where "overtly partisan stuff" is rewarded by its algorithms, and straightforward political reporting isn't. Adding: "The pieces that tend to do well out of straight-down-the-line reporting are ones where you hit a target hard, but fairly – which is probably what we need to concentrate on. I do think it's slightly unhealthy that people only want to read things that are really going for their opponent because it just becomes a boxing match."

However, he thinks his audience is cleverer than they're sometimes given credit for.

"Frankly, you've got to accept that a large chunk of your audience is just going to Google stuff if they want information, so unless you're the only place with that information, why would they read you when there's already a well-written resource out there?"

Suggested assignments

Creative analysis

You are asked to identify a technology problem; what would make life easier for you if only someone had invented the technology, or come up with a better way of doing something? The problem can be as large or as small as you want, but focus on something that is not just irritating but a real pain or annoyance for you right now. Present your problem to the class along with your suggestion or idea for how to solve it.

Research project and creative thinking

Research and propose your own idea for a new content-led product. It can be in any format (e.g. website, app, print, SMS) or on any platform (e.g. on YouTube, Instagram, Snapchat) and delivering news or information that is new, or otherwise difficult to access, or is delivered in a different way, or is aimed at a particular audience/market. You will deliver your idea both as a three-minute pitch (as if to potential investors) and as a written proposal to include an analysis of the potential market and competitors for your idea.

Group analysis and creative thinking

Your group has been given the name of a large media or news organisation. Imagine how your company will look in 20 years' time. Bigger? Smaller? Delivering pretty much the same products as now or different ones? To the same audience/customers? Think about the changes you are living through right now as consumers of news and information and be as creative as you can in imagining how consumption of news may change in 20 years.

Notes

1. 'The brain behind Netflix', Daniel Schorn, December 1, 2006, CBS News.
2. 'Google's YouTube to let users choose ads with TrueView', Arif Durrani, December 1, 2010, Campaign.
3. Including the first (possibly) UK user-generated news website; the first UK web-to-print self-publisher; the first cocktail party in a box service. I tend to be good at the new ideas bit, not so good at the business execution bit.
4. 'How we turned a world record in journalism crowd-funding into an actual publication', Ernst-Jan Pfauth, November 27, 2013, Medium.
5. 'Lenfest donates newspapers, website to new media institute', January 12, 2016, philly.com.
6. 'Get off the bus: The future of pro-am journalism', Amanda Michel, March/April 2009, Columbia Journalism Review.
7. 'Why I left the Huffington Post', from Mayhill Fowler's blog: www.mayhillfowler.com.
8. '"Hyperlocal" web sites Deliver News without Newspapers', Claire Cain Miller and Brad Stone, April 12, 2009, New York Times.
9. 'Patch Rebounds after split from AOL', Jack Marshall, February 2, 2016, Wall Street Journal.
10. 'Grown from Patch: A crop of new hyper-local news sites has sprung up from AOL's failed platform', Laura Hazard Owen, November 4, 2015, NiemanLab.
11. BackFence's co-founder Mike Potts wrote an interesting piece on why he believed his user-generated, hyper-local news project failed. Among the reasons he gave was an inability to leverage social networking. 'Co-Founder Potts Shares Lessons Learned from BackFence Bust', July 16, 2007, MediaShift. Potts founded two further hyper-local projects – GrowthSpur and NewsPeg, neither of which are still running.
12. 'A cross-platform, global network', Jonah Peretti, October 23, 2015, BuzzFeed.
13. For comparison BuzzFeed UK launched in March 2013 with three staff members.
14. A three-month investigation into working practices at the retailer prompted an investigation by MPs and improvements to staff contracts: 'Asos has told staff it is changing contracts following workers' allegations', October 4, 2016, BuzzFeed.
15. 'How the labour coup failed', Jim Waterson, September 23, 2016.

References and further study

Menand, L. (2009) 'It took a village: How the voice changed journalism', *New Yorker*, 5 January 2009.

Shapiro, M. (2012) 'Six degrees of aggregation: How the Huffington Post ate the internet', *Columbia Journalism Review*, May/June 2012.

Young, W. J. (first published 1940, but several revisions and later editions) *A technique for producing ideas*, McGraw-Hill, New York.

More on American non-profit journalism examples here, at: www.americanpressinstitute. org/publications/reports/nonprofit-news/ and http://gijn.org/resources/investigative-journalism-organizations/

Author interviews

Stuart Millar, Head of News, BuzzFeed UK, October 2016
Jim Waterson, BuzzFeed UK, October 2016

4
AUDIENCE CHASING

In the old days, the audience came to us. They walked up to a news stand or a vendor or into a store and bought a newspaper. Maybe they filled in a coupon to get it delivered; posting back a cheque every now and then, or popping into the corner shop to pay their bill. When radio arrived in the 1920s, they did the same thing – switched on the set and waited for the news programme to start. TV arrived and they sat down to watch the news at a time dictated by the schedule.

Obviously, the newspapers and broadcasters still had to attract that audience; persuade them to buy their newspaper rather than a rival's, or tune their radio to one channel rather than another. But they had habit on their side – regular newspaper buyers buy the same newspaper regularly. We don't generally flit between the Daily Mail one week and the Guardian the next; we pick a side.

In the 1950s our radios became small and portable and we began to take them with us. News on the radio travelled with us – in our car, on to beaches, into shops and workplaces. TV never had that same portability boom. Even the early "portable" TVs (Figure 4.1) were really just smaller, transistorised TVs used in secondary locations – like bedrooms or caravans; we didn't walk around with them balanced on our shoulders like 1980s boomboxes.[1]

While we may have watched films and boxsets on DVDs played on our laptops, or pressed into car players to keep backseat children amused, TV news didn't get its portability moment until the internet, and more specifically the development of wireless digital networks, made watching on our phones and tablets easy. Those big two wheels on the truck of change rolled in – technology and behaviour – and suddenly we're spending twice as long each day on our smartphones as on our laptops[2] – including catching up on TV news on our phones.

The technology changed to deliver mobile phones with massively more memory, with everywhere web access, cheaper data streaming – and our behaviours changed

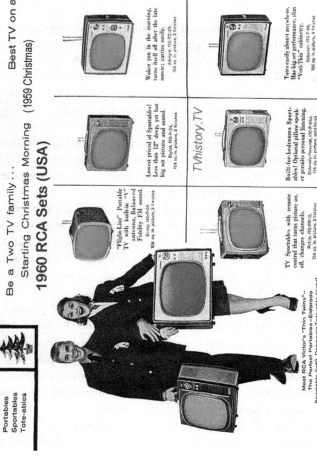

FIGURE 4.1 1960s' advert from RCA (Radio Corporation of America). Company no longer exists. Image supplied by www.tvhistory.tv

alongside. We demanded bigger phones with bigger screens (bye-bye, little clam phones); we demanded more and cheaper data (hello, mobile contract competition). We used our phones to seamlessly move between our social world – checking in with our Facebook Friends, and our inner world – watching that YouTuber who thinks like us; reading that book we don't want people to see we're reading.

Once we were out there, let loose on the World Wide Web with all of its sparkle and magic and madness to attract our attention, the news media had to come and find us. They had to come to where we were spending our time. As Ryan Kellett, in charge of audience growth at The Washington Post, put it when I interviewed him for this chapter's case study: "It's not going to happen naturally, there is so much information and news out there we [the publishers] have to think hard about what are the ways people find us?"

It's stopped being about building a website and trying to persuade your potential audience to visit it, instead – as the BuzzFeed case study illustrated – it's about getting your audience to find a particular story and read it, and share it, maybe follow a link back to another of your stories, or see an ad from one of your advertisers, or deliver a bit of tracking data your advertiser might find useful.

News, as Chapter 8 explores further, has become atomised. It's at the story level, even the sub-story level (headline and first par – that little clip that gives you the bones of the story without clicking "more") rather than at web page level.

News publishers have to persuade people to read their story or watch their video, effectively to access that publisher's version of the news or interpretation of what is news. And at the same time, that publisher has to find a way to make money from an audience that is likely already being milked by Facebook or wherever they came across the story.

I have this picture in my head when I think of trackers and cookies on web content of that scene in *The Matrix* film when reality is revealed to Neo as millions and millions of humans plugged into the alternate "life" of the matrix while their bodies are used as batteries to power the Machines and their world.

Dystopian analogies aside, the internet isn't an evil network but it has become a much more difficult space for news content to roam around. What we have today is a web packed with content that is increasingly tethered – hundreds and hundreds of invisible links between that piece of information and its publisher and its carriers and its trackers and cookies and all the companies and agencies that might have an interest in where it goes and who sees it and, crucially, what they do next.

SEO and "micro-propaganda networks"

So, you have that great story you produced as a freelancer for, say, Vice. A decent video about Europeans volunteering to fight on the Syrian frontline against Daesh, for example.[3]

It's a story that should be told, that you believe people should hear. Seeing the sacrifices of people who are like them might prompt your target audience to think deeply or differently about the Syrian civil war. Sure, your video will play on Vice's core site with its 25 million-plus monthly visitors.[4] But it'll be fighting for space in the News section with every other story; maybe not even get a front or top-of-page billing, particularly as it gets overtaken by newer news. And what about all those people out there who would be interested in this story but who don't visit vice. com – how do you reach them?

As soon as we started to look at content as something in itself, as the story separate to the news website (or newspaper or any other media), we began to look at how we could make it more likely that our story became the one that people saw at the top of Google's search results when they went looking for a news subject.

And so, SEO – search engine optimisation – was born.

Actually, it wasn't. No-one is quite certain when SEO became a thing or who invented the term[5] (although back in 2007, Jason Gambert caused a furore in webland when he tried to trademark the term) but there have been references to it as both a name and a concept since the mid-1990s, when website builders and marketers first began to realise there was a link between how often you used your client's name on their web page and how soon it appeared on the first page in Google in a search on that name.

However, it took a while before SEO became a whole industry and a while longer before news editors and journalists started crafting story headlines to get a particular story, rather than the name of their newspaper, into the top results on Google.

So, going back to that great video you made about Europeans fighting in Syria: obviously one of the things you'd do is SEO the heck out of it. What are your keywords, i.e. what are the nouns (mostly) and verbs someone might use if they were searching for a story on that subject? Syria, volunteer fighters, non-Syrians fighting, Syrian war, mercenaries in Syria, Germans fighting in Syria, Brits fighting in Syria, Kurdish resistance? You get the idea.

Google even helps you to find the most productive keywords, through tools such as Keyword Planner – designed to help small businesses get more benefit from AdWords, but just as useful when setting up a new website or checking you've picked the most likely or currently trending versions of keywords for your story.

The true art of SEO is second-person insight – what is someone who isn't you and doesn't think like you but who might be interested in what you have to say on this subject, likely to type into a search engine when they don't already know about your story?

Much of the time SEO is easy. Someone is searching for the result of the latest New York Yankees match. They could go to the Yankees' website but why bother? Just type "New York Yankees" into Google (Figure 4.2) and there it is. You don't even need to click on any of those news stories from ESPN or the New York Times because Google has helpfully given you the result at the top of the page, in a tidy little box-out, with a sidebar of further information. Just like it might look in a newspaper.

But perhaps better than newspapers because there's an embedded video with game footage, courtesy of YouTube (owned by Google) and MLB.com (Major League Baseball's official body). You don't get embedded video in a newspaper. At least not yet.

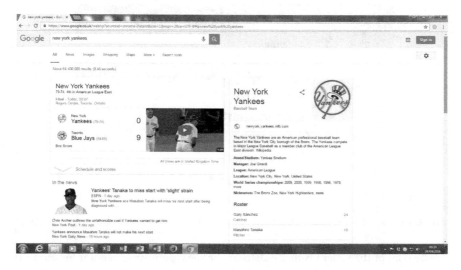

FIGURE 4.2 Googling "New York Yankees" delivers this helpful – or directed – grouping of results. Screenshot taken September 24, 2016.

As Google iterated and developed its search bar we got more and more used to asking Google to take us direct to the story and less likely to go via a news website. But with that power over which stories we choose to visit comes responsibility. Jonathan Albright is one of several academics currently researching how Google (and Facebook) algorithms drive us towards particular news stories and, more worryingly, how those algorithms can be "gamed" to push us towards false stories or extreme viewpoints.

Albright has written about a "micro-propaganda network" of thousands of small sites producing fake, misleading or hyper-biased news "bleeding through" the web:

> These sites have created an ecosystem of real-time propaganda: they include viral hoax engines that can instantly shape public opinion through mass "reaction" to serious political topics and news events. This network is triggered on-demand to spread false, hyper-biased, and politically-loaded information.[6]

Research psychologist Robert Epstein, who studies how search results might influence people's views and opinions, and affect voting patterns, has called Google "the most powerful mind-control machine ever invented."

That quote is from a feature by journalist Carole Cadwalladr (2016) which focused on the algorithms driving Google's predictive text search, whereby typing a word or two into the Google page title bar will "predict" what you are searching for. (See "References and further study" and Chapters 5 and 10 where I return to the issue of so-called fake news).

60 Audience chasing

FIGURE 4.3 Screenshot taken October 8, 2016, of results of Google search for "Syria".

The core of the system is that it delivers the most popular searches in relation to the words you've started to type. So, if we start typing "Syria" into the search bar at the top of the web page (see Figure 4.3), Google would predict what we're most likely to be looking for, based on what other people searched for. As an example, on October 8, 2016, Google told us that more people[7] were searching for information on Syrian hamsters than on Syrian refugees.

Anyway, back to our Syria fighters video: the one that took us months to set up, making contacts, organising trip details, persuading someone to cover the costs, convincing our partner and mother that we'd done everything possible to return alive. How do we get our video seen by that random person searching on Google for related subjects?

The point is that nowadays we don't. Google doesn't really factor in those circumstances. Just as I made the point earlier in this chapter that newspapers had habit on their side in their search for readers – both regulars and non-regulars picked the newspapers they usually bought – so our web behaviour has become habitual.

That's driven by the mobile technology we now mostly use to access the web. Small screens make browsing Google and typing in a bunch of keywords more of a pain. It's easier to download a handful of apps from sites we like or trust, built to make it easy to read and find stuff that interests us. In many ways, it's a repeat of picking a side in our newspaper reading or leaving our radio tuned to one favourite channel. Habit formation makes day-to-day living easier; it stops us wasting time on frequently made choices (do I have tea or coffee first thing in the morning?) and embeds new behaviours. We make our morning coffee; we switch on the computer; we check our email first. Before long that routine becomes a habit we have to consciously break: "I really have to get on with writing that book so when I switch on this morning, I will *not* check emails until midday."

Except the biggest habit news publishers are having to deal with is the 118 minutes a day[8] we spend checking in and browsing social media. If that potential audience for our Syria video is spending increasing amounts of their time on

Facebook, if two-thirds of them use Facebook for news[9] and one in ten people get most of their news from social media (and 28 percent of 18- to 24-year-olds), sticking our Syria video on our website and hoping potential viewers will come to us is wilfully ignoring how news works nowadays. It has to be found on Facebook.

Facebook: where our Syria video is fighting for attention among viral cat memes, and conversations between friends, and photos from that party everyone went to, and arguments about Metal Gear Solid, and mistaken facts and made-up stories and a whole bunch of true and untrue and truth-like content that means that, even if your target viewer watches your video via Facebook, they may have this little voice inside them asking: "Is this real? When did this happen? Who is this reporter? Who do they really work for? Can I trust what they're telling me?"

Hopefully, hopefully they will have that little voice.

Bursting filter bubbles

So, that "getting-on-Facebook" thing. That's where things really get messy. At least with Google you had two things on your side in getting your Syria video to your potential audience. Firstly, that your audience might be searching the web, via Google, looking for news stories similar to yours. Which gives you a fighting chance in getting your story found by using that second advantage – SEO and keywords – to push the story towards them.

But Facebook isn't a search engine and its mission isn't to deliver what its users are searching for; its mission is to encourage users to tell each other stuff they mostly already know, "to share and express what matters to them".[10] On Facebook it's Friends who "help us discover the world when we connect"[11] – not the media.

In theory, that should make sense – who is more trustworthy than a friend? In 2007, Zuckerberg told an audience of advertisers and press[12] that Facebook's commercial potential would be based on the "Holy Grail" of trusted referral: "Nothing influences people more than a recommendation from a trusted friend." And if a friend suggests we watch this video about Syrian fighters, or sign this petition about human rights or perhaps Like this meme about refugees "flooding" Britain, do we pay more attention?

Fernback (1997: 42) said that identity and democracy are found in cyberspace not so much in what we say in our virtual communities, "but within the actual structure of social relations". So, the relationships and networks articulated in Facebook have value alongside what we might say to each other. Who we listen to, who we trust in our social networks, is an important factor in how we think and act.

Katz and Lazarsfeld found we are more likely to be influenced by people we know if we associate with them frequently, and if they share our norms and standards, and if we have shared access to the same sources of information (1955, Katz, 1957). These three parameters apply to the majority of communication on Facebook where the architecture is designed to encourage us to interact and share content with friends and family with whom we share current or past association, or common interests.

Facebook is built in such a way that weak-tie links between people are encouraged (half of all Facebook users have more than 200 Friends on the platform) and Facebook itself determines the nature of the social contact (Lewis and West, 2009). Facebook is not just enabling communication with people users more or less know, it is giving users a route into a public sphere that traditional media had previously controlled. Kirkpatrick quotes Chris Cox, then vice president of product at Facebook, in an interview: "We want to give to everyone that same power that mass media has had to beam out a message" (2010: 296).

But what if that message is wrong, or misinterpreted – deliberately or otherwise? Several academics have pointed to our willingness to believe a convenient untruth or a truth-like statement, rather than have our biases or perceptions challenged. Psychologist Daniel Kahneman, in his book *Thinking, Fast and Slow* (2011) defined as "cognitive ease" our avoidance of facts that would challenge our brains to think deeper or work harder. Eli Pariser's "filter bubble"[13] warned against the race to personalise our web experience, arguing the result would be delivering a bias towards news we seemed to prefer, rather than stories that would challenge us.

That filter bias extends to social media – not only a growing source of the news we receive, but a source 24 percent of us already use to regularly share news stories – and predominantly sharing news we approve of or agree with,[14] according to a Reuters Institute report. Except, it seems, in the UK where we're more likely to share things we don't like.

So, back to our Syria video. We know we have to get it onto Facebook – it's where a big chunk of our potential audience, particularly our younger and female audience, is discovering news stories. We also know that at least a quarter of them will share our video with other people on Facebook who are likely to also be interested in our story. But how do we get it in front of that Facebook audience?

The first option is that we add it to our Facebook page – maybe our personal one as a journalist as well as our publisher's page. As the interviews at the end of this chapter explore, publishers such as the Guardian and BuzzFeed may use their Facebook site as a launch pad for stories into Facebook but are not able to rely on it as a route – not least because it's based on users Liking or following a page in order to have that content appear in their News Feed.

And there's no guarantee that any particular post will make it into a particular Facebook user's News Feed. Constantly tweaked algorithms select what Facebook believes will most interest each user – from posts by favoured Friends to news stories more of your Friends have shared to paid-for content Facebook thinks is more likely to be relevant to you. It prioritises "engagement" – content that will keep you coming back and spending more of your time on Facebook. Because if the algorithm can't do that, if it keeps showing content you're not interested in or posts from people you don't care about, you'll visit Facebook less often.

Facebook is pretty clear that its mission is to provide the most personally relevant content, and that means posts from Friends and family get a higher priority[15] than posts from organisations and pages users follow.

This focusing on share-able content, coupled with rising numbers of Facebook users and rising number of posts (i.e. competition for attention), means an inevitable decline in how many people will see a news story.[16] News organisations such as the Guardian and BuzzFeed try to tackle this by posting stories to Facebook frequently – roughly every half hour at the Guardian (see case study). Frequent posting also helps visibility because Facebook normally prioritises newness of posts, i.e. how "timely"[17] a post is in relation to an individual user, their Friends, and stories highlighted as trending topics on Facebook.

Thus, if things are happening in Syria to the extent that lots of Facebook users are engaging with the issues by posting what they think, sharing posts, Liking or commenting on posts, following related pages, clicking on related sponsored content (e.g. charity appeals) and watching related videos,[18] then you stand a decent chance of getting your Syria news story video seen and shared.

That is, as long as you repost it at least every hour during that "timely" window – and with a selection of titles which are different enough not to be spotted by the Facebook algorithm as trying to "game" the system, but which nevertheless contain enough of the keywords that mean the system will know your video is about that subject those users are interested in.

Oh, and add a big picture and some uppercase keywords. Sonya Song's research (2013) into which Boston Globe stories were shared most on Facebook found using words like BREAKING, WEATHER WATCH, MAJOR UPDATE, or NOW LIVE in your headline, along with a large-size image had a positive, direct effect on story traffic.

For the companies invested in getting our attention through social – not so much news organisations but the advertisers, government agencies and charities that see social as a more direct route to an audience, a whole new attention economy has grown up. Where we had SEO, now we have Paid Social and content segmentation for each platform. Different video clips for Facebook compared to Vine compared to Instagram compared to YouTube – all "native" (i.e. ads that don't look like ads), and talked about by social media "influencers" (often paid) with millions of followers.

Every story headline you write has to be written for both people and for algorithms. The algorithm will decide whether people get to see your headline; people will decide whether your headline is interesting enough to make them click to read your story or watch your video. Here's an example from my interview with Chris Moran, Editor Strategic Projects at Guardian News and Media:

> There was a real moment for me when I noticed a ten-year-old piece [a Guardian op-ed column] that never got any traffic at all before, so it was pre-optimisation, suddenly got a lot of traffic from Reddit.
>
> The headline in print, which had been naturally taken over into digital was 'Deep Thinkers', which is a lovely print line. The guy on Reddit who had made this suddenly be read had headlined it: 'If dolphins ever get out of

the water, we're fucked.' While obviously swearing is kind of cheeky, it's kind of wonderful. It sold the piece significantly better than we could have done.

For many news organisations, that extends to producing more than one headline for a story and A-B testing which gets the most attention and then, as in The Washington Post's case, using an in-house algorithm to pick the "winning" headline. And doing all of that in a space where clever dolphin features and Syrian fighters videos are competing for attention with advertising disguised as news, harrowing charity videos and spin-doctored political memes.

Truth, or something more comfortable?

If all of this sounds like a lot of work – multiple headlines, different keywords for search vs social, keeping up with changes to Facebook's News Feed algorithm – you're right, it is. And the job of the journalist has got tougher. Not only because we're competing on a playing field that levels out our Syria news video with "what I'm eating right now" photos from family and friends, but because we're often dealing with an audience who trusts their own judgement more than they trust ours:

> [I]t was clear that many active internet users now see themselves as editors – balancing and comparing multiple sources, multiple editorial judgements, and even multiple platforms.
>
> *(Reuters Institute, 2016: 12)*

Let's stay with that thought for a while longer. Is it a bad thing that a chunk of that audience for our Syria video thinks they're better placed to decide whether it's a story worth watching rather than us? That Reithian BBC mission to "inform, educate and entertain" implies a "we know what's good for you to know" approach that fell apart long ago, and perhaps never really existed in the sense of complete trust between news producers and news consumers.

Richard Sambrook, former head of the BBC's Global News Division, wrote of a modern, digital journalism concerned with verification, assertion, affirmation and interest groups. In relation to our Syria story, we might explain these as verification = this is proof this happened and why it happened; assertion = this just happened; affirmation = this happened because of this political point of view; interest group = this group paid me to make this video.

> In recent years, the journalism of verification has been in retreat as business models have broken down, traditional media have closed, and those that survived fought harder for a share of public attention. These conditions have encouraged the journalism of affirmation and assertion to maximise impact, leading to increased partisanship.
>
> *(Sambrook, 2012: 15)*

Craig Silverman went further in his research on how false stories spread around the internet:

> Rather than acting as a source of accurate information, online media frequently promote misinformation in an attempt to drive traffic and social engagement. The result is a situation where lies spread much farther than the truth, and news organizations play a powerful role in making this happen.
>
> *(Silverman, 2015)*

Indeed, the 2016 Reuters digital news report is one of several recent surveys pointing to decreasing trust in journalists, even when people say they trust the news organisation itself (i.e. we may say we trust the BBC's version of the news, but that we don't necessarily trust what its journalists tell us, or trust its editors' choice of what we should know).

Gallup found that Americans' trust in the mass media had declined from 55 percent having a "great deal" or a "fair amount" of trust in the media in 1999, to just 40 percent by 2015[19] – i.e. that one in six Americans didn't trust the media to tell them the truth (or perhaps to tell them an acceptable version of the truth). In the same period, Gallup found that Americans had also lost trust in federal government (only 38 percent trusted their government to tackle domestic problems). There's a similar pattern in the UK, with just 21 percent in 2016 trusting politicians to tell them the truth, against 25 percent trusting journalists.[20]

That loss of trust becomes a problem because the two are linked: journalists are the bridge between people and state, reporting what politicians do and say; reporting what voters think and say. Habermas (1962/1989) defined this as the public sphere: "people's public use of their reason" (1989: 26) within a network for communicating information and points of view between state and society, wherein public opinion is formed" (1991: 31). Or as James Carey put it:

> When democracy falters, journalism falters, and when journalism goes awry, democracy goes awry.
>
> *(2001: 19)*

If people lose trust in politicians as a result of stories by journalists (Watergate to Moatgate[21]) and trust in journalists, as the authors of truth, subsequently increases, that's a good thing. But if journalists and editors persistently tell the public that not only can they not trust their politicians but they can't trust any other professional group or "expert", the public will include journalists in that group of experts not to be trusted.

The job of journalists, as Chapter 10 argues further, is to report and inform, not to invent and direct. We're the Fourth Estate: our place is to stand in the middle, in between our public and the state. When journalists and editors decide it's OK to affirm that people who have spent their lives studying a particular issue are just

I AGREE THAT EACH IS A GOOD WAY TO GET THE NEWS
ALL COUNTRIES

36% Automatically based on what I've read before

30% Judgement of editors or journalists

22% Automatically based on what my friends have consumed

More people say that personalised algorithmic news is a good way to get the news compared to editors and journalists.

Algorithms based on friends' consumption least preferred.

People think *they* are the best judge of what's important to them.

Q10D_2016a_1/2/3: Indicate your level of agreement with the following statements: Having stories selected for me by editors and journalists is a good way to get news/ Having stories automatically selected for me on the basis of what I have consumed in the past is a good way to get news/Having stories automatically selected for me on the basis of what my friends have consumed is a good way to get news. Base: Total sample

Reuters Institute for the Study of Journalism

FIGURE 4.4 Reuters Digital News Report, 2015.
Credit: Reuters Digital News Report 2015.

making up facts to suit politicians, that those clever people in the class are really out to get you, we shouldn't be surprised if people decide it's safer to be their own news editor, or to replace editors with algorithms – as in Figure 4.4, from the Reuters report into digital news use.

Which brings me neatly back to the algorithms that control what news stories we get to see online, particularly via social media. If the Facebook News Feed gets its nourishment from user actions – Likes, shares, comments and how long we spend reading a story – it's inevitable that fake stories[22] that are "truth-like" stand just as good a chance of getting to the top of our News Feed or the trending topics list as real news.

Facebook's News Feed mission is to "connect people with the stories that matter to them most".[23] But what if what matters to you are the stories you'd *like* to hear – the news you wish was real, the stories that affirm your view of the world, good or bad?

> Our aim is to deliver the types of stories we've gotten feedback that an individual person most wants to see. We do this not only because we believe it's the right thing but also because it's good for our business. When people see content they are interested in, they are more likely to spend time on News Feed.
> *(Facebook)*[24]

Facebook provides advice pages and a video guide to help us get our Syria video to its users, including advising we write "compelling" headlines and using its Publisher Tools, particularly audience optimisation to suggest the preferred audience for a particular post. The system also asks you to use "interest-based tags" to reach people interested in that topic.[25] It's not perfect (and given Facebook's relentless new ideas turnover there's a good chance it may have gone or been replaced by the time you read this) but it can help.

Other things that may also currently help are posting a video, linking to content originated in Facebook (e.g. other pages, posts and videos) and responding to real-time metrics – Facebook, like Google, produces plenty of tools to help you find out not only how many people saw your Syria video but who they were (e.g. gender, age, location) and how much of the video they watched.[26] If it's not going well, you have the opportunity to re-headline it, re-tag it and re-post it. Think A-B headline testing.

So, having read this section, you may now be thinking that the best way to get our Syria video out there in Facebook land is to add a headline for the US such as: 'SHOCKING: the real truth about Obama and Isis in Syria', and in the UK perhaps: 'SHOCKING: how dogs are being forced to fight to the death in Syria.'

Except Facebook isn't keen on such "clickbait" headlines because its users don't like them:

> People have told us they like seeing authentic stories the most. That's why we work hard to understand what type of stories and posts people consider genuine, so we can show more of them. . . . We also work to understand what kinds of stories people find misleading and spammy to help make sure people see those less.[27]

How that works is that headlines where a user is likely to click, then discover the story isn't what the headline suggests and quickly stop watching/reading, are less likely to be distributed to users. In addition, Facebook says it's been trying to tweak its algorithm to weed out headlines with clickbait-y words or phrases (that "SHOCKING:" is probably a giveaway).

But none of that matters. There's only one reason why the headline we add to our Syria video will tell the viewer exactly what it's about, in a clear yet compelling way – because we're journalists, and we have a story people need to hear. So, here's our headline:

> 'VIDEO: on the front line in Syria with the international volunteers fighting ISIS'

We might A-B it to target particular groups or the demographics of particular platforms (e.g. 'with the Brit volunteers fighting ISIS', or 'with teenage volunteers fighting ISIS'), or perhaps go uber-social with something like: 'This mum left her children to fight ISIS on the frontline, here's why'. Just as long as our headline is supported by the video content.

For every new headline, hashtags and audience tags would also be tweaked and changed. And we would watch – and learn from – which ones were most effective.

As I said earlier: hard work. But also worth it. The one thing that all this thinking about keywords and headlines and tracking stats does for a journalist is make us really concentrate, more than we've had to in the past, on our audience. Who out there is going to be interested in this story? Where are they, what else are they into, how do they think?

Jim Waterson, BuzzFeed UK's politics editor told me he used to be "obsessed" with the stats on his stories, but not now: "I care much more if the right people are tweeting and sharing."

Social media has made the job of a journalist harder but also better. Our potential audience is massively larger, global, frequently more news "savvy" and encouraged to be more engaged with news. A strong story, with a clear and compelling headline, will be shared by people who believe that story and want other people to see it too. Our audience has become our publisher.

CASE STUDY: RYAN KELLETT AND CHRIS MORAN (THE WASHINGTON POST, GUARDIAN NEWS AND MEDIA)

Ryan Kellett and Chris Moran have pretty much the same job – at least that was how I saw it after meeting each of them, 3,665 miles apart. Basically, they measure audience, come up with better ways to measure audience, and help their colleagues get used to measuring audience. Kellett is Director of Audience Growth at The Washington Post; Moran is Audience Editor at the Guardian.

What they mostly have in common is the belief that it's not so much the numbers in terms of straight view count that matters, but the quality: how long did people read/watch that piece; what did they do next; when did they come back? The numbers should inform the journalism but not define it.

For Kellett and The Washington Post, it's about "entry points".

"We talk on my team a lot about entry points for the person who has never read a Washington Post article before; how did they find us? What is the very first time they interacted with something Washington Post–related?

"That first touch point is really important to me, and I think over time – this is a little bit of a business and marketing way of thinking about it – you want to surround people with touchpoints that make sense to them and give them other opportunities to come into our universe here."

Having found their way to The Post, they become part of what Kellett calls the "analytics narrative" of where that individual came from; what they did while they were on the site; and where they went next: "Especially numbers one and three in that equation".

And that's something The Washington Post expects its reporters to care about too: "If you're an everyday reporter who has a beat and covers something for us, we want you to know very clearly where people are coming from, where people are going to."

The goal is to encourage readers to move from one story onto another, to drive them "deeper into our universe, The Washington Post universe".

However, the journey to getting reporters to engage with that analytics narrative wasn't straightforward for either Kellett or Moran. When Moran started with the Guardian in 2009, there was a "huge amount of resistance" to the idea of driving traffic to the website and learning how to attract a web audience.

"My key job back then was to improve reach through Google chiefly, by making sure we were running headlines that made sense in search. What really fascinated me about that job was, we called ourselves the media, and we showed no inclination at all to treat this completely new medium differently from print. In fact, we defined a good headline as being a print headline."

The suspicion from journalists and editors back then was that driving audience through optimising headlines meant clickbait – something Moran dislikes too.

"We talk about something called 'responsible reach'. My belief is that people do want good journalism on the internet, but you have to let them find it. My job was never to warp our editorial mission. In fact, I had to be incredibly careful about not doing that. . . . I'm always incredibly careful about making sure that that input goes through editors. I've seen this story: it's knocking around; it's interesting; we haven't covered it; you make of that what you will."

Moran approached the small digital development team at the Guardian and told them he needed their help – he couldn't do his job pushing stories through search because he didn't know what worked in terms of audience because he couldn't see any audience data: "I realised that I needed the data first of all to establish best practice for me, and then secondly, to convince other people that it was actually worth doing this."

The digital approach back then was focused on Twitter: "One of the first things I had to point out to people was that Twitter was about a tenth of the size of our audience coming to us through search." Twitter was a useful tool for the Guardian's journalists but didn't warrant the effort being put into working it.

Moran approached Graham Tackley, then the Guardian's head of architecture: "His job was to sit next to the servers and make sure on a big traffic day they didn't decide to fall over. He said: 'I know who's coming into our site and I think, at the end of the day, I might be able to do something for you.'"

What Tackley did for Moran was build a simple SEO dashboard tool that meant he could see the last three minutes of activity data on every article on the website.

"I could launch a story on there and I had a little graph that said: 'That's Google traffic, and there's Twitter, and there's Guardian traffic.' It genuinely was like a light bulb being turned on. It was transformative."

They carried on working on and refining the dashboard, adding to it and changing it, gradually realising that what they were doing was key to understanding this digital media world, "and that really, almost every decision I was seeing being made was broadly speaking a weird gut instinct. Nobody actually knew."

Moran was working from his desk in the news desk area of the newsroom and people began to notice what he was looking at ("Wow, those people from Japan are looking at this article") and get involved – making suggestions, following stats.

"It turned into something which is now called Ophan," he said. "That's our real-time data platform. It now gives you 15 days of data. It has less than a two-second lag, so when somebody clicks, it's in there. It processed two billion pieces of data, I think, last week, and it's open to everybody at the Guardian. Incredibly, over 1,000 people a month at the Guardian use it. That penetration is unlike any other organisation in the world. What we tried to do is build a data tool that is not an act of aggression towards journalists – that is genuinely useful and supports them."

Access is simple; it's available inside and outside the Guardian's several offices, on mobile and desktop. It looks at page views ("pure reach"), attention time ("still a better indication of quality than anything else"), but also monitors activity by regular visitors (a key target demographic for the Guardian for conversion to membership).

What was clear fairly quickly was how much of the Guardian's output wasn't being seen at all online because no work had gone into promoting it. The story was written, published and then often ignored. But on Ophan, a journalist or editor could see exactly what happened to the story after it hit the web – which offices tweeted it, whether it went to Facebook – and push Moran and his team to promote it.

The section editors handle stories on the Guardian websites; Moran's team handles the main Twitter accounts and the Guardian's own Facebook account "which is a significant lever". Exclusive content works well on Facebook for the Guardian, as does content which has a longer shelf-life. Stories that may quickly die away on Twitter can live longer in the slower environment of Facebook.

"The news is not inherently share-able," Moran said. "In fact, quite the opposite. Generally, if you treat Facebook like Twitter and just post breaking news, you'll get a reaction like Twitter: big spike followed by an inevitable decay fast. To activate Facebook, you need a piece which will continue to run. That's why we often focus more on opinion than news [on Facebook]."

But it isn't enough to simply monitor the figures – stories colouring up green to show hits from search or blue for direct views on the Guardian's website or aquamarine for Twitter. As with Kellett at The Washington Post, Moran is looking for results that show a positive effect on audience growth as well as reach. How frequently a visitor comes back to the Guardian – on the day Moran and I looked at the figures, 34 percent had visited seven days out of seven.

"The ideal by the end of the day would be to have a lot of sevens, indicating it's quite good journalism, but also a lot of ones, as in a new audience who might start a relationship with us. Because my view is the best way of establishing new loyal readers is actually to give them our best journalism."

Other colours signify how long a reader stayed with a story, or whether a reader went from that Guardian piece to another – both key metrics for the team. Attention time is measured on an active basis – only counting when human activity is detected – and is contextualised against the average reading time of the piece. High bounce may not mean a story is boring, it may mean the story isn't what the reader expected, or that it's being shared a lot rather than read. "Data-informed, not data-led", as Moran says.

What is clear is that, at both the Guardian and The Washington Post, accurate audience monitoring has revealed how Google search and keywords have become part players in driving audience, rather than the lead player. Building a brand that brings people direct to your website, your Twitter feeds, your Facebook pages; driving people to stories through social media sharing and linking; pushing stories to subscribers through mobile apps or email – these are the new basket of audience drivers.

Moran said: "Five years ago, I was being asked in a conference, why should we be relying just on one major technical giant, and isn't it dicey that we're tagging along on Google? Now interestingly people are saying the same thing about Facebook. Of course, all of those concerns are correct, but at the very least, we now have somebody who is actually challenging Google."

He is critical however of Facebook's constantly changing algorithm and the company's lack of interest in the content they expect news providers to deliver. His argument is that quality journalism should matter to Facebook – that it improves Facebook's platform too, and should be made more visible: "They have to rethink it. I think we should be bullish about asking them to rethink it."

Moran's team may check headlines for stories and tweak them, but (unlike The Washington Post and BuzzFeed) they don't A–B auto-optimise them and journalists don't write multiple headlines for different output: "My view is this: first of all, we were already asking them to write a print headline. Digital and print, that's quite a lot. Secondly, I've never seen any search headline that didn't benefit from being interesting, human and raw. I've never seen a social headline that didn't benefit from telling you what it was about, which basically is the basis for search."

The Guardian's recent emphasis on "regulars" as the target market to tap into to build its membership has been added into Moran's team's priorities. There's a formula for "the interesting people" and monitoring both how many regular readers they have and how long the regulars stay with an article or video.

While Moran sees the regulars metric as crucial to the long-term aims of the Guardian, he also points out that it needs to be handled with care and nuance. For example, a piece about Michelle Obama's speech by Washington correspondent David Smith[28] that went "huge" on Facebook and on Spotlight search on Apple News, but views on the Guardian (and by regulars) were low – why?

"The answer to that," said Moran, "is simply it went beyond our site, i.e. very, very successfully travelled. That makes that number an excellent result. Probably being the first experience of our journalism for quite a lot of people out there in the world. The nuances around regulars need to be taken very carefully."

Ryan Kellett had been with The Washington Post over five years when we met in April 2016. He didn't see the same level of resistance to audience metrics that Moran saw, but he has seen the focus – and the definitions – change: "The Post has a very long-standing tradition of having audience-focused teams. When I started on the team here it was called 'interactivity' which is a word we don't really use any more. Then it was social, then engagement. Every year or so, you'll see a different prompt emerge out of the industry to kind of name what we would now call audience development. So this year, audience development largely because the New York Times uses that term."

For Kellett, that process of audience development starts long before a story is published. New "verticals" – topics or subject initiatives – begin by assessing who would be interested.

"One of the things we ask the people who are creating new verticals at The Post to do is to hear from our audience: what are they looking for, what is missing from that box? I'm a big advocate for asking directly the people who read us every day, so surveys I think are quite underestimated as a tool."

Looking at the existing audience for a particular journalist – Kellett gave the example of religion reporter Sarah Pulliam Bailey: "If you look at someone like Sarah, she has a very large Twitter following. Before she starts a new vertical you kind of want to say what are they looking for? What are the people who are around that person already? What are some of the lower-hanging fruit? It's not just saying, 'What does everybody want?' and it's not just three journalists talking to each other in back rooms."

Grouping content around a particular reporter or topic strand, rather than trying to attract people to The Washington Post as an entity, echoes the segmented content approach I saw at BuzzFeed and Vice.

"I think it's important to have goals," Kellett added. "There's a tendency in journalism, if you don't set goals, to celebrate the success of whatever." What's necessary is a clear target, established at the beginning of planning those verticals that success can be measured against.

"For me it's important to say: 'Hey, here's where we think we should be' and then to have a conversation around that. Just as we create an analytics narrative for every story or every individual in the newsroom. I think it's important to talk about those goals, because numbers lie in a lot of different ways and so you want to really understand the complex picture."

So, setting a goal for visitors to stay on the site for a particular number of minutes might encourage a reporter to add a video or reader comments, in order to hit that reading time metric rather than because the content would benefit from a video: "I do discourage the idea of minimums because that sort of misses the point a little bit; you're basically missing that conversation you would have. . . . Experience-wise I think that skews reporter's behaviour in a little bit of a perverse way."

The metrics Kellett and his team concentrate on are pretty much the same ones as Moran and his colleagues: unique visitors, page views, how much each visitor read, how long they stayed, where they came from and what they did next.

Said Kellett: "For us the page view is a measure of engagement of a certain kind. Again, it's not everything to everyone, but page views is one [metric] we look at and say, 'how much did someone read?' So, you're one unique visitor but did you read five pages worth, or 20 pages worth, or 50 pages worth as that one individual?

"Then we would move on to something like time spent, which is the average time spent across all the users of a specific article. We would also look at something like referrals. Re-circulation is our term for the people who are going to another Washington Post story, and people who leave us, so the percentage of people who make it from consuming one thing to consuming another – and that answers that second question for reporters, which is: where are they going to?"

There are more detailed, more specific metrics, but that "starting set" is not only what Kellett engages with but what The Post expects its reporters to engage with – "a foundational understanding so we're all talking the same language".

For The Washington Post, as with the Guardian, the job has got harder as stories have travelled across the social web and outside the company's own platforms. Facebook Instant Articles, Twitter Moments and Snapchat Discover all provide an additional challenge in determining measures of success – Kellett talks of going "one level up" from that starting set of metrics to determine what metrics matter on each particular platform, and whether The Post is over- or under-performing expectations on that platform.

Beyond that, there's the "not quite tangible" measure of whether more people are becoming familiar with The Washington Post: "are more people in our orbit, our universe?" Many of those people may not even know they're reading a Washington Post story, while others may be regular readers or subscribers and spend hours on the site every day.

"I care about the whole spectrum and want to see more people overall," Kellett added. "But I also want to see the most engaged segment of our readers get more and more out of it. [Are we] delivering on our promise that you've signed up to? If you're paying your money, you're putting it on the table for us, are we delivering it for you? What is the value you're getting? To me, as a person, in the newsroom, I want to say, 'Yeah, that person is getting a ton of content from us, they're really getting their money's worth.'"

Suggested assignments

Practical exercise

Take a story you've recently produced and which has been published on a website or blog. Note how many views that story has had to date. Next, using tools, such as Keyword Planner and the search bar "test" mentioned earlier in this chapter, research the most popular *and* relevant keywords/groups[29] for your story. Try to work more of those into the most important areas of your story in terms of search (in order: page title, story headline, first paragraph). Add them to tags and keywords in any story settings. Your headline should still say clearly what the story is about and be attractive to readers. Next, add a post to your Facebook page, Twitter and anywhere else you are on social media which promotes the story and includes a link to it. Make sure the headline on your Facebook post is attractive to people, rather than search engines. Encourage people to Like or share your post. Over two weeks, continue to talk about your story on social media and adjust headlines, etc. Regularly check story views and reflect on which actions to boost views have been most effective.

Group exercise and analysis

Take any tabloid newspaper[30] and select the top story on each of the first five pages (or a selection of pages). Individually or in small groups, come up with three new versions of the headline for each story. One should be pure clickbait, producing a headline designed to lure people into reading the story; one should be written for a Facebook audience and focused on making a human link with readers; one should be written for search and focused on getting the most relevant and popular keywords into the headline. In groups, discuss your choices and which headline would make you most likely to read the story and why, and which headlines would put you off reading the story and why.

Notes

1 There was, however, an ongoing battle between some US and Japanese manufacturers to build smaller and smaller TVs with the ultimate goal of portability and use where mains power was not available, including a tiny wristwatch colour TV around 2004. See 'Small (Micro) TV sets' article by Tom Genova at www.tvhistory.tv.
2 Ofcom's 2015 Communications Market Report found that we're spending two hours online on our smartphones every day: twice as long as on laptops and PCs.

3 Although not a direct reference, I had this video report by Vice journalist Sebastian Weiss in mind when I was writing this chapter: www.vice.com/video/vice-intl-international-fighters-isis.
4 Vice.com's monthly unique visitors have been difficult to measure, like similar sites that gain much of their traffic from social: http://money.cnn.com/2016/03/22/media/vice-media-audience/.
5 'Who invented the terms "SEO", "SEM", and "SEA"?', Rob Garner, October 8, 2008, MediaPost.
6 'The #Election2016 micro-propaganda machine', Jonathan Albright, November 18, 2016, Medium.
7 There are caveats attached. "More people" may have meant more people in the UK at that point because Google can filter results based on where your computer or device is. And it may also filter results as you do more searches in a session because it will try to reflect the things you personally seem to be interested in. I'm not personally interested in hamsters – Syrian or otherwise – and hadn't previously been searching for them.
8 According to statista.com: 118 minutes average in 2016, against 96 minutes in 2012.
9 Reuters Institute Digital News Report 2016, p. 10.
10 As of September 26, 2016, Facebook's mission statement is "to give people the power to share and make the world more open and connected. People use Facebook to stay connected with friends and family, to discover what's going on in the world, and to share and express what matters to them."
11 Facebook's own page on the platform.
12 'Liveblogging Facebook advertising announcement (Social Ads + Beacon + Insights)', Erick Schonfeld, November 6, 2007, TechCrunch.
13 Eli Pariser was an early developer of the concept of the filter bubble and its effect on what we get to see online. His 2011 book *The Filter Bubble: What the Internet Is Hiding From You* was a bestseller and his TED talk based on the book is in "References and suggested further study", above.
14 Reuters Institute Digital News Report 2016, p. 11.
15 'News Feed Values', newsfeed.fb.com
16 TechCrunch produced a useful guide to how Facebook decides what to prioritise in the News Feed, simplified as the equation News Feed visibility = creator x post x type x recency, i.e. interest of the user in that creator (e.g. you liked their page) x how the post performed among other users x type of post the user prefers (e.g. video) x how new the post is.
17 'News Feed FYI: Showing more timely stories from friends and pages', Erich Owens, September 18, 2014, Facebook Newsroom: https://newsroom.fb.com/news/2014/09/news-feed-fyi-showing-more-timely-stories-from-friends-and-pages/.
18 Facebook currently prioritises video – that may have changed by the time you read this.
19 'Americans' trust in media remains at historical low', Rebecca Riffkin, September 28, 2015, Gallup.
20 'Ipsos MORI veracity index 2015: Trust in professions', January 22, 2016.
21 Otherwise known as the UK MPs' expenses scandal. The story, prompted by files leaked to the Daily Telegraph in 2009, exposed misuse and fraud within the parliamentary expenses system (including a claim by Douglas Hogg for having his moat cleaned) and led to a number of MPs losing their posts, being prosecuted and even jailed. Subsequent stories by both the Telegraph and the Guardian have revealed continuing wrongful claims by individuals and an overall increase in the amount claimed by MPs.
22 In August 2016, the week after Facebook made its trending topics news editors redundant, the algorithm put a false news story about Fox News sacking anchor Megyn Kelly for supposedly backing Hillary Clinton in its top trending topics in the US. The badly written fake story originated on a pro-Republican blog.
23 'News Feed FYI from F8: how News Feed works', April 22, 2016, Facebook Newsroom.
24 'News Feed values', newsfeed.fb.com.
25 Audience optimisation advice pages on facebook.com.

26 'New video metrics: Understand the audience and engagement of your Facebook videos', August 10, 2016, mediafb.com.
27 'News Feed FYI: further reducing clickbait in feed', August 4, 2016, Facebook Newsroom.
28 '"She found her voice": Michelle Obama's DNC speech hailed as her boldest yet', July 26, 2016, Guardian.
29 Most searches are two or more words – often referred to as long-tail search or long-tail keywords. We long ago learnt that just searching on one word, e.g. "news" wasn't effective – we would be more likely to get the results we wanted by adding other, qualifying words, e.g. "news today", "UK news today", "latest sports news". We've become much more sophisticated as searchers as the volume of content on the web has grown.
30 This exercise can also work by watching a TV news bulletin and creating imagined headlines for each story.

References and further study

Cadwalladr, C. (2016) 'Google, democracy and the truth about internet search', *Observer*, 14 December 2016.

Carey, J.W. (2001) 'Lawyers, voyeurs, and vigilantes', in R. Giles and R.W. Snyder (eds.) *What's next: Problems and prospects for news*, Transaction Publishers, New Brunswick.

The Economist, 'Yes, I'd like to you, briefing: The post-truth world', 10 September 2016.

Fernback, J. (1997) 'The individual within the collective: Virtual ideology and the realization of collective principles', in S.G. Jones (ed.) *Virtual culture: Identity and communication in cybersociety*, Sage, London.

Habermas, J. (1962/1989) *The structural transformation of the public sphere*, MIT Press, Cambridge, MA.

Habermas, J. (1991) 'The public sphere', in C. Mukerji and M. Schudson (eds.) *Rethinking popular culture: Contemporary perspectives in cultural studies*, pp. 398–404, University of California Press, Berkeley, CA.

Katz, E. (1957) 'The two-step flow of communication: An up-to-date report on an hypothesis', *Public Opinion Quarterly* 21(1), 61–78, American Association for Public Opinion.

Katz, E. and Lazarsfeld, P.F. (2006) *Personal influence: The part played by people in the flow of mass communications*, Revised ed., Transaction Publishing, New Brunswick, NJ.

Kirkpatrick, D. (2010) *The Facebook effect*, Simon & Schuster, Pymble, NSW.

Lewis, J. and West, A. (2009) '"Friending": London-based undergraduates' experience of Facebook', *New Media & Society* 11(7), 1209–1229.

Pariser, E. (2011) *'Beware online "filter bubbles"'*, TED 2011 talk (video).

Reuters Institute for the Study of Journalism, Digital News Report 2016, compiled by Newman, N. et al. Research Reuters Institute Digital News Report 2016, at: www.digitalnewsreport.org

Sambrook, R. (2012). *Delivering Trust: Impartiality and Objectivity in the Digital Age*, Reuters Institute for the Study of Journalism, Oxford.

Scacco, J. and Muddiman, A. (2016) *Investigating the influence of "clickbait" headlines*, Engaging News Project, University of Texas, Austin.

Silverman, C. (2015) 'Facebook must either innovate or admit defeat at the hands of fake news hoaxsters', *BuzzFeed*, 30 August, 2016.

Song, S. (2013) 'Sharing fast and slow: The psychological connection between how we think and how we spread news on social media', *NiemanLab*, 15 November 2013.

TechCrunch, 'How news feed works': Facebook's own explanatory video, at: https://newsroom.fb.com/news/2016/04/news-feed-fyi-from-f8-how-news-feed-works/ and also *'How Facebook news feed works'*, 6 September, 2016.

Author interviews

Ryan Kellett, Director of Audience Growth, The Washington Post, April 2016
Chris Moran, Audience Editor, Guardian News and Media, July 2016

5
NEW NEWS GENERATIONS

I've been catching the same commuter train to work for the past eight years. About two stops in, it fills up with youngsters on their way to college. Really fills up, the aisle jammed; no bag given its own seat. I cannot, ever, recall seeing one of those young people reading a newspaper.

I see lots of older people reading newspapers – normally the free Metro or the Daily Mail – but not the follow-on generation. Now you may be thinking: "So what?", or ask: "Did teenagers ever read newspapers?", and those are both valid questions. Does it matter if teenagers don't read newspapers? Well, no. Not because reading newspapers would make them more informed or somehow better human beings, but because they don't need to read newspapers to know what's going on in the world, or to develop political awareness, or to pick a side in a debate.

The information that they will build their view of the world on is in their hands already – their smartphone doesn't just give them access to all the news and all the information in all the World Wide Web, but it brings news and information to them.

Why buy a newspaper, particularly a partisan one, when every news story you might be interested in will come to you? That Facebook feed, those Vines, that Snapchat thread, those YouTubers you like – those are the new news channels, and they're all in one place – on your phone. These channels don't only show what friends are doing and saying; they are infiltrated by media pushing out news stories and issue-based gifs and videos.

The average 18-year-old on my train sees more news and knows more about what's happening around the world than most 1950s teenagers, because the world is constantly interrupting them, constantly pricking their social bubble.

Their access to news is bigger and broader than that of many of their newspaper-buying, TV-watching parents. They are not only more likely to get their news, including political content,[1] through social media, but also more likely to see opposing views[2] than their parents will. Just because we don't see the newspaper, that doesn't mean they don't see the news.

The issue is not whether my train teenagers see what's going on in the world, but what they choose to take notice of. And how the news has been mediated before it gets to them.

The previous chapter looked at how stories might get to my train teens – how news organisations and journalists might optimise content for search or social to push their story up through a mass of competing material (I have that scene in my head from *Kill Bill Vol. 2*, where the Bride punches her way out of the coffin and scrambles up through what seems like acres of soil and roots to surface back in the world[3]). This chapter looks at the ways newer companies are "surfacing" content and getting younger audiences to engage with news, as they move away from the traditional news publishers that their parents use.

The new news environment is a tumultuous mish-mash of real news, fake news, sponsored news, partisan news (see Broderick, 2016), comment as news, lost news and ignored news, increasingly being delivered by companies that are not news producers and claim not to be news publishers.

More young people get their news from Facebook than from TV. It's the primary source of news for 28 percent of 18- to 24-year-olds. Across Facebook users, 44 percent rely on it for news (Reuters, 2016).[4] What we see on Facebook is incredibly important; what we do about what we see – the measures Facebook uses to show us more of what we seem to be interested in: the so-called "filter bubble" – is even more important.

It was disingenuous of Mark Zuckerberg to insist that the volume[5] of fake news pushed out by far-right campaign groups played no part in Trump winning the US presidency.[6] Facebook is the biggest global media in the world. It operates at a news scale we've never experienced before, but it is built on a commercial model that favours keeping users in their cognitive comfort zone. Neither we nor Zuckerberg yet know how influential Facebook's algorithms will prove to be in shaping cultures and politics in this decade.

However, Facebook is not the only gated platform reliant on algorithms to show us more of what we seem to be interested in. Other social media do the same – Twitter sends us posts by people we choose to follow; ditto Instagram with photos and video. WhatsApp and Snapchat encourage us to create conversational groups. And across all of them we're encouraged to share material from one social media to another – so we may see and share the same video on Instagram, Facebook and Twitter.

New and traditional media companies have jumped into this social media playpen, some of them deliberately creating filter bubbles. Upworthy,[7] New Republic and Flipboard curate news[8] – selecting stories from multiple sources according to what the user is interested in. Aggregators such as Google Currents, Feedly and Digg automatically pull together feeds of top stories from categories or websites selected by a user. Nuzzel puts together a personalised feed based on what news stories your friends – and their friends – think are good enough to share. Pocket lets you store stories and videos you come across to read later, while paper.li focuses on helping news publishers, rather than news consumers, by collecting content from social media and turning it into an online newspaper or newsletter.

Although by the time you get to read that last paragraph, at least one of those companies will have disappeared. The new news media landscape has its own fallen soldiers – news is a brutal battlefield whether you're a traditional or a new media company.

In 2013, natural language content aggregator Wavii was bought by Google then folded into Google's own work in AI. Circa had been the darling of news land because of its pioneering work on deconstructing story structures (see Chapter 8), but ran out of money and shut down in 2015. Pulse was bought by LinkedIn in 2013 as part of its move to develop news content on the site to encourage users to visit regularly. That same year, Yahoo bought mobile news aggregator Summly from its 17-year-old founder and then closed it.[9] And the Daily Mail bought Facebook news darlings Elite Daily in 2015, but wrote off its $31 million investment two years later. Prismatic, sort of like Nuzzel in recommending articles based on what people you know are reading, had been courted by the biggest tech companies but shut down its news reader in 2015.

It's important to recognise, however, that VC – venture-capital – funding, which underpins the early stage growth of most tech start-ups, is tied to an exit strategy which, in most circumstances, will see the acquisition of a small start-up by a bigger company (i.e. the examples of Wavii or Summly, discussed earlier) as a success; the investors get a financial return and the human talent or intellectual property may be acquired by a company with more development experience.

"We're not talking down to them. We are them."

So, news aggregators come and go. But the reason they arrived in the first place is because of one core problem that still needs solving – when we're swamped by news (including all that real news, fake news, sponsored news, partisan news, comment as news, lost news and ignored news), how do we get to the good journalism that might interest us? And how does it get to us? Systems that filter news based on recommendation – whether by curators or by contacts we trust – are technological attempts to deal with a new media problem by learning from traditional media's legacy of editorial judgement.

The phrase "the attention economy" is often used in relation to that problem. How, in a world in which our attention is the most difficult thing to pin down – with constant media distraction, and an explosion of competitors on the content landscape – does a story, an advert, a company, break through that noise to get our attention? The attention economy theory, first defined by Goldhaber (1997) and Davenport (2001), says that the scarcest commodity, in our internet-lived world, is human attention. The new economics of society are based on winning our attention.

> [E]conomies are governed by what is scarce, and information, especially on the Net, is not only abundant, but overflowing. . . . Furthermore, if you have any particular piece of information on the Net, you can share it easily with

anyone else who might want it. It is not in any way scarce, and therefore it is not an information economy towards which we are moving. . . . There is something else that moves through the Net, flowing in the opposite direction from information, namely attention.

(Goldhaber, 1997)

As people, we crave attention. As babies we needed it to survive ("Look at me, mum! Feed me!"). As children growing into adults winning attention from parents, then friends, then teachers and eventually colleagues and bosses is how we progress through life and how we measure ourselves. Are we popular enough? Are we respected by our peers? How do they show that – are they listening to us, watching us, following us?

And we give away our attention – watching how the cool kids dress, gossiping about TV stars, obsessing on favourite bands. Sometimes as a substitute for not getting enough attention ourselves, but always in return for receiving something: entertainment, information, belonging.

It's not surprising that social media exploded; it has the capacity to compensate our attention deficit in ways the one-way traffic (them to us) of traditional media never could.

So how, with those teenagers on my train already drowning in content, do we as journalists get their attention? And not just any old attention – real journalists don't do misleading and fake news; we care about getting the good stuff noticed.

There are two basic answers to that question. The first is, report on the subjects that a younger audience is more likely to be interested in. The second is to report on those subjects in an interesting way.

For example, both BuzzFeed and Vice target that Millennial audience and for both news operations, a key subject area has been mental health. "Mental health is a huge issue," BuzzFeed's Stuart Millar told me. "It's something that the vast Millennial audience is incredibly aware of and interested in and has a lot of personal experience of."

It's not that traditional media are not covering mental health issues, but that that coverage is focused on mental illness and disability – the experience an older audience may have of autism among their children and grandchildren, dementia among their parents and friends.

Jenny Stevens, Managing Editor at Vice UK (the case study at the end of this chapter), says their younger audience is "very savvy, and they don't like being talked down to".

"We are writing to people who are our age," she told me. "We're not talking down to them. We are them. We know what young people are interested in because we are all young people. I guess that is the crux of it."

To reach out to a younger audience, you start by covering the issues they care about. BuzzFeed's investigation into workers' rights at ASOS, an online retailer that targets the clothes-conscious, low-earning Millennial consumer. Vice's High Society video documentary series tackling drug use from a non-judgemental perspective.

AJ+ covering the Syrian crisis, or asking 'Is the South racist?'[10] in one of its most popular videos.

Then you engage them by covering those issues in a different way. A funny headline, a quiz, a game, a listicle, a video, these all help, but the core – as with all journalism – is to make people care about that story, that lived human experience.

"All the data shows that people will engage with stories and share them if they have that emotional reaction to them," said Millar. "That applies whether it's in news, or entertainment, or whatever. There's a second language of BuzzFeed where you sort of understand how to make a headline fly with a funny line but actually it's a serious story. Or different ways of treating a serious story in a fun way."

"All play means something"

Making serious news fun? Is that how we engage that younger audience?

Maybe. The big serious stories that that younger audience cares about – mental health issues, rental housing crisis, student debt, low-paid labour – they don't need to be dressed up with quizzes and funny gifs to be read. But they do need to be broken up with images and perhaps graphs and videos and subheads, because part of the professionalisation of journalism over time has been the development of our understanding of how people are attracted to a story by a headline or a photo, and how we break up that story to encourage them to read more, or to help them to remember more of it.

Channel 4 News, in the UK, made big changes in the way they delivered their content online (rather than on TV) and were massively successful in growing their online – and younger – audience. They ditched the traditional picture and words formats most news publishers took with them online and focused on video only – and "square" format video at that so it could be watched anyways up on a smartphone. They added subtitles so videos can be watched with the sound low or off (avoiding that annoying people on the train thing) and pushed everything out through Facebook. The result, according to Channel 4 and Digiday[11] was an increase in monthly views from five million to 200 million (overtaking the BBC), with two-thirds of viewers aged under 35.

Pictures are not just illustration, they attract attention to the story and engage the reader by humanising it – showing us a person directly affected by this story. They help slow our scrolling and improve eye tracking to keep us engaged for longer. Ditto video, graphics, subheads, quotes, quizzes, games, little bits of VR, and anything else the future journalism might add to keep us engaged with their story.

But how does that work with the really serious stories? Using a quiz as a fun explainer of negative media coverage of Jeremy Corbyn's leadership of the UK Labour Party[12] is one thing, but turning the torture of Syrian activists into a video-game, or the refugee crisis into a virtual reality experience?

Al Jazeera senior reporter Juliana Ruhfus used a mobile game[13] to tell the story of how Syrian activists were tortured to give up their passwords and security teams hacked networks to use the internet against the anti-Assad movement.

In the game, you message and interact with hackers, activists and cyber analysts, with individuals and conversations based on interviews the Al Jazeera team conducted while creating an earlier video documentary[14] on the Syrian cyberwar. The goal is to collect the maximum amount of information within a five-day "deadline", while protecting your sources by not getting "hacked" yourself.

It pretty much turns the process Ruhfus and other journalists would go through in researching a story like this into a game – you essentially become Ruhfus, trying to build a convincing web of information for her documentary.

> Turning journalistic knowledge that I acquired during the making of the film into message-based exchanges was probably the most gratifying part of the production. Confronting users with journalistic and security-related decisions in order to create a game environment felt absolutely instinctive.
>
> *(Ruhfus, 2016)*

In 2014, Ruhfus had produced an interactive story for Al Jazeera on illegal foreign fishing off the coast of Sierra Leone that was adding to the impoverishment of the country. The result 'Pirate Fishing' won multiple awards for its blend of traditional and radically different storytelling. At its core was another game where you are the journalist researching this story and making enough of the right journalistic decisions will reward you with promotion from junior to senior reporter.

The key difference between interactive storytelling and gamified storytelling is that element of reward. Games require something to be "won", some achievement to be gained by the playing. There is challenge, there is discovery, there is skill, but ultimately there is winning. We don't "gamify" journalism simply by sticking a quiz or a bit of an app game into a story to spice it up a bit. Those are decorative elements, useful in encouraging us to spend more time with the story, but ultimately only another type of interactivity. For journalism to really take advantage of games in storytelling it has to take advantage of what is fundamentally different about games, and play, in society.

"All play means something," Huizinga (1949) told us. It has a biological purpose which goes beyond the play itself. Fun is the essence of why we – and other higher species – play. If it was only about preparation for adulthood, animals would stop playing once they were mature, but dogs still chase and play-fight so long as their bodies will let them. We'll spend hours lost in a computer game; throw money into slot machines; take a pack of cards on holiday with us; buy a game for a family Christmas.

> The very existence of play continually confirms the supra-logical nature of the human situation. Animals play, so they must be more than merely mechanical things. We play and know that we play, so we must be more than merely rational beings, for play is irrational.
>
> *(1949: 3)*

According to Huizinga, play is something we need to do because we enjoy it. It is voluntary. It is a temporary stepping out of real life to pretend or to just have fun; it is a cultural function; it comes to an end; it can be repeated and, crucially, there is order – rules, turn-taking, time limits. Play creates order and is order: "Into an imperfect world and into the confusion of life [play] brings a temporary, a limited perfection" (1949: 10).

Which sort of makes it a bit weird that something so essential to humanity, something so important to how we experience life, hasn't already become part of the journalist's storytelling arsenal. We lose ourselves in play; we step out of reality into a more ordered world. If all we are shown is video after video of Aleppo's citizens being bombed into oblivion by their own government, and if all we hear about is how little our own government is doing to stop that, no wonder we eventually stop watching those videos – who wants to be constantly reminded of how powerless we are as individuals? But in a game, we get to have power because we make choices. Even if those decisions are the wrong ones and get us "killed", we get to play again to try and improve the outcome.

If we were able, in a game, to step in the shoes of those Syrian civilians, not just to feel what it is like to be bombed in a VR immersion but to feel we can take some control by making decisions that may help our family to survive, then we may feel we can take some control in the real world too. We can play a role beyond that of audience to the news story.

In 'This War of Mine' (11 Bit Studios, 2014), you lead a group of civilians trying to survive in a civil war. Inspired by the 1992–96 siege of Sarajevo, the videogame produced a 2016 sequel 'This War of Mine: the Little Ones' that focused on children caught up in civil war. It's dark – you're asked to prioritise each individual group member's survival as they became hungry, weak or sick. But the gameplay is strengthened by being based on research and interviews, effectively a blending of journalism and game making:

> We knew it was going to require research to know what people are going through. I don't mean political research to know how conflicts are raised or how they burst out or what are the physical needs, because they can be described easily. . . . What we were searching for were actual memoirs and stories from people who suffered in real conflicts, and to know the things that got stuck in their minds . . . or their inner feelings when they were describing what they went through.
>
> *(Pawel Miechowski, quoted in Gamespot article, 2016)*[15]

Game maker Lucas Pope's Republica Times (2013) forces the player into moral decisions on what information and content to "select" for a fictional newspaper, rather than purely journalistic choices.[16] Pope's work focuses on that element of choice in gameplay, but challenges players to consider what might force us to make unethical or immoral choices.

In his award-winning Papers Please,[17] you are an immigration inspector controlling the flow of people entering fictional Arstozkan. Sifting through documents provided by travellers and the Ministry of Admission's primitive information systems you decide who can enter your country and who will be turned away or arrested. The game forces the player to walk a moral tightrope – stop the suicide bombers and traffickers, spot the genuine refugees and visitors – while your decisions affect whether you'll earn enough to feed your family. The gameplay isn't perfect, but it does what games can do that other media can't – it makes us experience the decision making that might make us do the unthinkable.

The Westport Independent (2015)[18] tackles the issue of self-censorship in news – you play as editor-in-chief of a newspaper about to come under new, draconian media laws and deciding what direction your publication should take. In Jeu d'influences (Game of Influences) (2014), you step over the fence to play as a spin doctor for a controversial French building company, trying to prevent journalists getting to the truth.

Richard Hofmeier's Cartlife (2011; see also Hofmeier interviewed by Donlan for Eurogamer, 2013) tackles the everyday issues faced by working-class Americans – you are a street vendor trying to keep health and family together at the bottom of US society. While one of my personal favourites (and my students') – Inside the Haiti Earthquake (2011) by Andrea Nemtin and Ian Dunbar – places us in the roles of aid worker, journalist or survivor caught up in the 2010 disaster.

The Haiti example is one of several that mixes gameplay with original video to create a more immersive experience. In Fort McMoney (2014), David Dufresne created an interactive, game-led narrative that tackles environmental issues by putting the fate of oil-rich Fort McMurray, a real Canadian town, in your hands. In many ways, it follows on from what's possibly one of the earliest examples of interactive narrative, filmmaker Glorianna Davenport's Elastic Charles (1989) about Boston's Charles River. The "hypermedia" experience lets viewers add text and graphics to video content or edit and add additional video to create their own documentary.[19]

Videogame creators have been building storytelling into games pretty much from the start of the medium. They've included news – and occasionally journalists – in games but as bit players, a background to the gameplay. But the work being done by independent game creators such as Pope and 11-Bit Studios in tackling serious issues, or the ability of indie game makers such as Camp Santo (Firewatch) or Chinese Room (Dear Esther) to build emotionally immersive worlds, show how games might be used to deliver empathic journalism using games as the medium.

VR – virtual reality storytelling – can also deliver that "walk in their shoes" element, albeit without videogames' agency element – the ability to affect what you see. In that sense, VR storytelling can be no different to showing news report after news report of the same humanitarian disaster. Eventually we get bored or we become immune. However, VR isn't just a different form of video, good VR steals from games to deliver interactive storytelling. It gives us choices to make and enables us to participate in, rather than just observe a scene.

Game designer and academic Chris Crawford defines interactivity thus: "A cyclic process between two or more active agents in which each agent alternately listens, thinks, and speaks – a conversation of sorts" (2013: 28).

VR without that "conversation" is missing a trick.

The Economist used VR to walk viewers around destroyed artefacts from the Mosul Museum. Using crowd-sourced images, interviews, records and eyewitness accounts of the museum's layout, the project aims to preserve the cultural heritage of Mosul for generations. It's a very important piece of work, but my students rarely spend more than a few minutes with it.

Newsweek reporter turned documentary filmmaker turned "immersive journalism" pioneer Nonny de la Peña creates VR projects to give people first-person experiences of a situation. "It creates a real sense of being present on the scene," she told the Guardian.[20] "It puts the audience in a place where they can experience the sights, sounds and even emotions as events unfold. This is unlike any other medium."

Project Syria (2015) puts you in the middle of a rocket attack and a refugee camp; Hunger in LA (2012) places you with homeless people on the virtual streets of Los Angeles; Use of Force (2013) takes you to the US–Mexico border to live the story of a man beaten to death by Border Patrol agents. From de la Peña's website:

> Immersive journalism is distinct from news games in that news games embrace gaming protocols. . . . In contrast, a participant in immersive journalism isn't playing a game but is put into an experience where she is participating and affected by events but may or may not have agency to change a situation.[21]

She adds that immersive journalism is analogous to traditional journalism in that, even if the experience starts from different points, "the story itself should not shift".

Palmer Luckey worked on the prototype goggles for Hunger in LA, alongside de la Peña at MxR lab. In 2012, Luckey raised $2.4 million through a Kickstarter campaign to develop his Oculus Rift virtual reality system. Facebook bought his company for $2 billion in 2014. Meanwhile, Google partnered with the New York Times to give away one million Google Cardboard "VR" viewers so readers could experience the Displaced, a NYT VR project following children caught up in the global refugee crisis (2014).

"The power of VR is that it gives the viewer a unique sense of empathic connection to people and events," Jake Silverstein, editor in chief, the New York Times Magazine, said announcing the project. "In the context of international reporting and conflict reporting . . . this has huge potential. Through this immersive video experience, we can put our readers at the center of the most important story of our time."[22]

However, VR is expensive and time consuming. And while both costs and time taken are likely to come down in the future, in the meantime news organisations have shown more interest in 360-degree video – less expensive than VR and closer to the tradition of documentary filmmaking that is a more traditional partner to journalism. 'Millions March NYC' (2014)[23] the collaboration between film maker Spike Jonze and 360-degree innovator Chris Milk, is possibly the best example of that filmmaking link.

In their report for the Tow Center for Digital Journalism, Fergus Pitt and Taylor Owen tracked the production of a VR documentary for PBS's Frontline series. They concluded that VR is still in its infancy as a medium and a technology with "tradeoffs that sit on a spectrum of time, cost, and quality" but its value to journalism could be immense:

> Fifty years of research and theory about virtual reality have produced two concepts which are at the core of journalistic virtual reality: immersion, or how enveloped a user is, and presence, or the perception of "being there." . . . The authors' hypothesis is that as the separation shrinks between audiences and news subjects, journalistic records gain new political and social power. Audiences become witnesses.
>
> *(Pitt and Owen, 2015: 4)*

They warned that the rush to invest in VR by tech's big players – Facebook, Google, Sony, HTC – is driving the development of the technology along paths set by each company. Journalism needs to be at the table, articulating its distinct needs, or the products they build will only properly serve other fields such as gaming and productivity.

For journalists navigating the world of VR, 360, algorithms, games, immersion and interaction, what matters isn't the tech but the purpose. Can this technology help us to reach a different (particularly a younger) or a bigger audience for that story we have to tell? Will it help them to understand and consider the issues? Will it encourage them to act – if action is needed – in our role as interlocutors between public and state?

CASE STUDY: VICE

Jenny Stevens is Managing Editor for Vice in the UK and also reports on identity politics, mental health, arts, culture and books. Her background includes a career in Westminster before becoming a music journalist at NME, then commissioning editor, culture, at the Guardian.

She followed Pussy Riot for NME as they energised people to challenge Russian authority and power ("inspiring") and reported on feminism in music and is interested in the legacy of the Riot Grrls scene ("exciting – this idea that girls could spearhead a revolution"). For her, music and politics have always been linked and she believes that's true for much of Vice's audience.

"I think it felt for a while like there were lots of old people telling young people that music wasn't politicised anymore," she told me. "There were lots of people moaning about the days of Red Wedge or Rock against Racism, [that] it had kind of disappeared. I didn't think that that was true. In some sense, it was true, but I think I was just really passionate about politics and I was also really passionate about music and I really cared about where those two sections meet."

Growing up on a council estate, the music of protest and of aspiration were equally important – bands like Oasis, but also the Girl Power "mission" of the Spice Girls. Her piece for Vice[24] talks about the jolt their music delivered to a generation of teenage girls:

"But that generation grew up. And we grew up entitled. We were the girls who were told we could all have it all, but were tossed into a world where we couldn't."

Stevens is her Vice audience, albeit in a more "mature" role: "I think it would be wrong to say that I'm still 22 years old going to gigs every night. I'm in a managerial position at Vice now, but then I'm still young. Everyone here is young, and that's the point of Vice. It's about young people telling their own stories and being immersed in the culture that they're writing about, so yes, I don't feel like I'm approaching retirement age in terms of youth culture. I think I can still write about it and I understand it and I'm part of that culture."

Vice itself isn't that young even if its staff and editorial stance is. The business started back in 1984, when Shaun Smith and (then) friends Suroosh Alvi and Gavin McInnes took over a government-funded community magazine called Voice of Montreal. They made it more street-cred, more music-led, shortened the name to Voice then Vice, before relocating to hip Williamsburg in New York in 1998.[25]

Vice magazine grew and expanded into Vice Media, jumping onto the web and betting on online video well before traditional media noticed where the cool crowd had gone. They launched VBC.tv in 2007, initially in partnership with Viacom's MTV before buying them out. "We saw that everyone was building a YouTube or a Hulu or a Facebook," Smith told Forbes.[26] "Everyone was spending all their money on platforms but none of it on what you put in the pipe. So we said, "Okay, eventually the market's going to catch up, and everyone's going to need content."

That content increasingly moved towards news and documentaries and across multiple media, business partnerships (including Intel, CNN and Disney) and countries – Vice Media currently operates in 30 countries around the world and Vice TV ("*60 Minutes* for young people", according to Smith) is currently into its fourth season with HBO, while Vice News on YouTube has over two million subscribers.

In a speech at the 2016 Edinburgh International Television Festival, Smith warned: "Baby Boomers have had a stranglehold on media and advertising for a generation. That stranglehold is finally being broken by a highly educated, ethnically diverse, global-thinking, hard-to-reach generation, and media is having a hard time adapting to this rapid change."

It was time, he said to break rules, to open up: "Media today is like a private club, so closed that most young people feel disenfranchised. You have to hand it over to the kids."[27]

Handing it "over to the kids" at Vice means distinctive, personal, irreverent journalism.

"Vice has a really strong identity," said Stevens. "[In] the kind of areas that we cover, the angle. We're always looking for an outsider youth-orientated angle. The way that politics is covered in newspapers is incredibly different from the way that we cover it. We cover protests quite heavily. Our commentators are just turning things on their head a little bit.

"Brexit was a really good example of this. We published a piece that I think is quite great, and it was called, something like: 'Oh my god, Grandma, what the fuck have you done?'

"I think it really reflected the kind of shock amongst young people who voted to stay because that was a shocking result and it was definitely shocking to a younger generation. Also, I think we do tell stories that other people are not telling, so we did stuff like 'The Vice Guide to Liberia' and our coverage of the Ukraine and Greece. Lots of young people in Greece were in kind of a youth culture movement. The idea of Vice is just having something different to say."

That Vice "difference", in particular in video, is to be very "gonzo", very personal. It's about what the journalist is experiencing – going out to where the story is happening, saying what they see, what they feel about what they see – very different to the third-person, impartial "straight" journalism of traditional media.

"I guess lots of our journalism really, we're going somewhere and we are telling a story and we're also kind of enabling people to tell their stories, as well. Our journalism is more immersive in that way."

Stevens commissions articles and pieces ("I don't like the word 'content'") that fit that Vice News "difference". Often from new writers: "Our writers are young and are perhaps not as experienced as writers for national newspapers, so I think we do a lot of nurturing. We will commission people that have never written an article before and we will help them with that. In many ways, it's a lot more of a dialogue with our writers.

"If we have a newer writer, then we might give them a bit more advice about exactly what we want from them, and people are new to journalism, so we do have to give them more advice about what they might want to get out of an interviewee, the actual practicalities of the job that they're doing."

She gets a lot of pitches ("way more" than in her previous jobs), a lot of the time from people sharing their experiences: "I look after mental health pitches here, and we get an overwhelming volume of young people just wanting to tell their stories."

The structure has become more formal as the team has grown. Stevens and editor-in-chief Rebecca Nicholson, who also joined from Guardian News and Media, run a morning news conference, with editors outlining the stories they've got coming out that day.

"I think that was definitely what I found quite challenging at first. Vice is a new company. We don't have sub-editors. We don't have a picture editor, so you are very much working across all areas and trying to organise that, and then at the same time it's kind of dynamic and fluid and you can get things done a lot quicker."

Stevens organises the story flow: "I guess my job is to organise the editors to make sure we are publishing the right things at the right time and that they're going out on social media, again at the right time, that we're commissioning the right things for our audience.

"Our readers come to us via many different platforms. They might watch a video and then they'll want to read about it, so we try and do what people call packages now, so we will publish either a film or something, and then we will commission around that so we will make sure that there is a package of pieces all together."

Does it matter whether the audience knows that the content – that package – has come from Vice when they come across it on social and or the general web?

Stevens: "I think people definitely look to us for an alternative take, and young people do. It's a tricky question to answer, really. The thing for us is that it doesn't really matter what medium we publish on as long as the content is good really. Is the Vice brand and what we do well known? Yes, I think it is."

Right now, Stevens is working at Vice in a period of expansion, with new channels (verticals) building their own distinct audiences: the TV channel Vice Land; Noisey, the music channel; Munchies, food; Broadly, for women ("not as niche as it sounds", said Stevens, "but it covers feminism and those kind of areas"); Thump, dance music; a games channel; Vice Money; Vice Travel; as well as Vice News online and the HBO Vice News documentaries.

She's proud of bringing ex-Great British Bake Off contestant Ruby Tandoh on board, not to write about baking cakes but taking a Vice sideways look at food, writing about body image and food culture.

"I think it's so important and it was something that personally was quite important to me in my experience in my life. I really, really wanted to get her to write for us. She did a fast food column for us, which I thought was great, and again, quite an alternative take.

"Getting Ruby to write for us is really great because I think she definitely opened us up to a very new audience. What she was saying was exactly spot on. She wrote a big long read for us about clean eating and the damage that that is doing in culture, and I just feel really proud that she was able to do that piece for us because I think for me, it was just something that needed to be said."

And for the future? "The thing I find a bit sad about journalism, there is this perception that online journalism is all churn," she said. "That it's all traffic chasing and it's all clickbait. I don't think that we do that here. Personally, I think we're just doing really good quality journalism. We've

FIGURE 5.1 Photo of Jenny Stevens, then Managing Editor at Vice UK. Credit: Ed Miles

got great columnists. We've got writers like Joel Golby, who people really care about his writing, and I think just to continue what we're doing.

"I just want our journalism to continue to be really good and really tight, and explore issues that people aren't exploring, and being able to send writers out to do really brilliant things."

Suggested assignments

Group exercise and creative thinking

In groups, imagine you've been given £/$10 million to launch the best global news service you can imagine. Discuss and agree what your news service would deliver. What does it need? What are your spending priorities? How much do you need to spend on journalists, editors, managers, interns, etc.[28]? What about kit and facilities? Office space/s? Promotion? You need to plan for the launch year and to keep it going for a couple of years (at least) until revenue kicks in. What are your spending priorities?

Practical exercise and analysis

(For individuals or small groups.) Play one or two of the free games listed in "Games for further study".[29] Discuss afterwards and report back to the class on your game/s. Was it fun? Did it make you think about the situation you were in? Did you feel you played "in character" – that you were making decisions as the character you were asked to play? How did that feel? How might the game be improved to make it a) more fun and b) more thought provoking?

Games for further study

The Republia Times, Lucas Pope: http://dukope.com/play.php?g=trt
Fort McMoney, David Dufresne: www.fortmcmoney.com/#/fortmcmoney
Inside the Haiti Earthquake, Andrea Nemtin, Ian Dunbar: www.insidedisaster.com/experience/Main.html
#Hacked, Juliana Ruhfus: https://syhacked.com/
Jeu d'influences, Julien Goetz, Luc Hermann: http://jeu-d-influences.france5.fr/
Cart Life, Richard Hofmeier: https://indiegamestand.com/free-games/2199/cart-life/

Notes

1 Reuters Institute for the Study of Journalism, Digital News Report 2016. The research found that 61 percent of Millennials mostly got their news about politics and government from Facebook, against 39 percent of their parents' generation (60 percent of whom got their political news mostly from TV).
2 Pew Research in 2014 (American Trends Panel) found older Facebook users are most likely to see political content on the site that supports their own views: 31 percent of Baby Boomers (over 50) Facebook users say the posts they see are mostly or always in line with their own views, against 21 percent of 34- to 49-year-olds and only 18 percent of 18- to 33-year-olds: www.journalism.org/2015/06/01/millennials-political-news/.
3 You can watch it here: www.youtube.com/watch?v=JnXi3SVJXbM.
4 Reuters Institute for the Study of Journalism, Digital News Report 2016 looked at sources of news used across age ranges, and in 28 countries including the UK and the US: www.digitalnewsreport.org/.
5 A BuzzFeed investigation in October 2016 showed that hyperpartisan right-wing sites published double the amount of false or misleading stories to left-wing sites, and that the more extreme the false story, the more likely it was to be shared.
6 Zuckerberg was responding to questions at the Technonomy conference in November 2016, arguing: "Personally I think the idea that fake news on Facebook, which is a very small amount of the content, influenced the election in any way – I think is a pretty crazy idea. Voters make decisions based on their lived experience."
7 Upworthy founder Eli Pariser was an early developer of the concept of the filter bubble and its effect on what we get to see online. His 2011 book *The Filter Bubble: What the Internet Is Hiding from You* was a bestseller and his TED talk based on the book is in "References and further study" in the previous chapter.
8 News aggregators are not the same as news curators. Basically, aggregators pull in news sources, which the user then assembles into the feed they want to see. News curators add in editorial judgement – whether human or AI/algorithm led – to quality-control content and highlight or package interesting stories for the user.

9 According to Yahoo in a report on Business Insider, Summly was swept up as part of a more complex technology deal: www.businessinsider.com/why-marissa-mayer-bought-a-30m-startup-2013-4?IR=T.
10 'Is the South racist? We asked South Carolinians', June 30, 2015, Video: www.youtube.com/watch?v=h2TPlxBIvOQ.
11 'How Channel 4 News grew its monthly Facebook video views to 200 million', Jessica Davies, August 9, 2016, DigiDay.
12 As BuzzFeed did brilliantly: 'Can you survive a week as Jeremy Corbyn?', October 3, 2016.
13 https://syhacked.com/
14 'Syria's electronic armies'. Juliana Ruhfus, June 18, 2015, Al Jazeera.
15 'How This War of Mine goes even darker with The Little Ones', Alexa Ray Corriea, January 20, 2016, Gamespot.
16 You play as the editor-in-chief of a trusted newspaper, forced to select stories which would encourage readers to see the authoritarian government in a more positive light.
17 www.youtube.com/watch?v=_QP5X6fcukM
18 www.doublezeroonezero.com/westport.html
19 http://ic.media.mit.edu/icSite/icprojects/ElasticCharles.html
20 Source: '"Godmother of VR" sees journalism as the future of virtual reality', Edward Helmore for the Guardian, 11 March, 2015: www.theguardian.com/technology/2015/mar/11/godmother-vr-news-reporting-virtual-reality. See also Video[0]: Nonny de la Peña's talk for TEDWomen (May 2015) *The future of news? Virtual Reality*.
21 www.immersivejournalism.com/about/
22 'The New York Times launches NYT VR: Delivers over one million google cardboard viewers', October 20, 2015, NYT Press Release.
23 See https://with.in/watch/vice-news-vr-millions-march-nyc-12-13-14/.
24 'Was girl power just a lie?', Stevens for Vice, November 4, 2016.
25 Interview with Shane Smith, Spike Jonze for Interview Magazine, April 4, 2013.
26 'Tom Freston's $1 billion revenge: Ex-Viacom chief helps vice become the next MTV', Jeff Bercovici, for Forbes, January 3, 2012.
27 Video of Shaun Smith's speech: www.youtube.com/watch?v=ZSdkxXGQAPA.
28 Tutor's note: When I do this exercise with my students, I produce a series of picture print-outs to represent different options, e.g. "a battle-hardened foreign correspondent", "an enthusiastic citizen journalist", "the free but inexperienced intern", "the cool New York headquarters", and attach an annual cost to each option. Using these visual aids usually prompts more interesting discussions as students argue over cost vs benefit.
29 Tutor's note: I can't guarantee that the games I've suggested will still be available at these locations to play for free. You may need to substitute others – a good source is http://docubase.mit.edu/project/ (filter to select "games") but also look for games that could be played within the session (e.g. free Flash games).

References and further study

Broderick, R. (2016) 'This is how Facebook is radicalizing you', *BuzzFeed*, 16 November 2016.
Crawford, C. (2013) *Chris Crawford on interactive storytelling* (2nd ed.), New Riders, San Francisco.
Davenport, T.H. and Beck, J.C. (2001) *The attention economy: Understanding the new currency of business*, Harvard Business Press, Brighton, MA.
Donlan, C., (2013) 'Cart life: "The only thing that changed was me"', *Eurogamer*, 25 January 2013.
Goldhaber, M.H. (1997) 'The attention economy and the Net', *First Monday* 2(4–7), April 1997. Accessed at http://firstmonday.org/article/view/519/440
Huizinga, J. (1949) *Homo Ludens: A study of the play-element in culture*, Routledge and Kegan Paul, London.

Knight Foundation, 'Viewing the future? Virtual reality in journalism', 13 March 2016.

Pitt, F. and Owen, T. (2015) 'Virtual reality journalism', *Report for Tow Center for Digital Journalism*, 11 November 2015.

Reuters Institute for the Study of Journalism, Digital News Report 2016, compiled by Newman, N. et al. Research Reuters Institute Digital News Report 2016, at: www.digitalnewsreport.org

Ruhfus, J. (2014) 'Why we decided to gamefy investigative journalism at Al Jazeera', *Medium*, 1 October 2014.

Ruhfus, J. (2016) 'Gamifying the Syrian cyberwar: 6 important lessons I learned', *Medium*, 3 October 2016

Wakefield, J. and Cellan-Jones, R. (2016) 'Social media 'outstrips TV' as news source for young people', *BBC Online*, 15 June.

Author interviews

Jenny Stevens, Managing Editor Vice UK, November 2016

6
THE NEW (HUMAN) JOURNALISTS

There's a line I like. Misty Knight says it to Luke Cage[1] in an argument about the role of vigilantes: "They have no training. No responsibility. . . . They don't have the right to just start meting out justice."

It's a line I come back to often when I'm thinking about bloggers and vloggers (video bloggers i.e. YouTubers, Periscopers, etc.). I come back to it because I can never really decide what I think. On the one hand, I believe journalism training matters. You're less likely to end up getting sued; you're more likely to be able to put a balanced piece together that will get attention. On the other hand, passion for your subject and natural communication skills (written or verbal) underpin the better blogs and vlogs.

Is that enough? Does what you're blogging or vlogging about matter, or is that where Knight's "no responsibility" bit comes in? Who should have the right to mete out justice online? When anyone can find a platform (particularly in social media) to say pretty much anything they want to say, no matter how biased or bizarre or offensive, do we live with it as part of an "open" web?

Temple (2014) argues that the media should provide space for these wider viewpoints – even those of "fruitcakes and fascists", rather than leave them to the internet's filter bubbles. Open debate in an inclusive new public sphere would weaken claims by populist groups and politicians that they alone represent the disaffected and the disenfranchised.

The arrival of the internet itself, as I noted in Chapter 2, created a shift towards interconnectivity between people – friends and strangers – that has undermined the power of the traditional mass media in favour of the individual and an enhanced sense of empowerment (Flanagin et al., 2009) through seeing collective action via the internet.

Most blogging and vlogging isn't like that of course. Most bloggers, including myself, write about things we're interested in – hobbies and passions, maybe even as a business. Over 300 million blog accounts have been created on Tumblr (Statista, 2016) and tens of thousands of new Wordpress blogs are set up every day. Alongside the hobbyists and diarists, there are bloggers delivering hyper-local news in spaces the traditional media have left behind (Williams et al., 2015), and there are bloggers delivering polarising rants and twisted takes on the news.

On YouTube, top-earning bloggers such as PewDiePie and Lily Singh earn millions of dollars a year. While others – journalists Martin Lewis (MoneySavingExpert) and Michael Arrington (TechCrunch) for example – have turned their blogs into profitable businesses and sold them to bigger media groups (£87 million for Lewis in 2012, $30 million for Arrington in 2010). The Young Turks, launched in 2002 by Cenk UyGar, started as a liberal politics radio show before moving onto the web and, in 2005, launching what has become the TYT Network and "largest online news show in the world", covering politics, pop culture, sport and lifestyle.

Statistician turned writer Nate Silver took his FiveThirtyEight blog, focused on baseball and election stats and predictions, first to the New York Times[2] then, in 2013, to ESPN. At the time of the move to the Times, Silver was looking forward to being part of a traditional news team, writing (on FiveThirtyEight): "I very much see what we are doing as a type of journalism, in the sense that it consists of doing original research on a timely basis to help inform the public discourse. Thus, the Times' unflinching commitment to quality journalism makes for a natural fit". Adding that he was excited about the relationship with NYT evolving as FiveThirtyEight was "incorporated into a 'traditional' newsroom setting".[3]

But he was also seen as disruptive by some of that "traditional newsroom", particularly when he criticised the value of political punditry ("fundamentally useless") against hard facts and statistics. When he left for ESPN, the (then) Times public editor Margaret Sullivan wrote

> I don't think Nate Silver ever really fit into the Times culture. . . . He was, in a word, disruptive. Much like the Brad Pitt character in the movie *Moneyball* disrupted the old model of how to scout baseball players, Nate disrupted the traditional model of how to cover politics.[4]

Silver, whatever you might think of his style of reporting[5] or the value of a statistics-led approach to politics (and baseball), is one example among hundreds of thousands of bloggers challenging the profession of journalism and traditional journalism training by delivering information and analysis in different – and often deeper – ways.

Eliot Higgins – the case study at the end of this chapter – is another example – up-ending everything we believed as journalists: that you have to be there "on the ground" to report a story; that you need to be a proper journalist to know how to tell it well; that the public can't be reliable sources on their own.

His work, first with his blog Brown Moses, then with the citizen journalism extension of that, Bellingcat, and then in partnership with other groups via First Draft News, focuses on citizens monitoring and reporting on events they're living through. It challenges the idea that the pro-journalist is the first and most reliable deliverer of the news.

On July 7, 2005, Rachel North started to blog.[6] She started writing just before 11pm that night and finished in the early hours of July 8. She wrote about being on a tube train earlier that day, a train that was bombed as it left Kings Cross station. She wrote eloquently about the experience and of her joy at living through that day. She wrote because she had to. She told a story that was unique because it was hers.

> In the pub [later] I found out there had been many bombs. I went into shock – I probably still am in shock. It took another two hours to get home after a friend managed to pick us up in her car. I am very lucky. I feel euphoric. I'm sure I'll crash soon, but right now, I'm so glad to be alive.

Four years earlier, the web was younger and very few people caught up in the 9/11 attacks blogged about their experiences. Most accounts came via the traditional media – interviews with journalists, interpretations by commentators. Those that did use the web to give first-person accounts used forums and guest posts on pioneer blogs, such as Adam Oestreich, guest-blogging on the Ideapad[7] about watching the plane hit the Twin Towers:

> I ran to the other side of my office and saw fire raining down. Parts of the building was falling and on fire along with paper and other things. We had to look way up because the plane hit in the higher floors. The impact hole was huge – it looked like 10 stories were burning. The fire seemed to crawl around the tower. The winds were so high it caused the smoke to spin in a large swirl.

Oestreich recounts grabbing "bag, palm pilot and my juice" as he escaped his building, and how everyone's first instinct was to try to phone family and friends.

In 2005, people caught up in or witnessing the London bombings also called family and friends, but this time took another step – they took photos and videos as eyewitnesses and sent them to the media, or uploaded them to communal areas such as Moblog.[8] This was pre-social media (pretty much), pre-smartphones, but many had mobile phones that could take a photo. Within an hour of the first bomb going off, the BBC had been sent 50 photos – 300 photos in the day – and witness media led the BBC's main evening news that day:

> [It was] the first time such material had been deemed more newsworthy than the professionals' material. They not only conveyed the choking, claustrophobic atmosphere but also provided significant evidence, helping identify the time of the explosions.[9]

Newsrooms – and the Metropolitan Police – began asking the public to send them pictures and eyewitness accounts. The idea of citizen media, user-generated content, crowd-sourcing – whatever phrase you choose to use – became a part of the newsgathering process.

Rachel North carried on writing and made contact with other victims of London's 7/7 terrorist attack. The blogging was cathartic, for a while, but it also attracted the interest of the mainstream media. North was eloquent and her first-person blogging told the story better than a journalist's interview could. Soon, her prominence as a blogger (her BBC posts attracted almost 400,000 hits in the first week) and as the media's "go to" spokesperson for survivors, attracted conspiracy theorists and trolls. She received death threats, her parents were phoned and abused, she was cyber-stalked. Even in December 2016, a Google search on "Rachel North 7/7" brought up three conspiracy/troll sites alongside North's own blog, in the top five results (see Chapter 4 on the dark side of Google's search algorithm).

North's experience is not as unusual as we might hope, particularly for women bloggers. But there are other problematic issues around the use of eyewitness or citizen media – namely attribution, verification and authority. As researcher Claire Wardle noted (see "References and further study") ten years after 7/7, most news-rooms still paid no regard to the ethics involved in using eyewitness media:

> I would have thought that . . . every newsroom would have guidelines for crediting and labelling eyewitness media, ethical standards would be agreed and adhered to, and there wouldn't be scrums of journalists asking the same poor eyewitness "can we use your photo?"

She adds that licensing agencies should recognise that "financial incentives could encourage eyewitnesses to run towards an explosion and not away from it".

Wardle has a long background in researching witness and citizen media, co-founding EyeWitness Media Hub, leading research at the Tow Center for Digital Journalism, and then joining First Draft news, via founding partner Meedan, as research director.

First Draft is one of a growing group of journalism-led organisations focused on verification of open source content and professionalisation of witness and citizen media. First Draft focuses on verification – delivering tools, guides and training to help journalists verify content shared online, check the provenance of images and identify fake and hoax stories.

Founded in 2015, it's a coalition of organisations involved in aspects of that work, including Bellingcat, Google News Lab, Reported.ly and Storyful. Core partners include news organisations such as The Washington Post, BuzzFeed, Al Jazeera, NBC News and Witness, and media-ish organisations such as Facebook and YouTube, plus media activist organisations such as the American Press Institute, ProPublica, and Amnesty. It's a "who's who" of journalistic intent.

Not all of the organisations on those lists will survive the next year or two (Reported.ly has already folded due to funding cuts[10]) but the legacy of that work means that all journalists – future and now – must learn how to verify content found online or sent to them. Moreover, the work of these organisations is a reminder of what being a journalist is – a responsibility to report truth and facts, not an opinion.

Like First Draft, WITNESS focuses on better journalism through verification. However, as its name suggests, WITNESS concentrates on eyewitness media, training and helping people to use video to fight for their human rights. Its online resources teach people on the ground how to document protest, abuse and testimony, and how to shoot and archive that video so that is easy to verify and capable of being used in evidence. WITNESS (Figure 6.1) launched in 1992, begun by musician Peter Gabriel after he'd documented the stories of witnesses he met on an Amnesty International tour. Gabriel had used his own Sony Handycam and WITNESS grew with the rise of domestic camcorders and the explosion of smartphone video.

Sometimes the filming happens as a result of WITNESS's support, sometimes WITNESS partners people already trying to record abuse. As with Papo Reto, a collective of volunteers "armed with little more than their smartphones and tablets" documenting police brutality in Brazil's *favelas*, according to a New York Times Magazine article (Shaer, 2015), listed in "References and further study":

> No newspaper or television reporters would set foot in Alemão, so they would take it upon themselves to report the news from their favelas. Their intention was to draw attention to the conditions in Alemão – the blackouts, the curfews, the suffocating police presence – and to warn residents to avoid particularly volatile areas.

WITNESS is not alone in giving cameras and guidance to help people record what's happening around them. In 2014, the Guardian gave a camera to 13-year-old Mohammed Saleh Tuaiman,[11] whose father and older brother had been killed by a US drone in northern Yemen in 2014. Helped by a Yemeni journalist, Tuaiman documented life for children living under the shadow of the military drones. A

FIGURE 6.1 WITNESS supports people in using video and technology to protect and defend human rights.
Logo image credit: WITNESS

few months later, Mohammed was killed by a drone himself.[12] It was an incredibly complex issue – the only support the Tuaimans and their neighbours had come from al-Qaeda, as the war destroyed their farms and ability to earn. The story was not an easy one to tell then and became more complex as American, Saudi, Yemeni and rebel factions collided in a comparatively unreported war.[13]

That people have smartphones and can film what's happening around them isn't enough. The web is packed with images of beatings and bombings and abuse. These stories are no longer hidden because "the media doesn't go there", but they are hidden because as audience we can't find – or don't want to find – those stories. It's not enough to film what's happening if no-one who has the power to create change sees your video. The concept of the public sphere still applies: the media as conduit between the people and the state to effect change. Better democracy, engaged citizens and holding the powerful to account is journalism's job.

Bloggers like North, experts like Silver, citizen investigators such as those Higgins and enabling NGOs such as WITNESS have become part of the new journalism matrix. That matrix delivers multiple versions of news, not all of it trustworthy or unbiased, and journalists and the public work together and separately in navigating through the media to their acceptable truth. To be a good journalist in the 21st century is about adding value to the matrix, not trying to control it.

A report by WITNESS in 2011, 'Cameras Everywhere', noted five challenges for journalism and human rights in an era when everyone carries a video camera: privacy and safety; network vulnerabilities; information overload; authentication and preservation; ethics and policy, and that "as the store of human rights content grows, curating and aggregating it in ways that are clear and appealing becomes a major challenge" (p. 11).

Storyful is doing the gathering and curating bit – tracking down, verifying and obtaining the rights to great user-generated content. Its journalist-led team concentrates on finding compelling stories – even if the story is that the content is actually fake.[14] Effectively, they are a traditional press agency – finding and re-selling content to media publishers or advertisers, but concentrating on user-generated content and content found on social media.

Founded by journalist Mark Little (RTE, The Washington Post) in Ireland in 2009, the video of a speech he gave on the background to why he founded Storyful is in the "References and further study" list at the end of this chapter. He talks about his horror at the waste of content he saw as a foreign correspondent, hours of great footage discarded and deleted because the news organisation only needed a few edited minutes: "It was just like buying a cow, and taking a piece of steak and throwing away the rest of the carcass."

With Storyful, Little wanted "to prove that the eternal values of quality journalism mattered more than ever in the age of social media."[15] Storyful was bought by NewsCorp in 2013 and Little left in 2015, joining Twitter as Vice President of Media for Europe and Africa.

Storyful and WITNESS raise an interesting question – which one of them is a news producer? Neither are news publishers – they don't run a newspaper or a news website; the content they gather or encourage goes out through other media – sometimes, only through social media. Do we define journalism by where the content is published, or by who produces it, or by whether the content has been turned into a compelling story, a verifiable narrative?

Eliot Higgins of Bellingcat told me he sees himself as "an occasional journalist", depending on who is paying for that work. But if that work is proving Russian involvement in shooting down MH-17, how much more "real" journalism is Higgins doing than the journalist repurposing PR about whether two reality TV show stars dislike each other?

I keep returning to this point but, if we only see journalism as a profession, as a job someone is paid to do, then it is a set of activities supported by a set of skills which change over time and technology. The quality of our work and our individual skill level can be as good or bad as in any profession – we are the accountant serving our anonymous clients, the lawyer working equally well for the innocent or the guilty. But if, as Chapter 1 explored, we see journalism as a set of ideal attributes, objectively engaged in a public service, then we have to define journalism as an activity, not a profession. I'll return to this issue in the final chapter.

Can't stop the signal

I started this chapter talking about the millions of bloggers and vloggers writing and talking about the things that interest them. That's the reality of most user-created content on the web, not the work of Papo Reto in Brazil's *favelas*, or Bellingcat's dogged pursuers of Russian armament. Mostly it's hundreds of thousands of bloggers producing their own sports sites or beauty blogs or gaming channels or hyper-local news.

Their passion, their level of expertise in their subject, can give them a perspective that is uniquely attractive to their followers. Particularly if that's aligned to a natural storytelling ability or a compelling on-screen personality. Our hobbies and interests are being served by an army of individual writers and producers, some building decent incomes from influencing our taste and opinions on that shared interest.

But I'm going to stay on the more traditional journalism side of blogging to wrap up this section and focus on two particular stories to highlight how bloggers helped shift traditional journalism standards.

Matt Drudge is the journalist who, in January 1998, broke the story about then-US President Bill Clinton's affair with White House intern Monica Lewinsky. Actually, scratch that; it wasn't Drudge's story – his story was that Newsweek reporter Michael Isikoff had the story but that Newsweek editors had blocked publication. I've reproduced part of original report, taken from an independent archive.[16] The story, headed 'Newsweek kills story on White House intern', begins:

BLOCKBUSTER REPORT: 23-YEAR-OLD, FORMER WHITE HOUSE INTERN, SEX RELATIONSHIP WITH PRESIDENT

> **World Exclusive**
> **Must Credit the DRUDGE REPORT**
> At the last minute. . . . NEWSWEEK magazine killed a story that was destined to shake official Washington to its foundation: A White House intern carried on a sexual affair with the President of the United States!

I thought it was worth looking at that opening in detail because of the reporting style (I suggest you follow the end note to see the full post). Matt Drudge wasn't a journalist, he ran a one-man news aggregator passing on gossip he'd picked up and hyper-linking to stories elsewhere.

Newsweek didn't "kill" the story; they held off printing because they felt they didn't have enough at that stage to corroborate what they saw as the much bigger story that Clinton and his aides had coerced Lewinsky to lie under oath, i.e. to obstruct justice:

> Contrary to expectations, the 90-minute tape the magazine heard neither confirmed nor disproved the most explosive legal allegation – obstruction of justice. Apart from Tripp's [Lewinsky's friend] accusations, the magazine had no independent confirmation of the basis for Starr's inquiry on that subject.

Newsweek reporters had never spoken with Lewinsky and did not know whether they could trust her story. They were concerned that putting her name in print would change Lewinsky's life and felt they needed to know more before proceeding. "In the end, time ran out."[17]

As a weekly magazine, time running out meant losing a whole week on a story. Not for the Drudge Report, able to publish straight to the web 24/7. Being on the web gave Matt Drudge a time advantage over both Newsweek and his traditional competitors, tied as they were in 1998 to rigid print or broadcast schedules. Had Drudge done a similar thing today, broken a story about a president and an intern, other media outlets would be linking to his report within minutes, or simply rewriting it and posting it on their own site and social media. The technology and the behaviour has changed.

Newsweek's reasons for holding the story will be familiar to anyone who has been through journalism training: the need for second sources, "independent confirmation" and credible witnesses, and that ethical concern for a young woman for whom publication would "inevitably change her life forever". As the case studies throughout this book show, these issues are still important today. The source of a story still matters, and issues of ethics, accountability and credibility are perhaps even more important in a world in which news can be attacked by governments, PR agencies, big businesses and minority political groups.

The Drudge Report is still going strong with over ten million unique visitors a month but nowadays has a lot of competition. In political blogging alone, it was preceded by David Talbot's Salon in 1995, and followed by Josh Marshall's Talking Points Memo and Andrew Sullivan's (Daily) Dish in 2000; Eliot Gorn and

Adam Hochschild's Mother Jones in 2001; The Daily Kos in 2002; Paul Staines with his alter-ego Guido Fawkes in 2004; Wonkette (linked to Gawker) in 2004; the Huffington Post in 2005; Breitbart News in 2007 – and I could go on, for several pages.

A 2010 study of the 25 most popular websites in the US found the right-wing Drudge Report was a key driver of traffic to news sites, providing over 30 percent of traffic to the Daily Mail's mailonline.co.uk, 19 percent of the New York Post website's traffic and 11 percent of traffic to FoxNews.com.[18]

However, while that may have been true in 2010, social media is winning the influence battle today. Andrew Sullivan, who gave up his political blog the Dish in 2015, lamented how social media had delivered "more and more eyeballs but less and less loyalty" for online journalism. But, he suggested, we may have reached "peak scale" in terms of opinion, aggregation, curation-type websites and predicted a resurgence of blogging as readers seek a return to the trust, intimacy and distinctiveness of the early blogosphere.[19] To journalists thinking of blogging, he suggests: "Be yourself. Do your work. And they will find you."

But what about bloggers for whom being "found" is that bit more difficult because they live in a more repressive country or time?

Salam Abdulmunem, better known by his pseudonym Salem Pax, started blogging in 2002, and, like some human version of charades, became a book and then a film, as "the Baghdad Blogger". His witty and personal posts[20] about living in Iraq before and after the 2003 invasion attracted global attention (although few Iraqis would have been able to access his blog). He became a columnist for the Guardian and went on to publish a book about his life and the risk he'd taken as a gay young Iraqi blogging about the reality of living in a regime where hundreds of thousands of people "disappeared."[21] Nowadays he works as a communications officer for UNICEF in Lebanon.

Abdulmunem found his voice in blogging under a repressive regime, but other bloggers and vloggers have been jailed or killed for fighting back against fascism.

Saudi blogger and writer Raif Badawi was imprisoned in 2012 (and as I write is still behind bars) after criticising Saudi religious leaders. In 2015, he was publicly flogged – 50 lashes – and is still sentenced to a further 950 lashes. Blogger Abduljalil Alsingace has been in a Bahraini jail since 2011, after writing about human rights abuses in the country. He's been tortured, beaten and spent most of 2015 on hunger strike. Alsingace was one of seven journalists in jail in 2016 in Bahrain (259 globally), according to the Committee to Protect Journalists.

And it's not only governments that might seek to silence bloggers. The Hindu Times has produced a timeline of bloggers and journalists hacked to death in a wave of killings by religious fundamentalists in Bangladesh, starting with the murder in February 2015 of US-based blogger Avijit Roy.[22] Roy was one of 84 people, most of them secular bloggers and writers, on a hitlist circulated by al-Qaeda–backed militants.[23] The list included bloggers in the US, UK and Europe.

Bloggers can bear witness to who we are and what is happening around us in ways that social media chatter cannot. Good bloggers, like good journalists, go beyond social media's "here's what I think, tell me if you agree" conversations to tell a compelling story or make a convincing argument, to inform and engage an audience beyond their own social network. They are modern-day diarists, recording how it is to be human in this place and this time.

Within the journalism matrix, passionate bloggers are testimony to the things we care about, but also to the things that anger us, while some – like the secular bloggers killed by fundamentalists – give testimony to the ideas we are prepared to fight to express.

CASE STUDY: ELIOT HIGGINS (BELLINGCAT)

The audience for news may also be active participants in it, helping to deliver a story through eyewitness testimony or media, as outlined in the first half of this chapter. Some go further – actively searching out new stories, using complex investigative tools to interrogate the information that travels around the web and social media.

Rather than passive recipients of the news from "authority" sources, they may contribute as co-writers or researchers within open journalism, or use open source investigation techniques (sometimes called open source investigation (OSINT) or open source social media intelligence (OSSMINT)) to gather the news and information that interests them from multiple sources. This is more than citizen journalism, more than the monitorial citizenship promoted by media organisations such as WITNESS; this is part of the new journalism of verification.

Operating under the pseudonym Brown Moses (a Frank Zappa song), Eliot Higgins hung out on forums and chat threads focused on the Arab Spring and Middle Eastern politics, before starting his blog in March 2012. He kept the name ("It was a hobby, and I assumed very few people would read [my blog], so why spend time thinking of a clever title?") and within months the site became the go-to source for information on the weaponry being used in the Syrian conflict, a key resource on the UK media phone hacking scandal, and Higgins has broken dozens of stories about who is firing what and at whom, both in Syria and elsewhere.

He is not a journalist, has never worked in a war zone, is not a weapons expert or a human rights worker, but over four years he's become an indispensable part of the reporting of Middle Eastern conflict. New York Times war reporter C.J. Chivers wrote about how Higgins broke the story of Saudi-bought arms from Croatia ending up in Syrian rebel hands:[24]

> Thank you, Eliot, for your patience, and your fine eye, and for creating an opportunity for merging new and old forms of reporting into a fresh look at recent events in what is becoming a more active regional war.

FIGURE 6.2   Eliot Higgins speaking at the SKUP festival of investigative journalism in Norway.
Source: SKUP.no

A Kickstarter campaign helped Higgins mutate Brown Moses into Bellingcat and launch its open source investigative reporting team of around 30 to 40 volunteers, with a core team of 10 to 15 investigators actively pursuing stories – including Higgins and four full-time staff. He is also a founding partner in First Draft News, which trains journalists in verification and open source investigation techniques.

All begun by a personal interest in news happening in countries he'd never visited and involving people he had no connections with. "When I was looking at Libya", Eliot told me, "I was just consuming it as news rather than writing about it. I saw through social media, that there was a lot of information that was being shared and put out there that seemed relevant to a lot of other stuff [but] was just being ignored. What could you do to a) verify it, and b) bring it together and actually understand what it means?"

One story stood out for him: Tawergha in Libya, just south of Misrata. The pro-Gaddafi town of around 30,000 people was largely occupied by black Libyans, a legacy of its origins on the 19th century slave trade routes. As anti-Gaddafi Misrata rebels pushed through the town, in August 2011, they systematically bombed, killed and captured Tawergha, forcing survivors to run away, and effectively ethnic cleansing the town, according to human rights groups.[25]

"The foreign journalists in the area were busy driving off to look for Gaddafi, so they would tweet occasionally about, oh, the rebels are firing artillery into this town [Tawergha], or they're firing at this town, but that wasn't their primary interest," he said.

Journalists would tweet about seeing these things in passing but the story was not important enough to include in their report. Higgins would piece together these "lost" bits of information: "These individual tweets didn't mean too much, but when you see the entirety of it from a macro view you can actually see there's a lot of connections there. You could see something was happening in that town, but it was just being completely overlooked. So, that was my drive to become my own media in a way, and figure out what was going on in these places."

"Figuring out what was going on" meant developing the early verification skills that would become part of his work, and that of an increasing number of journalists: using Google Maps to identify locations from photos and videos, checking the veracity of social media accounts against a web of news reports, systematically scanning hundreds of YouTube channels every day. In 2013, Higgins wrote:[26]

> Syria has produced vast amounts of information on social media. It's estimated over half a million videos have been produced and posted online during the conflict; hundreds, if not thousands, of Facebook and Twitter accounts exist, many of which belong to armed opposition groups and local civilian media collectives. Social media has become the key way for people inside Syria to communicate with the outside world, but for the most part it had been widely ignored by the mainstream media. Occasionally a video might go viral, and get picked up by the mainstream media, but generally all this information was ignored, in part because of the fear of writing about videos that would later turn out to have been faked.

In those early days, Higgins would investigate the stories that interested him. Now ideas are brought to the table by others in the Bellingcat team, or suggested by partner organisations. When I spoke to him, in December 2016, he'd just completed work on a report for the Atlantic Council into Russia's role in Syria and was now following up "interesting parts" of that:[27] "So, for example, I've just looked at the chemical weapon attacks that happened at Aleppo in this last six months. And then we're now looking at all the hospital attacks in the last six months, and just systematically looking at the different areas and then going off and researching it."

With Syria the approach is fairly methodical: "There's only so many places you can go internet-wise for information coming from Syria, so that's actually not too difficult. And then we'll reach out to organisations who work on the ground. So with the hospital attacks we've been contacting all kinds of groups running hospitals in Aleppo. And then we'll reach out to groups like the White Helmets and media outlets on the ground for additional material they might have, and then build it all up from there."

Part of that work is finding out who to trust, which reports are real: "We are looking for someone to say, this thing happened. We're looking for the video of it. We're looking for their past activity. We're cross-referencing that up against other material. It's not about one piece of information. It's about the network of information around it that supports whoever knows it's true."

He's shocked by how few journalists know how to do things like reverse image search, "the basics" of verification, as well as the more complicated ways to verify a source, and feels basic open source investigation techniques should be part of journalism training. "[Verification] is the skill that maybe not everyone needs as a journalist, but it's nice to have. But even the most basic verification stuff just still isn't happening. We're seeing that a lot with universities."

He's excited by work that's starting to happen using students to crowd-source material for verification and investigation projects.

"The Berkeley School of Human Rights, Amnesty International, the EyeWitness Media Hub and the University of Essex, and I think another university, have created something called the Digital Verification Corps,[28] where they're trying to verify videos from conflict zones using open source analysis. And the idea is that the students will get trained in the basics and have live cases that are feeding into real projects and work. Over time they'll get more skilled at doing it and be able to do more in-depth investigations."

Bellingcat gets involved in investigations in different ways. Sometimes, something interesting happens and Higgins or one of the team will follow it up, like the ISIS social media campaign in May 2016[29] when ISIS members in Europe ("fanboys, basically") posted photographs of themselves holding messages of support for ISIS, at locations around Europe, the aim being to suggest ISIS was everywhere.

Higgins says he was home doing the ironing and just thought it'd be a "fun thing" to use social media to track down where these photos had been taken: "The thing is, they left quite a bit of the background visible even though it was out of focus. And I basically asked my followers on Twitter, challenged them to geo-locate them all, which they went off and did. But they did that as I was at home doing my ironing. And then they came back and I wrote an article about how it was done." A few months later, he would use similar techniques to track Anis Amri, the Berlin Christmas market attacker, through social media.[30]

While Higgins's army of Twitter followers are generally helpful, as in the ISIS story, he also attracts critics and trolls, particularly from the conspiracy theorists, who leave comments on his website, social media accounts and wherever he appears online.

"The self-described anti-imperialist community," he said. "That kind of crowd has already existed, and there's a big market for that. When I appeared and started getting quite popular and recognised, their first call is that I must be some sort of propaganda campaign or something. As time has gone by, with Syria and then Ukraine and now Russia, because there's a pretty active conspiracy community around that, they came together and fed off each other, so I have my 'anti-fan club'. And because of the internet, they can network together and share their hatred of me!"

He moderates comments on Bellingcat but there are too many to block them all: "I would spend all my day moderating if I tried to be more systematic. Each day I'll have maybe a thousand comments."

They've also had more sinister attacks ("all kinds of fun stuff") including Denial of Service attacks after producing reports on ISIS. "By people claiming to be supporting the Islamic State but I think are just random idiots who have access to a botnet."

"We've had the CyberBerkut, the Russian hacking group, attack one of our contributors and access his email account and his son's account. We've had the FancyBear hacking group, also linked to Russia, try to do phishing attacks on us. And they were the ones who did the Podesta emails and the DNC hack as well. So yeah, we've been targeted at a quite high level." He said cybersecurity firms had investigated and confirmed the attacks came from those groups and, as a result, had given Bellingcat protection software for free.

He added: "It's like I had around the second anniversary of the MH-17 disaster on July 17th, there were over thirty separate articles written about me on various Russian websites, many of which we knew were linked to troll factories. So, it was a clear campaign of a troll factory trying to attack me.

"But what was interesting, we knew just over half of those were definitely linked to troll factories. We were 100 percent sure. But it meant that we could not be sure that all the other ones were also linked to troll factories because all these posts appeared around the same time. So, this told us that they're part of a wider network. For us, in a way, it's free data for our research when they attack us."

Bellingcat runs on project funding from various sources, including running training in OSSINT techniques, carrying out investigations for open society foundations and funding to set up a Russian version of the website. Google Digital News Initiative has given grant aid to carry out projects on the Syrian conflict and Higgins is currently talking to the BBC about running a course for their journalists in his investigation methods.

"What we struggle with", he said, "is getting core funding, because all of these funders want to fund all the fancy projects, but they don't want to pay your rent and keep the lights on." So 2017 will see another crowdfunding bid.

He tries to find paid work or funding for his volunteer contributors with partner organisations or as contractors or consultants. "One guy who's done a lot of work, I got him in contact with the Syria team at the OHCHR[31] and now he's interning there for six months. That's great for me because he gets experience and contacts but he also gets to take the Bellingcat methodology to a big organisation."

Higgins feels that this mix of crowdfunding, commissions and project funds is the way to keep Bellingcat's investigations team going. The website doesn't have the views to support a subscription model, such as that of the Texas Tribune or the Correspondent. Their busiest day saw 170,000 views but a slow day may only get around 4,000. Nor does he see what they produce as journalism and able to attract subscribers: "I see ourselves as an NGO with a focus on open source investigation and everything comes from that, so the journalism is a product of that rather than the purpose of it.

"Bellingcat is really about spreading the use of open source and promoting it, rather than journalism being a product we're trying to aim for, which makes it difficult for funders."

Does he feel there are enough journalists doing the verification work he does in their coverage of stories?

"I don't know. There are very few people doing this, but there is a huge amount of potential in all kinds of different areas to use this information. I go out and work with all kinds of organisations, to show them how to do it. NGOs and thinktanks and all kind of things.

"Sometimes we do work with journalists. With the MH-17 case, initially we wrote all these articles and then the journalists would go out and look at past stuff without having talked with us. But as it went on they began to trust our information a lot more, because they could check on the ground. So, then they contact us and come and ask us if there's anything that they could do on our behalf on the ground, and we'd cooperate together.

"A big part of what we do is about working together with other people, and not wanting ownership of something. For a traditional journalist model, that is very unusual spirit in the field."

Suggested assignments

Practical training

Learning how to verify sources and potential material for stories has always been a key journalistic skill. Techniques change over time and with new technologies but core skills you should learn in verifying open source and social media material are reverse image search and geo-location verification. Use the resources below to learn these skills.

> 'How to verify images like a pro with Google Earth', in First Draft News resources, along with 'Piecing together visual clues for verification'. Also read: 'A Beginner's Guide to Geolocating Videos', 2014, on Bellingcat.

'Search for images with reverse image search', Google Help, along with 'Manual Reverse Image Search with Google and TinEye', 2015, on Bellingcat.

'Verification', Google News Lab online training course (nine lessons over three sections/courses).

Video verification and reverse image search. Use Amnesty's YouTube Date Viewer (www.amnestyusa.org/citizenevidence); copy and paste a YouTube video URL into the box to display video meta data. The Viewer will automatically link to Google's reverse image search tool; click on the link beside the photos to find further information.

Training into practice. Once you're comfortable using the techniques above, use it on a story. First, look for a breaking story and set up keyword alerts to monitor it (use Google Alerts for the web, Tweetdeck for Twitter, Facebook Signal for emerging trends on Facebook[32]). Once you see a video or image or tweet that interests you, start using the tools above to verify it. Work through as many images and videos you feel you need until you have a story, then write that story up – even if the story is how the video/image turned out to be fake. These guides from First Draft may be helpful in assessing how strong your story evidence is: https://firstdraftnews.com/downloads/firstdraft-vvg-photo-ALL.png and https://firstdraftnews.com/downloads/firstdraft-vvg-video-ALL.png.

Class discussion

"Reporters. Journalists. Witnesses. Citizen journalists: What are they good for?" As a group, discuss what you think defines each one – a journalist vs a reporter, or a witness vs a citizen journalist, for example. Is there any crossover? What do you think each of them is good at, in terms of the contribution they might make to delivering the news?

Notes

1 TV series produced for Netflix, based the Marvel comics. Misty Knight is Detective Mercedes Knight, Luke Cage the super-powered vigilante.
2 The blog launched in 2008 and, after correctly forecasting 49 out of 50 state results in the 2008 US presidential election attracted massive traditional media interest before signing a partnership agreement with the Times to join its online stable.
3 See https://fivethirtyeight.com/features/fivethirtyeight-to-partner-with-new/.
4 'Nate Silver went against the grain for some at the times', Margaret Sullivan, July 22, 2013, New York Times.
5 As chapter ten explains, I was trying to complete this book during a weird year. As example, I think this is (mostly) excellent reporting and analysis: http://fivethirtyeight.com/features/the-real-story-of-2016. In particular, how "public opinion was sensitive to news coverage." But Silver is preaching to his particular choir. For journalism to do its job, ideas have to travel. Which means gifs and animated charts and games and 360-video and anything we can and should do to attract attention to the stories that are truly worth the telling.

6 Original posts on the Urban75 blog here: www.urban75.org/london/bombs.html, reposted to the Blogger blog: http://rachelnorthlondon.blogspot.co.uk/2005/07/kings-cross-bomb-my-eyewitness-account.html and also to a "survivor blog" on BBC online: http://news.bbc.co.uk/1/hi/uk/4670099.stm.
7 The Ideapad, founded by David Wertheimer in 1998 and "one of the world's oldest continually publishing blogs": www.netwert.com/ideapad/sep11_adam.html.
8 Founded by Alfie Dennen in 2003, Moblog was a mobile social sharing platform: "It had the crazy idea of uploading mobile phone photos and commenting on them . . . way before Instagram, Facebook, et al. We learned how to talk to each other, how to be on the web, we argued about what was acceptable and what was not (no driving and taking photos), and we went on to live and do other things online. . . . Moblog is still alive and well": http://moblog.net/news/.
9 'How 7/7 democratised the media', Torin Douglas, July 4, 2006, BBC online.
10 'Reported.ly says goodbye for now', August 31, 2016, from the website: https://reported.ly/2016/08/31/reported-ly-says-goodbye-for-now.
11 '"My father was martyred by a drone": Yemeni teenager records life months before suffering a similar fate', February 10, 2015. Video.
12 'Yemeni child killed by US drone "lived in fear"', Abubakr al-Shamahi, February 10, 2015, New Arab.
13 'The world needs to know about Yemen's war: But journalists are being silenced', Charlene Rodrigues, October 26, 2015, Guardian.
14 See case studies, including the "twerking girl on fire" story on Storyful's website: https://storyful.com/case-studies/.
15 In a blog post by Little on the company website, announcing he was to leave Storyful, June 2015: https://storyful.com/blog/2015/06/25/mark-little-on-leaving-storyful-stronger-than-ever/.
16 Excerpt from drudgereportarchives.com, an anonymous, independent archive begun in 2001 and registered in the US. The site archives screenshots of Drudge Report posts. The link below includes subsequent follow-up posts, which named Lewinsky as the intern involved with Clinton: www.drudgereportarchives.com/dsp/specialReports_pc_carden_detail.htm?reportID=%7B48035CE9-3FF3-4BD6-83BE-9B9C0A960C7B%7D.
17 Quotes from 'Newsweek's decision', editorial in Newsweek, February 2, 1998 – see http://www.newsweek.com/newsweeks-decision-169856 Linda Tripp was a Pentagon co-worker Lewinsky confided in over several phone conversations which were recorded the "90-minute tape". Excerpts playable from here: http://news.bbc.co.uk/1/hi/events/clinton_under_fire/tapes_and_transcripts/216333.stm or here: https://partners.nytimes.com/library/politics/111898trip-tapes.2a.ram.html.
18 Pew Research Center report 'Navigating news online', 2011, based on 2010 Neilsen statistics.
19 'The online conversation that's dying out', Sullivan, February 2, 2015, on the Dish.
20 https://salampax.wordpress.com/
21 'Salam's story', Rory McCarthy, May 30, 2003, Guardian.
22 'Timeline of Bangladeshi bloggers hacked to death', April 24, 2016, thehindu.com.
23 'Militant group publishes global hitlist of bloggers, activists and writers', Jason Burke, September 23, 2015, Guardian.
24 'For Syria's antigovernment fighters, a Saudi purchase of Croatian arms', C.J. Chivers, Gun blog.
25 'Ethnic cleansing, genocide and the Tawergha', September 26, 2011, humanrightsinvestigations.org.
26 'How I accidentally became an expert on the Syrian conflict', Brown Moses, July 20, 2013, for Sabotage Times.
27 'Distract, deceive, destroy: Putin at war in Syria', Atlantic Council, April 5, 2016.
28 'Human rights squad detects abuse in warzone social media images', November 11, 2016, Aviva Rutkin, New Scientist.

29 'ISIS had a social media campaign, so we tracked them down', May 22, 2016, Bellingcat.
30 'Hunting the Berlin Christmas market attack suspect on social media', Daniel Romein, December 22, 2016, Bellingcat.
31 Office of the High Commissioner for Human Rights.
32 Teacher's note: I often find it easier to do a three-step process in introducing new students to verification tools: 1) teaching them to use the tools, 2) giving them images and/or videos that are potentially fake (I research this bit according to current news stories) and getting them to use the tools on the image/video, 3) setting the "find and verify a story" exercise as homework with a class follow-up, to allow time to find a story that will pique their interest.

References and further study

Flanagin, A. J., Flanagin, C., and Flanagin, J. (2010) 'Technical code and the social construction of the internet', *New Media & Society* 12(2), 179–196.

Shaer, M. (2015) 'The media doesn't care what happens here', *New York Times Magazine*, 18 February 2015. https://www.nytimes.com/2015/02/22/magazine/the-media-doesnt-care-what-happens-here.html?_r=0

Sullivan, A. (2015) 'The years of writing dangerously', *Dish*, 6 February 2015.

Temple, M. (2014) 'A forum for fruitcakes and fascists: The saviour of mainstream journalism', in A. Charles (ed.) *The end of journalism version 2.0*, Peter Lang, Oxford.

Video: '*Eliot Higgins demonstrates geolocation for #FDlive at the Guardian*', May 14, 2016. On YouTube at: www.youtube.com/watch?v=D7zvsXv2ECI

Video: '*Mark Little – the future of news*', Dec 11, 2009 for IIEA1 seminar. On YouTube at: www.youtube.com/watch?v=lSYp0rtKTLM

Wardle, C. (2015) '7/7: Comparing the use of eyewitness media 10 years on', *First Draft*, on *Medium*, 7 July 2015.

Wardle, C., Dubberley, S., and Brown, P. (2014) *Amateur footage: A global study of user-generated content in TV and online news output*, Columbia University's Tow Center for Digital Journalism, New York.

Williams, A., Harte, D., and Turner, J. (2015) 'The value of UK hyper-local community news', *Digital Journalism* 3(5), 680–703.

Author interviews

Eliot Higgins, Founder, Bellingcat, December 2016

7
THE NEW (NON-HUMAN) JOURNALISTS

Among the umpteen things robots struggle to do are climb stairs and show empathy. CoBot, developed at Carnegie Mellon University's Robotics Institute, deals with the stairs issue by waiting by the lift and begging passers-by to press the button for the floor it needs.[1]

In asking for our help, the robot is tapping into the empathy most of us feel when we see weakness in another. Even an inanimate other. Obviously CoBot doesn't know it's tapping into the core of our humanity – it's a robot: it would fail the Voigt-Kampff.[2]

I touched on the importance of empathy in Chapter 5 and how immersive journalism, using games, VR or AR can create an emotional link between subject and audience. In Chapter 6, I talked about the new journalists – the bloggers, witnesses and investigators whose passion for an issue or their subject was delivering deeper or more engaging journalism.

But what if your new "journalist" is incapable of empathy or passion? What if, like CoBot, they are a limited-skills-defined robot? Or an artificial intelligence (AI), or an algorithm?

I once worked with a promising young cub reporter. When the newsroom emptied into the local pub at the end of a long shift, he'd work the bar, glass of Coke in hand (he wouldn't drink alcohol), and chat to everyone – hunting out stories and gossip and contacts. While we sat in "our" corner, moaning about editors and readers and the unrealistic expectations of both, he would still be working. I once asked him why and he was confused by the question: "Why wouldn't I?" he said.

Nosiness; curiosity; a need to know what others know; always wanting to ask the question beyond the comfort zone; being the stranger that people open up to in a bar, on a train, at a crime scene – are these journalistic skills or personal attributes? And can they be taught?

I tell my students that the most important skill a journalist can have is curiosity. Not only about the big stuff – who owns what, why that war started, who's spying on who – but curiosity about the everyday. What's going on with that couple having the whispered argument? What brought that old guy to counting up pennies to buy his pint?

News is what's happening; journalism is discovering what might be happening.

The stories that young reporter picked up were sometimes great, sometimes dull and often needed rewriting. But he quickly got better; he improved – as most of us can – learning from each other and from our own mistakes and successes. Within a few years, he was the foreign editor for a national newspaper. And he could still talk to anyone in any bar.

But robots and algorithms work with what we give them. They need us to push the button to get them to the right floor, or at least to start them travelling. And no matter how many buttons we press, we can't make a robot empathic or curious.

What we can do is teach a robot or AI to mimic curiosity using techniques of discovery or interrogation to find out what's going on – teach them the five Ws effectively. So, put Intelligent Systems Informatics Lab's "journalist robot" in a room and it'll work out what's going on by autonomously exploring its environment – gathering data to assess what's unusual in the room – the "anomalies" that all journalists look for. It'll even question people to gather information, and search the internet to find out more. If something seems newsworthy, the robot will write a basic "story" and publish it to the web.[3]

That was back in 2010. And robots have got better.

Let's wander back to that pub and imagine my junior reporter being replaced by a story-seeking robot. Our robot would have sensors so it could manoeuvre around the bar without bumping into people or knocking over drinks. It could use facial recognition tools and access social media accounts, news reports and public records to be able to identify, say, the local councillor or retired footballer, and ask them tailored questions. It would use natural language processing to ask questions that sound relatively normal and be able to respond, mostly appropriately, to the answers it gets. These things are possible now.

It would probably struggle to "hear" answers in the noisy buzz of a bar, but don't we all, and as long as the robot was cute rather than creepy, people would generally be willing to answer questions. Filmmakers Alexander Reben and Brent Hoff used story-gathering robots to document the things we would be willing to tell a robot. Their experimental Cubies[4] were small and cute with smiley faces drawn onto their cardboard shell and voiced by a young boy.

A combination of cute and fallible – more CoBot than Darth Vader for instance – would get our story-seeking robot a long way. Add in a natural language question-asking programme based on Weizenbaum's "ELIZA" test[5] – asking follow-up questions mostly based on rephrasing answers ("Hi, how are you today?" "I'm depressed, that's how I am!" "I'm sorry to hear you're depressed. Does being in the pub help you?") and, Bingo! As long as no-one pours a beer over our robot's head, it'll find a story. Of sorts.

Because that empathy thing is still an issue. How does a robot know when to make eye contact and when to look away?[6] How does it know when it's better to change the subject? When to press for a response and when to let someone be? When to ask a different question to get a better answer? When the answer is a lie?

A better use for our story-gatherer robot might be those situations where the reporter's role is more note taker than interrogator – court rooms, big press conferences, event launches, council meetings, etc. – anywhere where being there to gather details, a photo, and a couple of quotes is better than not sending a reporter at all.

We could send our robot to situations where it might be dangerous to send a human journalist – war zones for instance. Almost a thousand journalists have been killed in the last ten years (to time of writing), so why not send robots into war zones instead? A robot can capture pictures, record what people say and be controlled at a distance by a journalist-operator, perhaps feeding it questions to ask people the robot meets. Safer, remote gathering of what's happening on the ground could mean we get closer to the reality of those trapped by war or disaster.

Back in 2002, Chris Csikszentmihályi's Afghan eXplorer challenged us to consider that issue by suggesting his robot[7] would report from the war in Afghanistan as an alternative to endangering the lives of journalists. As BBC News reported at the time:

> Robo-journo has one big advantage over its human counterparts. There will be no-one back home worrying about its safety. "They can imprison it, shoot it. I don't care. It is just a robot, its feelings can't get hurt," said Dr Csikszentmihalyi.[8]

In a later interview, Csikszentmihályi criticised journalists' willingness to pick up on that idea that sending robots to report from war zones was a safer – therefore better – option than sending journalists "to report where our tax dollars are going; whether the government is taking care of our kids; who we are there to fight; whether we're choosing the right strategies; and to let, in a democracy, people know which politicians to vote for based on those problems."[9]

Drones, news and helicopters

There are things robot "reporters" are already doing pretty well – like providing cheaper disaster footage or data-dependent stories for tiny audiences, but these are not robots as we might imagine them, but AI and drones.

Media outlets are using algorithmic software to produce stories and drones to capture eyewitness footage. Data is fed in, the algorithm adds structure and an acceptable story is produced. Narrative Science's algorithms (see case study) filled the reporting gaps left by a contracting news industry – in school sports reporting, business data crunching and so on.

In 2002, scenes of flooding in Wiltshire were captured by a viewer with his own drone and sent to – and used by – the BBC.[10] Now every man and his newsroom seems to own a drone and footage of floods and other disasters, and incidents taken from the air by drones has become an everyday part of newsgathering. In the US, media companies filed court documents in 2014[11] arguing the Civil Aviation Authority was "hindering" free speech and press freedom by restricting the commercial use of drones (i.e. use by newspapers but not by government agencies or hobbyists).

FAA regulations[12] (the "Part 107" rule) came into effect in August 2016 limited to "non-hobbyist" drones weighing less than 55 pounds. The rule requires the pilot to have a special licence (or be supervised by someone with the licence); to be aged over 16; to keep the drone within visual line of sight; to limit height to 400 feet and speed to 100 mph, and operation to daylight (or twilight if drone has anti-collision lights) hours only. Flights over unprotected (i.e. out in the open) people on the ground who aren't directly participating in the drone operation are banned, but the FAA rule does not specifically deal with privacy issues or regulate how drones gather data on people or property.

In the UK, rules are similar. The "Dronecode", operated by the Civil Aviation Authority (CAA) also requires the operator to keep the drone within view, under 400ft high and, if it has a camera, at least 50m away from a person, building or vehicle not directly linked to the operator. Camera drones also need to stay at least 150m away from congested areas or events or large groups of people. So, no fans filming football matches from above the ground.

While the Dronecode is written for non-commercial operators, the rules are pretty similar for commercial flyers[13] (e.g. newsrooms), with additional requirements on holding licences (permissions) relative to size of drone and type of operation.

However, Part 107, Dronecode and similar country-based rules are just that – country-based. What's most interesting about drones is where they are being used and by whom. This isn't only an issue about whether journalists should be sending drone-carried cameras over celebrities' backyards,[14] but about how we report the use of drones by governments and other agencies around the globe. What's most interesting about the use of drones in newsgathering is not where you fly and how high, but why the drone is being used. Drones (and robots and algorithms) are what we make them to be, and whether a drone is an eyewitness, a spy or a killer is a decision made by humans.

In December 2013, drones were used to gather footage of clashes between protestors and Thai police. In a country in which media reporting of the government is fairly restrictive, drone footage published by some Thai media and circulated around the world delivered an independent perspective on the scale of the protests.[15]

Drone footage shot by UK journalist Lewis Whyld for the Telegraph mapped the devastation of the city of Tacloban, after Typhoon Haiyan swept through the Philippines in 2013, killing more than 6,300 people. Six months later, he returned and re-shot the area with his drone to document Tacloban's recovery.[16] While in 2015, a drone-shot video by news agency RussiaWorks showed the destruction of Damascus – set to an upbeat music track.[17]

In 2005, Danny Schechter coined the phrase "helicopter journalism" in criticising media coverage of the tsunami that killed hundreds of thousands of people on Boxing Day 2004. The lead story from The Washington Post, opening, "From the skies above Aceh's devastated western coastline", was an example, he said of helicopter journalism, of: "'outside-in' reporting that accesses few if any sources in the country itself, does not speak the language, and does not explain much about what is going on" and drew an analogy with the correspondent who "flies into a conflict zone for an afternoon and gets most of his information from a taxi driver".

Schechter criticised the "endless stories" by Western media of Colin Powell or Kofi Annan visiting scenes, when local reporters on the ground were documenting chaos and disorganisation in the relief effort: "As the crisis deepens, the journalism has not. . . . The reporting is often more graphic than informative."

We might reasonably substitute drone journalism for helicopter journalism if the aim is only to show scale – of destruction, devastation – the graphic rather than the informative. But sometimes the scale is the story and the journalism is in adding the why to the what, where and when – why this happened, why this story is important, why you should care.

Going back again, as Whyld did with post-typhoon Tacloban, can be a crucial part of telling the story and is something as journalists we're frequently – and rightly – criticised for not doing enough.[18] The advantage of using a drone is that it can deliver that grand-scale before and after footage cheaply and relatively safely. The technology means it can even follow the same flight path to show us exactly what has changed. The job of the journalist then becomes one not just of showing us the footage, but of asking questions about whether things changed for the better for the people on the ground.

Here to witness a "man-machine marriage"

However, at least drones help us gather the story we're after as journalists, rather than write that story for us, or instead of us.

Back in 2013, Narrative Science's algorithms produced and published around 1.5 million sports stories. In 2015, it was over four million.

That those sports reports were largely of Little League games is actually what's most important here. Because your response might be "Little League games, so what?" Important to all the players, parents, staff and friends caught up in each game, yes; but important on a global news stage – of course not. Which is why you'll rarely see a paid reporter covering a Little League game, or any other kids' sports team or adult amateur sports league.

Millions upon millions of events happening every single day are never reported because the small target audience means the cost vs benefit to the news industry just isn't worthwhile. Until computer software started writing individual match reports, with a bit of input from the mums and dads watching the match.

Narrative Science's algorithms are not replacing journalists, they're producing the stuff journalists don't do because it's boring or involves masses of data or isn't economically viable to report on. Narrative Science doesn't do as much news reporting as it used to (because "that's sort of at the low end of the technology's capabilities" – see case study at the end of this chapter), but its pioneering work in using algorithms to write news, business and sports reports is part of a surge in algorithm and AI-written news[19] in the last few years.

Automated Insights produced 1.5 billion "narratives" in 2016. Most of that was internal information for companies and individuals (e.g. using their natural language generator to automatically update reports attached to Excel spreadsheets, or tell your MapMyFitness friends what you did on your last workout), rather than news reports. However, the company helped Associated Press produce 12 times more company earnings reports for their business customers. That led to an increase in trading activity for those companies,[20] according to research by Stanford University and the University of Washington. In the Associated Press press release, researcher Elizabeth Blankspoor said: "It's an exciting first step in what is possible with automation technology. It's not about displacing journalists from their jobs – it's about providing coverage for firms that were not previously in the news."

The Washington Post used AI software "Heliograf", developed in-house, to automatically produce short, real-time news reports about the 2016 Olympics and automatically publish the reports to its live blog and some social media.

Jeremy Gilbert, director of strategic initiatives (see Chapter 1 case study) said automated storytelling had "the potential to transform The Post's coverage. More stories, powered by data and machine learning, will lead to a dramatically more personal and customised news experience." Heliograf would free The Post's editorial staff from the drudgery of manually publishing results to concentrate, he said, on "analysis, color from the scene and real insight to stories".[21]

Syllabs, based in Paris, automatically produced 150,000 web pages for Le Monde in four hours during France's 2015 election, reporting highly targeted results from France's 36,000 municipalities. Syllabs's co-founder Claude de Loupy said on Twitter (June 16, 2016): "Robot writers are definitely the future of hyperlocal [journalism]."

It isn't just about automating the story writing. I talked about news aggregators and curators in Chapter 5, but at the cheaper end of that spectrum are chatbots, such as Facebook Messenger, which can automatically send personalised stories – chat – to individual subscribers.

In the US, the New York Times created the NYT Politics Bot for Messenger, sending users text messages with the latest information on the 2016 presidential election, numbers, forecasts, comment from their political team – and the ability to ask questions and receive an (automated) reply. According to TechCrunch:

> While many news bots rely solely on users clicking on prompts or texting pre-configured commands, what's interesting about NYT's Politics bot, which was built by Chatfuel, is that it's powered by an A.I. engine that also lets you talk to the service more conversationally. That is, you can say things like "Will Hillary Clinton win?" or "I live in Texas," and it will return the Upshot forecast or the state's forecast, respectively.[22]

In the UK, the Sun used Messenger to send subscribers football news on their chosen club. The initial experiment was targeted around the transfer period when news about which players might move where was constantly changing. Users received general stories every day, and could subscribe to get stories about particular clubs. According to the newspaper, 95 percent of users chose to subscribe for the personal club updates and they saw higher than usual rates of users clicking through to the main site from stories plugged on the bot.[23]

While user numbers are small (subscribers to both the NYT politics bot and the Sun's football chatbot are a fraction of the users of their Facebook or main news sites), Facebook has made it possible for Messenger users to pay for things within Messenger itself,[24] rather than going to a third-party website such as PayPal, and ramped up its support for Messenger. This may make it easier for newspapers to sell subscription add-ons or products within Messenger, making it more viable to serve those smaller, but more engaged, chatbot audiences.

The key question is not what can robots, drones, algorithms and chatbots do now, but what might someone make them do in the future? And that includes how we choose to use them as journalists. We shouldn't see these as technologies that will take jobs from journalists (the job losses are happening in any case) but as tools that could help us report more of what's happening in the world – and perhaps push journalism to concentrate a bit more on the "why", rather than the "what" or "who".

In the future, human and automated journalism will likely become closely integrated and form a "man-machine marriage." Journalists are best advised to focus on tasks that algorithms cannot perform, such as in-depth analyses, interviews with key people and investigative reporting. While automation will probably replace journalists who merely cover routine events, the technology is also generating new jobs within the process of developing news-generating algorithms (Graefe, 2016).

It is when we stick to the traditions of journalism – the structured story forms, the fact-based reporting, the focus on speed and "new" news – that we make journalism vulnerable. AIs can produce more copy, faster and with fewer errors. And, as the next chapter suggests, by passing embedded traditions such as the five Ws and the inverted pyramid on to the next generation of journalists, we may be weakening our profession.

More automation of journalism is inevitable, not least because there is more data available to us in which to look for stories. Our ability to "crunch" that data as humans is limited, but as humans controlling increasingly capable AIs, we can spot needles in haystacks.

CASE STUDY: NARRATIVE SCIENCE

Kris Hammond works two jobs – Professor of Computer Science at Northwestern University, and Chief Scientist at the company he co-founded – Narrative Science. When I spoke to him, in spring 2016, he was in an ebullient mood. Two jobs clearly agreed with him.

The company, like much in his life he said, arrived accidentally. He'd been working at Northwestern within the artificial intelligence (AI) field, in particular natural language processing: systems that can work with human language.

He and fellow professor Larry Birnbaum ran an incubator called InfoLab and brought together students from computer science and journalism in a research project called StatsMonkey: a prototype that automatically generated baseball game recaps. Two of those students subsequently joined Narrative Science as its first employees. In January 2010, Narrative Science was incorporated, and the business grew, moving away from the StatsMonkey prototype to build a new, patented artificial intelligence authoring platform they named Quill.

Hammond's early interest in AI was on the generative side – generating plans of action to satisfy goals automatically. He began to focus really on information systems, based upon the same principles that he'd been working on within AI – that there are certain things that people are really good at, and certain things that people are really bad at. He was particularly interested in the things people are really bad at, such as being able to articulate what they want, what they are looking for.

"There are a suite of technologies that flow from that basic premise," he told me. "One of the things that we did, in my lab, was we started working on the idea that, when you present someone with information based upon their implicit needs, that is what they care about, you probably don't want to give them a list of things. You don't want to Google-ise the entire experience."

FIGURE 7.1   Kris Hammond of Narrative Science.
Credit: Kris Hammond

They started thinking about how to present information in the ways that we present information to each other: with stories, with explanations, with descriptions: "That led us to start thinking about the notion of narrative, and, in particular, the idea of a narrative arc, defining how computers interact with people."

They built a system called "News at Seven" (Figure 7.2) to present material as a news show:[25] "It was a really fun project, and a really interesting project for us, where, essentially, we were building out narratives on a substrate of search."

He sent a handful of his computer science students to take classes over at Medill, Northwestern's journalism school, in order to better understand the narrative, journalistic process. That attracted the interest of the dean of the school and they began working together. Hammond became a faculty member in journalism and started teaching in journalism.

"It was that sequence that led to us becoming part of the journalism school, and, in fact, working on the core technology that, eventually, became the Narrative Science technology. That is storytelling, but not on the basis of search, but really a basis of having data, analysing the data, figuring what's true in the world and then explaining to somebody what's going on, based upon [the AI's] understanding of how narratives work."

Narrative might just as easily be explored through fiction – film for instance. But there was a key factor that drove Hammond and the InfoLab team towards news: "Because news is based on what is true". That created a natural link between the data and the storytelling.

FIGURE 7.2   Screenshot of News at Seven, taken February 26, 2017.
Credit: Kris Hammond

"For example, one of [News at Seven's] dynamics was it would do film reviews. It would do so by going to reviewer sites, looking up scores, and actually figuring out from that what the sort of zeitgeist was, to do with a movie. Then, based upon that zeitgeist, it would say: 'Oh, if there are two extreme points of view, we're going to have an argument. We're going to build an argument. If there's a strong view on one side, we'll try to find counterpoints. But if there's sort of an average view, we're going to just sort of describe things.'"

Depending on what the system saw as true in the world, it would make decisions about how it would structure the narrative. "It was interesting," said Hammond. "It was less: 'We're going to do journalism,' and more: 'We're going to build systems that can look at what is available to the machine, figure out what's true, and then explain it to people' because people can't look at that data on their own and figure it out."

The system was about truth based on the data that's already out there, so the information, the numbers, the perspectives, the understanding that people have. It's a reflection of the world as we see it as truth, but without the bias (largely) that a journalist or an editorial stance might bring into it. A reflection of the world through its data.

He added: "Sometimes, it's a bad reflection. I mean, there's bad data, and there's good data. It's a reflection of the world, and what Quill does, what News at Seven was aimed at doing, is really finding the truth in that data, and then giving voice to it."

As an example, Hammond describes the investor who wants to know how their investments might be doing: "You want to know how the market is doing, but you don't want to know how the market is doing in the abstract. You actually want to know how the market is doing with regard to your investments. That doesn't just mean the value of your investments. It means the market as it relates to them. If you have a lot of technology stocks, you care about how those stocks are doing, but how, actually, technology stock is doing in general, and then how the market is doing in general, and maybe how developed world stocks are doing. There are all these different things that you might look at, but they all kind of converge on you want to know about the things that are important to you."

Those, says Hammond, are editorial decisions: telling that investor what they want to know relative to what stocks they own and what might impact on those stocks: "They're based upon, really, two ideas. One is, what's genuinely important in the world? For example, I don't own any Apple stock, but if Apple stock dropped in price 50 percent, that's like astoundingly important – that comes to the surface. Then, tied to that is, what is interesting or impactful to the audience? If there are stocks that are less important to the global world, but actually impactful on you, those will also come to the fore."

Likewise, you might want to know how the game went for the sports team you follow but you don't want to be told that the other team absolutely beat the hell out of them: "That would be me not paying attention to what you care about."

"I might tell you that they lost, and I'll tell you why they lost – I will not withhold anything from you. But what I will do is, I will tell you about where they struggled, where they were striving, where they did well, even in the face of a failure. That also has a very editorial feel. I'm a big believer in data systems having an editorial point of view, but one, it's got to be transparent, two, it can't be built by engineers. That's an important thing."

He is critical of systems that are pure algorithm, pure engineering. For example, Google News which might deliver news stories related to a particular search – a collection of keyword-related stories. These are editorial-related decisions, in that some stories are shown rather than others: "I love Google News, but those editorial decisions are not particularly transparent, and they're made by someone whose goal is to have you click on something, not to give you multiple points of view. . . . [E]ditorial control should be in the hands of people who know how to provide editorial control."

What Hammond is describing is a service, a deliverer of content, which is personalised, which is curated in the sense that it's gathering information that the receiver might be interested in, but which also has the potential to be "spun" towards the user's particular viewpoint and interests. It goes beyond Google News collecting information related to keywords that an individual may be interested in to delivering information that reflects their thinking as well as their interests.

That makes it less about algorithms versus journalism, I suggested to him, but something additional to journalism. News which is based not only on my interests, but on my perspective, is quite a seductive and efficient way of articulating that information.

"I would say that there is an interesting difference," said Hammond. "Between for example, a site or a service that curates news based upon your interests, and creating news stories that are attending to your interests or attending to what is impactful to you. The first creates news bubbles, so that no matter how many times I go to The Washington Post, I either see very conservative or very liberal stories, because that's what they think I care about; then that's what I'll see.

"If I see only stories having to do with Chicago, and I never see anything having to do with Bosnia, or Syria, or Turkey, that's easy to do. That's what Facebook is. Your news, the news on Facebook is highly curated, but it's highly curated based upon algorithms associated with your interests. That creates a bubble. You only see those things."

But news created based on an understanding of the individual, or group of individuals, could deliver a deeper, more meaningful version of the news. Not personalised news stories, but a personalised explanation of the news and information – news that resonates: "News and information that's related to me because the system has struggled to relate it to you. That, I think, is the promise of news and information being more algorithmic."

Narrative Science – and Hammond – had attracted a lot of press because of that interest in algorithmically generated news using narrative techniques. Major news outlets were experimenting with using the Quill software to generate news reports, largely hyper-local, amateur sports reports and stock market reports – stories that were data heavy and narratively simple. Hammond was being quoted saying around 90 percent of journalism would be written by computers by 2030. However, the company had stepped back from journalism in the last year or so: "We don't do a lot of media work. We do some work for Forbes,[26] we do work for the Big Ten Network. We do the Sports Network, so we still do a little bit, but it's certainly not our focus for a couple of really straightforward reasons.

"One, the big one, is that just in terms of what the technology can do, writing a single story about an event, even though we write either hundreds or thousands or tens of thousands of similar stories about similar kinds of events, is sort of at the low end of the technology's capabilities. Taking a single event, and then writing literally a million stories associated with it, that are aimed at particular constituencies, and particular individuals, particular organisations, that's a much more powerful use of the technology.

"The second thing, and this was something that we always knew, is that we're living in, I think, a fascinating world. We have a genuine wealth of absolutely marvellous data about ourselves, about our government, within organisations. But the problem is that data is in a form that very, very, very few people can understand. Even things like business data, there'll be parts of an organisation that they build business intelligence tools for, so other people can understand what's going on, but those tools are really hard to understand."

So, the mission became about making people smarter by helping them understand the data: "That was not in the realm of journalism anymore."

Journalistically, he loves the work they still do with partner company Game Changer, which has a scoring app for Little League baseball games. People at the game input information and scores, that data is passed to Narrative Science and Quill writes a game story – about four million of them in 2015.

"Not many people read any given story," he said. "It's mostly eight-year-olds and their dads. There isn't a journalist in the country that's covering that, but we're able to turn something that is of marginal value into something that, for any given individual who's reading the story, is incredibly valuable, incredibly valuable.

"That's actually the promise of the technology, to create that value by letting people understand what's happening in the world."

A lot of their work ("our bread and butter") is now in the financial sector, around 40 percent of their customer base at the time we spoke: portfolio analysis, producing personalised quarterly portfolio reports and impact narratives. It still excites Hammond, however. It's still on the path to the core mission, which is to make people smarter by explaining the data.

"We have a path. Part of that path is making enough money so that the company can thrive. Part of that, part of what we're doing now, is building out the next version of the technology, which is really aimed at having it be available to a much broader audience. . . . We have this notion that we tend to refer to as narrative analytics, that is when you tell [the system]: 'Here's what I need to say, here's the kind of story I want to tell,' the system knows the kind of analysis it needs to perform in order to build up a knowledge that we'll then use to generate the story.

"You can change a whole bunch of things along the way," he added. "But the place where you can't change things is where it's preserving the truth."

The company had submitted a set of new and renewal patents in 2016; it was maturing and shifting – and the focus on what will pay is neither surprising nor unnecessary. What is of interest in what Narrative Science is doing however is the potential to use their software to go beyond telling stories from data but to investigate data – to find stories within the numbers. Would that get lost in the need to make money and expand?

Hammond said the goals were not in conflict with each other – it was possible to do both. He gave as example the data associated with the Chicago beachfront, from sensors up and down the beachfront that deliver data about the water quality.

"It turns into a big spreadsheet, and there are very few families that have somebody [who] is a data scientist! We take the same data, do the same kinds of analysis, and then for every single beachfront, say something about the water quality, how it's doing, how it's changed and what the alternatives are for anyone who wants to go to the beach that day."

The future aim is to open up interaction with the system to enable other people to build their own stories and their own data connectors, to tell stories about the data that they care about. But that means building a system that is easy to interact with.

"My particular goal is that by the time I die . . . I want people to look at spreadsheets in exactly the same way as they look at computer punch cards, that is, this used to be the way we communicated with the machine, and the machine communicated with us. By humanising the machine, and having it come to us with: 'Here's what's happening in the world,' we can, I think, slow down the process of mechanising people."

Everyone in the company, he said, had their own area that they wanted to apply the technology to "outside of the realm of the core business, and how we make money. We're all dedicated to getting there."

Which sounds worthy and fabulous, but could Narrative Science just be another company collecting lots and lots of data to use, or for other people to use – more commercialisation of data, rather than have a genuine desire to tell us more about the world?

"In terms of the data that is coming up, we will always have clients who have commercial interests in our generating things for their commercial use," said Hammond. "Usually, our clients provide us with whatever data they have, but the technology will also be there so that groups that are looking at other kinds of data, for other reasons, will have the technology available to them.

"So that, if someone who has a treasure trove of data having to do with income levels, demographics, socio-graphics, government services, transportation services, food services, you might have this massive database that goes all across the United States, but then what do you do with it? Do you write one story about it, or do you have it be that you can write a story for every single neighbourhood? In fact, a critical story of every single neighbourhood, with comparison, and finding correlations, and all of that. You need this technology to be in a mature state so that anyone can do that, and that's the issue.

"I think there's a wealth of change that can come from that moment where we realise that, in order for people to make informed decisions, they have to be informed. But almost no one is being informed by raw data."

Suggested assignments

Practical training

The National Institute for Computer Assisted Reporting has been supporting journalists in finding stories in data since 1989. Its website includes an excellent library of resources and tools. At https://learn.ire.org/free-videos/ you'll find videos introducing you to a range of data journalism tools. Browse through them until you find a tool that you'd particularly like to try. Follow the link underneath the video to further information to help you learn how to work with that tool.

Practical exercise

Most of us are lazy searchers. We'd rather make multiple ineffective searches than learn how to use specific Boolean operators or other techniques. However, Google's Advanced Search page can help you improve your search skills. Go to www.google.co.uk/advanced_search and work through what each different box does to a search. Carefully note the text to the right of each check box; this explains the indicator that you would use to force a search of this type in Google without having to use the Advanced Search tool – for example, putting a minus sign in front of word to stop those words appearing in a search. Practice using the operators until you've memorised the ones that will be most useful to you in the future.

Notes

1 'CoBots: collaborative robots servicing multi-floor buildings', Veloso, M. et al. (2012), Carnegie Mellon University, School of Computer Science. Videos of the CoBots (collaborative robots) and further links at: www.cs.cmu.edu/~coral/projects/cobot/.
2 Philip K. Dick's fictional test of whether someone is human or a replicant (robot) using the Voigt-Kampff machine and a series of questions designed to test empathy levels, from 'Do Androids Dream of Electric Sheep?' and Ridley Scott's film adaptation *Bladerunner*. Take the test yourself at: www.bfi.org.uk/are-you-a-replicant.
3 Source: 'Robot journalist takes pictures, asks questions, publishes online', Aaron Saenz, Mar 18, 2010, for SingularityHub. Original paper 'Journalist robot: robot system making news articles from real world', Matsumoto R. et al. (2007) Tokyo University.
4 Video of 2013 documentary project at Tribeca Film festival: https://vimeo.com/57930115.
5 In 1966, computer scientist Joseph Weizenbaum developed the chatterbot ELIZA in an early and important piece of work in AI and natural language development. He discovered one language script he created – the DOCTOR script which parodied psychotherapist techniques, was unexpectedly successful. Users began to unconsciously assume ELIZA's questions implied interest and became emotionally attached to the chatterbot, even when reminded it was a robot hardwired to a script.
6 There's a fair bit of work going on around teaching robots when to hold a human's gaze and when to look away; see: 'This robot's been programmed to look you in the eye at just the right times', May 6, 2014, Jason Dorrier on Singularity Hub.
7 Despite being reported by media outlets around the world, the Afghan eXplorer never existed as a working robot "reporter", it was created as a media artifact to challenge the way we think about journalism. The article 'Robots for Resistance', in "References and further study" includes Csikszentmihályi interviewed on his eXplorer.
8 'Robo-reporter goes to war', Jane Wakefield, 28 March, 2002, BBC News Online.
9 See "References and further study": 'Robots of resistance', Luke Yoquinto, October 9, 2014.
10 'UK flooding: Malmesbury seen from a drone camera', 25 November 2012, BBC News Online.
11 'FAA's drone policy is having "impermissible chilling effect" – News Media', May 6, 2014, Tow Center.
12 'Summary of small unmanned aircraft rule', www.faa.gov.
13 'Unmanned aircraft: requirements for operating in airspace', www.caa.co.uk.
14 In 2015, California signed into state law an extension to privacy and trespass law to make it an offence to send a drone into the airspace above someone's property to capture picture, video or sound of that individual or his/her family.
15 Several sources, including: 'Bangkok's unlikely embrace of drone journalism shows the extent of the government's problems', November 25, 2013, Newley Purnell, Quartz.
16 'Typhoon Haiyan six months on: two 360 panoramas show Tacloban's recovery', Lewis Whyld, May 6, 2014, Telegraph.
17 'Russia release terrifying high quality drone footage of Damascus devastation', Charlie Atkin, October 21, 2015, Independent.
18 Here's an example. During the research for this chapter, I came across the story of Uplift Aeronautics and the Syria Airlift Project's bid to use drones to drop humanitarian aid into difficult locations in Syria. The issue of whether drones could be used for that purpose was one that came up time and again in news and comment during 2016. However, this crowdfunded attempt to use drones to deliver aid had been barely reported, aside from initial interest in it as a concept. Perhaps because, as a follow-up story, it was messy – the project had failed after running out of funding and the volunteers were "burned out" (http://uplift.aero/?p=324). No-one went back and covered why it had failed. There have been a handful of successful uses of drones in aid, but the investment isn't there. Yet both Amazon and Google are racing each other to use drones to deliver our shopping, and Facebook is working on solar-powered drones to connect the developing world to the internet.

19 Also called automated journalism or automated storytelling, but it is *not* "robot journalism"!
20 'Study: News automation by AP increases trading in financial markets', Associated Press press release, December 8, 2016.
21 'The Washington Post experiments with automated storytelling to help power 2016 Rio Olympics coverage', August 5, 2016, The Washington Post.
22 'You can now get daily election updates on Messenger, with NYT Politics' new chatbot', Sarah Perez, October 20, 2016, TechCrunch.
23 'The Sun's Facebook chatbot drove nearly half users back to its site', Lucinda Southern, September 14, 2016, DigiDay.
24 'Facebook Messenger now allows payments in its 30,000 chat bots', September 12, 2016, TechCrunch.
25 http://infolab.northwestern.edu/projects/news-at-seven.html
26 http://resources.narrativescience.com/h/i/83535927-case-study-forbes

References and further study

Graefe, A. (2016) *Guide to automated journalism*, Tow Center for Digital Journalism, New York.

Schechter, D. (2005) 'Helicopter journalism', 9 January 2005, ZNet: https://zcomm.org/znetarticle/helicopter-journalism-by-danny-schechter/

Yoquinto, L. (2014) 'The Robots of Resistance', *Big Roundtable*, 9 October 2014.

Author interviews

Kris Hammond, Chief Scientist and Co-Founder Narrative Science, August 2016

8
NEW NARRATIVES IN NEWS

In the early hours of April 15, 1865, a telegram was sent by the US Secretary of War, Edwin Stanton. It began:

> This evening at about 9:30 P.M., at Ford's Theatre, the President, while sitting in his private box with Mrs. LINCOLN, Mrs. HARRIS, and Major RATHBURN, was shot by an assassin, who suddenly entered the box and approached behind the President.
>
> The assassin then leaped upon the stage, brandishing a large dagger or knife, and made his escape in the rear of the theatre.
>
> The pistol ball entered the back of the President's head and penetrated nearly through the head. The wound is mortal. The President has been insensible ever since it was inflicted, and is now dying.

The telegram continues, and Stanton was to send further messages as events unfolded that day, but what makes this first telegram particularly interesting (aside from the historical significance) is that it was used pretty much verbatim by most newspapers (Figure 8.1).

There are several reasons for that. Stanton wasn't there, so he can't be counted as an eyewitness, but his high-ranking role carries authority. And the telegram is a public statement – effectively a government press release on what is believed to have happened. Then and now that would make Stanton's telegram a primary source and reason to quote from it.

But to use it all? In large part that's about the relationship between press and government in the 1860s. Stanton himself introduced censorship and restricted press access into war reporting and filled the news gap by sending his own official War Diary to newspapers during the civil war (Mindich, 1993). It may also be

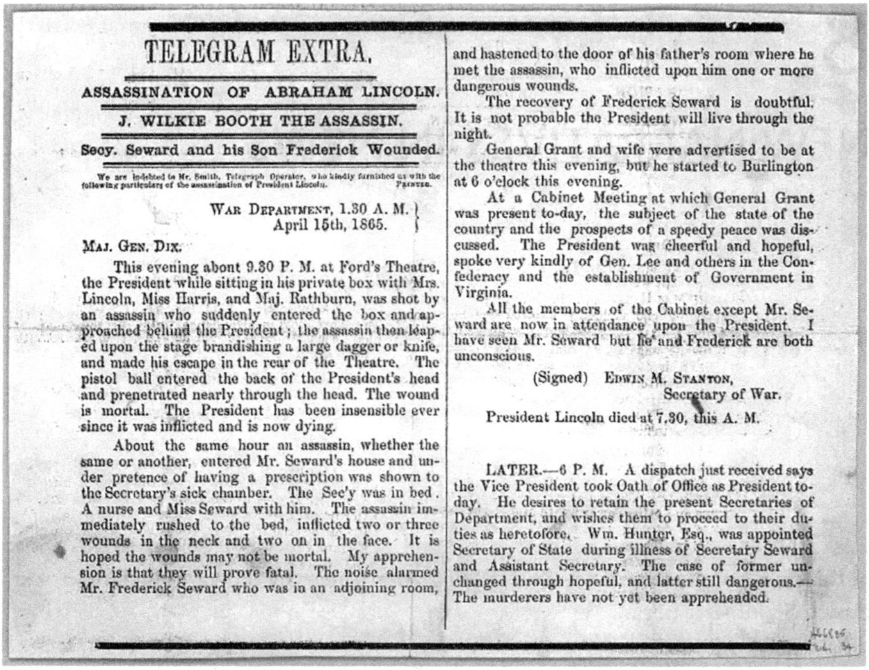

FIGURE 8.1 Telegram detailing the assassination of Abraham Lincoln. J. Wilkie Booth the assassin. Secy Seward and his son Frederick wounded . . . War department, 1.30 A. M. April 15th, 1865. Pdf.
Retrieved from the Library of Congress, www.loc.gov/item/rbpe.12601000

about adding gravitas to the reporting – this is the Secretary of War writing about brandished daggers and mortal head wounds, there is no need to add extra drama.

But it's also about a profession that had not yet developed the structured ways of delivering a story that we work with today. The invention of the telegraph in 1845 had already forced a more economical way of writing (when each word costs money, each one has to be worth paying for), but according to Mindich, the inverted pyramid "was born with the coverage of Lincoln's death".

Stanton wasn't a journalist, but note how those Ws are neatly encapsulated in the first paragraph – when, where, who, what. A journalist might have got to the lead line – that the President was dying – rather sooner than the third paragraph, but Stanton is doing what most journalists still did at that point, which was to tell the story of what happened as a chronological narrative. Reporting then had been largely "stenography, observations, and sketches" (Schudson, 2008: 81) without the structures we use today.

Obviously, we still put the best line first in a story because we want to attract an audience, but we have to ask, what is the point of an inverted triangle of importance based on, essentially, assuming our audience will gradually get bored with our report and drift away? If we put all the good stuff in the first three paragraphs – the line/lede/lead, the key Ws, the most important facts, the best quote – why bother producing more?

The answer is that we are writing not only for our audience but often for an employer that needs us to fill a pre-determined space – whether an empty box on a newspaper page or fixed minutes for a radio or TV report, the length set by a mixture of editorial space available around ad space, and self-imposed limits by which we expect to hold our audience's attention: this many items, this many words, broken up in these ways.

The focus becomes on news as series of isolated reports on events, rather than as interconnected and ongoing stories that may need explanation as well as information.

As news migrated online, we should have expected that to change. There are no boxes to fill on pages, each story has its own web page and each can be any length we want it to be. Videos can be as long or as short as we like: the ads, if we have them, will largely top and tail our report. Story length is limited by the delivery technology – storage space, download speed, memory power – not by the software.

And yet. As the web became professionalised, journalism took those same offline structures to its new online home. Even as least as I write this, the BBC Academy instructs new journalists on its "Online journalism tips" page that:

> Online reporting demands certain techniques to engage the reader . . . key skills [are] ensuring headlines grab their attention, keeping language simple, sentences short, and telling the story in the first four paragraphs.[1]

In case you didn't get it the first time, the way to ensure the story works across all media platforms, particularly in a mobile-first world, is to tell it in four parts, around 70 words. The rule is "a staple of writing for the BBC News website. The piece needs to be balanced and legally sound. It must also give the mobile reader a bite-size version of the story in case they do not want to read any further."

I wouldn't disagree with that per se, but "in case they don't want to read any further"? Shouldn't it be about the ability to decide what an audience wants/needs to know, and the skills to engage and interest them in a story that's as long as it needs to be?

My problem with any "rule" that starts by insisting every story is told – even in essence – in four paragraphs, is that you don't need a journalist to do that job, just a reasonable writer. Human or AI.

It shouldn't be about fixed structures for stories, but about what works for that individual story. To re-quote Stuart Millar, from the Chapter 3 case study, it's about knowing how you create content to give it the life you want it to have online: "Is it a 600 word post? Or is it a video for Facebook? Or what is the thing that will make this fly on Facebook as opposed to on Twitter, say? Those are editorial decisions as to the best way of doing a story."

The issue isn't how many words but how many stories we produce. Too much of the time we're producing what Millar's editor-in-chief, Ben Smith, calls "commodity news" – stories everyone has and all we're trying to do is get a fresh quote for our own media outlet.

In 2011, Twitter founders Biz Stone and Ev Williams launched Medium. Williams had form – he also co-founded Blogger (sold to Google) and podcasting pioneer Odeo (sold to Sonic Mountain), before starting Twitter in 2006 with Stone and others. While Twitter taught us to tell stories in 140 characters, Medium was built for long-form writing.

Stories were measured by how long they would take to read, rather than how many words. Like all the great ideas, that was simple but also revolutionary. By saying how much time a story would take to read, they were putting the reader in charge of deciding whether they had that time to give, whether they would skip the story or save it to read later.

As a young broadcast journalist, I was taught to mark up my scripts by dividing up each group of three or so words as one second of airtime. I might properly time the script later, but that three-word marker was a quick reckoning tool to assess the time my story would take up. It took Williams and his techy mates to recognise that the audience was constantly having to make that same assessment themselves: "Have I got time to read/listen to this story I'm interested in?"

It was a couple of years – 2013 – before Medium opened its doors to the public to produce their own stories, and a couple more years before it started to develop as a sort of department store of better blogs, attracting small, esoteric publishers to its platform, with a focus on longer, compelling stories, a design aesthetic influenced by broadsheet newspapers, and a degree of curation to help users navigate to stuff that might interest them.

There are plenty of places now to read longer articles, deeper thinking and complex explainers. From The Washington Post to the Conversation, from the New Yorker to the Big Roundtable, from Vox to Upworthy and many more.

Even YouTube has enabled unlimited length for videos (from verified users) since 2010, and rather than flood YouTube with 25-minute videos of your cats playing, what that move enabled was independent feature-length programmes and original drama. Streaming video technology (and behaviour) has enabled YouTube, Netflix and Prime producers to create programming that isn't limited by traditional broadcast schedule ideas or ad breaks.

The story structure rules have been subverted in the past, for example in gonzo journalism, but it is the intersection between technologists, entrepreneurs and journalists in new media that is underpinning the experimentation with news narratives that this chapter focuses on.

There's a word that has become both praise and critique among journalists – "snowfalling" or "to Snowfall". It refers to the 2012 New York Times Pulitzer-winning feature Snow Fall[2] about a group of skiers caught up in an avalanche. It is gorgeous-looking interactive storytelling. Seamlessly integrating words, pictures, video, explainers, graphics, links, maps and audio into something that only the web makes possible. And it puts the long in long form.

I remember being blown away the first time I saw it and every group of students I've shown it to has been similarly mesmerised. But, despite the majesty of John Branch's writing ("Snow filled her mouth. She caromed off things she never saw, tumbling through a cluttered canyon like a steel marble falling through pins in a pachinko machine."), I've never yet met anyone who has read the whole thing. Hence "snowfalling" which in journalism circles has come to mean taking time and people (six months involving up to ten staff for Snow Fall[3]) to create something which wins awards but not necessarily readers.

The New York Times has produced other stunning interactive multimedia stories – my personal favourites are The Jockey, with its use of live audio to create atmosphere, and Tomato Can Blues which uses videogame-style parallax scrolling to "animate" the illustrations and a neat audio option.

The NYT is not the only traditional newspaper to play at the edges of what the web can bring to storytelling, but what is important in the context of this chapter is how these new forms go beyond 600 words and a picture, to deliver something much more elastic in structure.

Way back in 2008, the Tampa Bay Times produced 'The Girl in the Window'[4] about the rescue and rehabilitation of an abused and feral child. Journalist Lane de Gregory got the story through her local contacts and, through them, access to child's new parents and her story. It is a strong story in itself but that decision – in 2008 – to create an interactive multimedia piece with audio, slideshows and video is even more remarkable.

What makes the story compelling however isn't its interactivity (that's looking a bit clunky nowadays), but the journalism. DeGregory and her colleague photographer Melissa Lyttle worked together, gradually building up trust with the child and her family, spending time with them, interviewing other actors. Long-form journalism is also about the time put into building relationships and gathering the story, not just the time it takes to digest it. From a 2008 interview with Lyttle:

> While Lane got to know the parents and was sitting there with the caseworker . . . I had about three hours with Danielle. And I got her really comfortable in front of the camera because I sat there for so long and I watched the same movements over and over.[5]

DeGregory spoke of her and Lyttle spending time with the family together, over four or five months, when one of them "could be a fly on the wall while the other person asked the questions".

What 'The Girl in the Window' shows is that a strong story is a strong story, it doesn't have to be a new story. I've noticed that my students – particularly the women in the class – always spend longer with 'Girl' than with 'Snow Fall'. It's that empathy thing.

"Stories don't end when the article is done"

I used the word "long form" in relation to journalism in that previous section, and a couple of other words – interactive and multimedia. Here are two more – structured and atomised.

If the journalism of the past was about creating structures that work – the five Ws, the inverted pyramid, the telling the story in four pars, and so on, the journalism of now is about deconstructing the story into discrete parts that can be reassembled in different ways.

What I mean is that, instead of seeing the story as one thing – a 600-word article or a three-minute report, for instance, we see it as a group of things: paragraphs that deliver different elements of the story (this happened; because of this; then that happened; this quote), and assets such as video clips, pictures, etc., which can combine to produce one or several articles. Those things, parts, can be switched around or dropped as the story updates and develops.

One of the start-ups that did this first and best was Circa. Launched in 2011, it closed its doors in 2015. My interview with David Cohn, former Chief Content Officer, is in the case study at the end of this section, but essentially Circa's editors took each paragraph and tried to make it a discrete unit that could be understood apart from every other paragraph. In doing so they made a much more flexible version of the news.

As Cohn explained it to me, each paragraph was a type of paragraph: "This is a fact. This is a quote. This is a statistic. This is an event. This is an image." And each type required different information. "So, a statistic is a fact as a number. An event is a fact that we place on a map in time and space. An image was the fact of the image." The paragraphs – points, they called them – operated independently so they could be dropped (as the story moved on), brought back or reassembled into a different story, theoretically according to what the reader already knew.

"Stories don't end when the article is done," said Cohn. "It is kind of like, 'Oh. It is done. We finished.' When in reality the story continues. Articles don't reflect that nature." Whereas the "little bits of information" in each point can be linked to previous bits of information, and the ongoing story. As a story "forks" – for example the Boston Marathon bombing – the bits of information can go in different directions.

Cohn again: "There was the day of the bombing which was one story. Then there was a manhunt which actually forked, we called them forks, and was its own story. Eventually they found him in the boat [new story]. Then there was a trial, and the trial got its own story as well."

"Bridges" linked story forks so the end of one story – for example Zarnoff's arrest, becomes the top of the next new story, say announcing the trial date. But if the reader was confused by the new story, they could follow a bridge to another point. "You are like, 'Well, who is this? What is the background?' and you could go to the story that was the manhunt. All of these stories had bridges. Bridges are basically links, but they were literally facts or data points that existed in multiple stories."

Circa was not the last to attempt to deconstruct stories into component elements in order to make them work better. BuzzFeed builds its stories from "blocks" (also in the case study), AJ+ (spun out from parent media publisher Al Jazeera) works with "cards" of elements which "stack" to build the story. Vox[6] does a similar thing – grouping cards of related stories into a subject stack. The BBC has experimented with "elastic" news and "object-based broadcasting" to deliver mobile news of "atomised and adaptive experiences, based on assembling items of content at the point of consumption."[7]

That each publisher uses its own words to define this deconstruction process is an indication of how new it is as a concept. When everyone is doing it, we'll all start using the same terms to describe it. But regardless of whether we all end up working with cards or blocks, it's that overturning of journalism's 200-year-old inverted pyramid concept that is the takeaway.

As Mark Coddington (2015) says in his piece on structured news (see "References and further study"), Circa's human editors were actually re-aligning the news universe:

> Circa's branch system required its journalists to view every event as inseparable from some broader social or political context, which seems much closer to the way things function in reality than the way they have traditionally been presented in news.

Approaching news as multiverse rather than universe (this subject channel, that distinct story) is something we're not yet doing in journalism, but the more we play with news structures and storytelling formats, the closer we'll get to delivering news as something we experience rather than watch.

As Chapter 10 explores further, one barrier to that is processing power. That Circa, AJ+, Vice, BuzzFeed, Vox et al. are mostly using human editors and journalists to create their story stacks limits the scale of that news multiverse and the ability of each piece of news to travel on its own around the web, attracting its own linked stories.

CASE STUDY: TOM PHILLIPS ON BUZZFEED'S "BLOCKS" AND DAVID COHN ON CIRCA'S "POINTS"

Experimentation with story formats is a particular focus for Tom Phillips, BuzzFeed UK's editorial director leading its New Formats team (less a "team" more a permeable grouping of creatives). Phillips was one of BuzzFeed UK's earliest hires, "its seventh or eighth", he said, brought in in 2013 by BuzzFeed UK founding editor Luke Lewis, from Trinity Mirror's UsVsTh3m.

Phillips said the process of developing UK rather than US-friendly content took time – a learning process: "There were certain kinds of things that would do well in America that wouldn't work over here, like broadly things in the 'inspirational' category, uplifting inspiring tales. If there was a difference in tone it was that ours was slightly, cynical isn't quite the right word, but ours was very much focused on humour, a bit of sarcasm, slightly more piss-takey, slightly less 'hugging'."

That issue of what differentiated BuzzFeed UK content from BuzzFeed US – that British tone of voice – was and is something that exercises the editorial team. Phillips said the early days were characterised by playing classic tropes – "the Queen and corgis, that sort of thing". Danny Boyle's work for the 2012 London Olympics opening ceremony was a key moment: Boyle's focus on aspects of British culture and history that were not the standard tales, pushed the BuzzFeed team towards a Britishness that was "young and liberal and open".

Much of Phillips's work in 2016 had been around "upping their game" in being funny about the news – explainers, quizzes, new ways of telling news stories that play on that British, self-deprecating, aware of the absurdities but not nihilistic, funny approach. The "news jokes, we keep trying to come up with a better name".

One of the key formats he and his team worked on was quizzes – not just as a structure but as an intuitive, fast-turnaround tool for all journalists. The aim is to build a new tool or format in a day or so "while a story is still a story" rather than the six months' development time a traditional news publisher might consider. Phillips said that was partly a reflection of BuzzFeed's younger editorial team's "let's do this now, let's do this now!" approach.

What's driving his team is not just fast turnaround – creating something new in hours rather than days – but creating something evergreen that can be used time and again, iterated on, developed and become part of the toolkit for writers, rather than build spectacular one-offs.

He's critical of the news industry "award culture" that encourages big showcase projects to win awards and grab attention: "They're not actually very useful in the long term to the future of journalism. Nothing that takes three months to build from scratch, custom every single time, is the future of journalism – it's *part* of the future but it is not *the* future of journalism. We're not going to be making Snowfalls all the time."

He adds: "There is a side of this where you want people to experiment with things as much as possible – find out things early on – but I do have this worry when I see people putting lots of money into virtual reality experiences, stuff like that, and I just think, 'no'."

Phillips walks me through the story creation process within BuzzFeed's custom CMS (content management system). It starts with the writer choosing one of two options – Article or List. Article has further options – article or feature. Feature has a particular, long-form layout (very Medium-like, with screen-wide feature image options), and List can be numbered or not. New formats that Phillips's team have created, such as their quizzes, are often created in a separate editor tool and then dropped into the article as a block of code.

Non-numbered lists tend be used more as a design tool, particularly for explainers such as Phillips's piece on Theresa May,[8] because the block-based layout is friendlier to breaking up text with lots of dropped-in pictures and gifs.

"The atomised story thing is a large part of how we work," he said. "And also how we construct our stories. There's a fascinating extent to how much does our CMS influence our approach to news because it's entirely constructed around "sub-buzzes", as we call them. Each thing is a block and you can move them around in the content management system.

That comes from the List background basically, but it crosses over into the news side as well."

Phillips said a journalist may still write 800-word stories, but that atomised approach to crafting a story means each of those story chunks, those "sub-buzzes", could live separately somewhere else; stories are assembled and can be reassembled. The question, he said, then becomes how do you drop "a little bit of VR" into an article, rather than how do you create a stand-alone VR piece?

The threat to that process comes from new distributary platforms such as Facebook's Instant Articles or Google's Accelerated Mobile Pages (AMP) initiative[9] which strips out code and custom design elements in favour of quick-loading for mobile and a degree control of experience from those platforms.[10]

"I think that there are legitimate concerns," said Phillips. "That they're actually holding back the development of certain newer forms of journalism because you can't do it because it'll get stripped out. . . . You're not going to get traffic from Google basically unless you are stripping it down."

He understands the push to "clean out" web content from the massive overloading of cookies and Java script that has slowed the experience for users, but worries about the effect on innovation if Google and Facebook are prioritising a return to a basic format of picture-plus-words news story, and pre-approved code.

Phillips believes it's less of an issue for BuzzFeed because the company is social rather than search-focused, which means changes Facebook makes to Instant Articles matter more than what Google is doing with AMP. But he can see a point at which news publishers need to become "white-listed" by Facebook and Google so that more of their content makes it through the filters.

As example, one of the pieces Philips is proudest of is a memory-led timeline of the London 7/7 terrorist attack[11]: "Rossalyn Warren put a call-out on the site for people's memories on that day and we constructed this timeline composed of memories. . . . That one we pulled out all the stops.

"I was proud of it because it got an amazing response, it genuinely connected with people. It wasn't just that it did well in terms of readership, it was the fact that when people were sharing it everybody was sharing it with their own thoughts. Usually when you share something it pre-fills with the headline of the piece, and that's the default share text, but almost nobody was sharing it with the default headline; everybody was taking the link and writing their own thoughts. I'm proud of that because it was technology in service of a creative and emotive idea."

David Cohn,[12] first with Spot Us, then Circa, then AJ+, now with Advanced Digital, had been involved in innovation around journalism for around ten years when I spoke with him. His role at Advanced is as Senior Director in a new division to incubate and develop ideas. Our conversation focused on ideas around deconstructing news.

"I would put it this way," he told me. "Different organisations have different base units of journalism. So, a broadcast company is going to produce video segments. The majority of news organisations are like the children or grandchildren even of newspapers, and in newspapers, the base unit of journalism was an article.

"That has changed a little bit as we went from desktop to mobile. I think that that could change even more as we continue to receive information from different places. So, for example, push notifications . . . an art form that did not exist, certainly not 20 years ago, and now it does. News organisations have to create content for it. That is new even within phones, and that is increasingly becoming a space where people get attention."

In world in which we have lots of different web-connected devices – from phones to refrigerators – there may be new opportunities to push out information in the future, but those opportunities are unlikely to suit that article base unit.

"Don't misinterpret me by saying: 'I predict that people are going to be getting their news from refrigerators.' My point here is just that attention will be scattered through different devices – all of which could be conduits of news and information, but won't be until we explore well beyond the confines of the article."

News organisations are already tuned in to the concept of an atomic unit of information in the form of a tweet, he says, where someone might tweet an image and that image gets picked up and retweeted and embedded in lots of other tweets.

FIGURE 8.2 David Cohn pictured at work at Circa.
Credit: David Cohn

These atomic units of story – on whatever platform – can be threaded together to tell a story over time. As example, he talks about the story thread of Donald Trump's campaign and election.

"An election is a story that occurs over, in the US, a year and a half, two years. So, for the last two years we have kind of been part of a story which ended in November. Now a new story is kind of coming out of it which would be the actual presidency. Which is maybe a four-year story, and there are going to be sub-stories in that.

"Every atomic unit of news that came out during those two years could all be threaded together to kind of tell this story. The idea that you have to write an article every day to kind of summarise what was already said, and then catch people up with one or two bits of new information. At Circa, the idea was if someone is following the story. Then they only care about what is new."

Someone who has been closely following the election story doesn't care about the background, they know it. All they want is the one or two bits of new information from that day. Whereas another reader may have been away, or only dipping in and out of the story, and may want more. "The inverted pyramid is this like dance of trying to catch people up to where they should be. They do want to be caught up, and not be treated like an idiot. But like, 'Hey, there is stuff I don't know. Can you help me figure it out?' The classic inverted pyramid tries to do this dance of treating both [readers the same]."

The issue becomes whether you can keep track of what someone has read and only deliver what they don't know: "At Circa we kept track of basically everything that somebody read. So, we could treat them accordingly."

Cohn says they didn't get to the level of personalisation they would have liked at Circa – "feasible, because of the structure of the information" – not at the granular levels of being able to deliver more of a type of content (e.g. less comment or more pictures). By keeping track of what users had read, they could say: "'Okay. Here is what you missed while you were gone or since you last checked in.' We could also do things like, if for example you read a fact that turned out later to be untrue or fact checked, we could actually alert every person who read that fact."

Circa's editors worked as if every reader was a brand new reader, ordering and adding the content accordingly, and the technology would reorder it based on the individuals.

There was much that Circa didn't get to do with the tech the company had designed (see also Coddington, 2015). Particularly around that ability to order content by type as well as by date – so being able to pull up all Obama's quotes in a particular date range, or on visits to a particular location, for example, or "show me all of the events that took place in Chicago. Show me all of the events associated with crime."

He added: "I always kind of had dreams of what we would be able to do. We never really got there, but that is another interesting side effect of having really structured information."

In the early days, all the work of assigning and cataloguing those different types of information and different story points was done by Circa's human editors ("part of the process of writing anything on Circa was also the creation of the database").

"You are looking at a blank canvas, and you say: 'Create new unit.' What type of new unit? An event. What is the date of the event? You put in the date. Type the text, and then where does the event take place? Then you put it on a map. A longitude, and latitude or use Google Maps.

"So, the act of telling the story of [the] Inauguration, we would say: Event, BC, January 20th, 10am. Here is the location. Then we would just write the text. Donald Trump was inaugurated in Washington, DC. Done. Next thing, quote. Then we would put in who said the quote. Donald Trump. What was the quote? He says: 'I am such a great guy.' Then there is a quote. Next thing, fact or maybe it would be an image of protests. There were also protests that happened.

"It was very tedious, but in some respects, all of what I just described is the same stuff that a reporter would have done. It is basically the same labour of like a human interpreting the world. It is just that we kind of created a little bit more structure."

They had critics: "People would say: 'Oh, it is not good journalism. What you guys are doing is so short. It requires no thinking.' Actually, it was like this really deep, rich tangle that required a human to make really confident decisions. Again, stories here are not articles, but stories. So, you had to have a really good sense of where was the story going to start and stop? When do you fork a story?"

The staff of 12 or 13 people could handle ("touch") 150 stories on a good day: "I use the word 'touch', because we didn't write 150 new stories. Half or more of those were just updates to stories. So, it could have been something as simple as one new fact on a story. So, you could actually get a lot of content out in the world."

Cohn said others were working with similar ideas – cards and stacks, atomic news – but he didn't think they were keeping track of the data at the same level that Circa had. He mentioned the work of David Caswell at Structured Stories (see "References and further study") and Bill Adair, PolitiFacts's creator.

"I would actually argue PolitiFacts is also an example of structured content in a way. Because you can [say]: 'Show me all the claims from Hilary Clinton. Show me all the claims from Hilary Clinton that are deemed: Liar, liar, pants on fire.'"

Does he still get excited about the new ideas and the future of journalism?

"It kind of depends on the day. I want to say yes, I am still excited and I think there is a lot of potential in stuff. [But] especially lately, it just feels like the rug has been pulled from under us."

"Tech companies", he adds, "are becoming media companies, and media companies are slowly becoming tech companies. They might not know it.

There is some future where the two are indistinguishable. I don't know how or what they look like. I think they will probably look a little bit more like Facebook. Just because that is where the money is.

"My worry is that the traditional publications won't move towards that weird future. So a lot of the values and ethics and traditions will get lost. I am not saying that we need to keep all that for no reason, but some of it I think should be shepherded into that future."

Suggested assignments

Practical exercise

You've been given a copy of the Stanton telegram referred to at the start of this chapter.[13] Rewrite it as a modern story, deciding what you think should go where. You may want to try this in several formats – for example how you might write the story for mobile vs how you might present it as a TV report. Think about what makes each of those media different and consider what other elements you would add to the story as a journalist today – for example who might you try to get quotes from? What images, video or explainers might you use?

Analysis and practical exercise

Take a story which is on a major news website. Pick one which you know to be a long-running and complex story – perhaps one which involves lots of agencies, countries or key players. Look very carefully at each paragraph in that story and break each paragraph down to identify the role it serves. Which paragraphs introduce the newest elements to this long-running saga? Are any paragraphs discrete, i.e. they could tell the gist of the story on their own? Which are new quotes? Which paragraphs are background information? Which are likely to become part of the background as the story moves on? What could happen next in the story? What other news stories might this relate to? Breaking down the story in this way will help you in understanding what is meant by "atomised" news.

Notes

1 'Online journalism tips', BBC Academy website.
2 'Snow Fall' the project is here: www.nytimes.com/projects/2012/snow-fall/#/?part=tunnel-creek. For examples of criticism of 'snowfalling' and 'to Snowfall', see the Twitter conversation captured at: https://storify.com/macloo/pros-and-cons-of-snowfalling-stories
3 'How we made Snowfall', January 1, 2013. Source: https://source.opennews.org/articles/how-we-made-snow-fall/.
4 www.tampabay.com/specials/2008/reports/danielle
5 'Looking through the girl in the window', Steve Myers, August 5, 2008, Poynter.
6 www.vox.com/cards
7 http://bbcnewslabs.co.uk/projects/atomised-news/
8 Phillips produces a lot of content himself, including this list-format piece: 'Why Britain suddenly has a new prime minister, explained for Americans', July 13, 2016, BuzzFeed.

9 The system prioritises stripped-back, fast-loading content, initially in Google's "Top Stories" list, but extended in the summer of 2016 to organic search for news content.
10 'Report: AMP causing monetization frustration among some news publishers', Greg Sterling, October 28, 2016, Search Engine Land.
11 'These are our memories of London's terrorist attacks': www.BuzzFeed.com/BuzzFeed UK/these-are-our-memories-of-londons-terrorist-attacks?utm_term=.bibbKM0b1#.nj4VK9JVn.
12 His blog – Digidave (tagline "Journalism is a process, not a product") – is well worth exploring, not least for his insights around technology and future journalism.
13 Available on the New York Times website: www.nytimes.com/1865/04/15/news/president-lincoln-shot-assassin-deed-done-ford-s-theatre-last-night-act.html, or Google this intro: 'WAR DEPARTMENT, WASHINGTON, April 15–1:30 A.M. Maj.-Gen. Dix'.

References and further study

'*Atomised news – with BBC R&D*' (ongoing research pages), at: bbcnewslabs.co.uk/projects/atomised-news

Coddington, M. (2015) 'One thing we can learn from Circa: A broader way to think about structured news', *Nieman*, 26 June 2015.

Mindich, D.T.Z. (2000) 'Edwin M. Stanton, the inverted pyramid, and information control', in D.B. Sachsman, S.K. Rushing, and D.R. van Tuyll (eds) *The civil war and the press*, Transaction Publishers, Picastaway, NJ.

Schudson, M. (2008) *The sociology of news*, Norton, New York.

The structured stories project, led by David Caswell, previously a director of product management at yahoo, has a video demo and FAQs that help to explain atomised story structures on its main site, at: www.structuredstories.com, while Caswell's blog (http://blog.structuredstories.com) outlines development work within journalism.

Author interviews

David Cohn, Senior Director, Advanced Digital, January 2017
Tom Phillips, Editorial Director, New Formats, BuzzFeed UK, October 2016

9
YOUR TURN

I've taken you through a heck of a lot of journalism formats and a heck of lot of models for funding journalism – paywalls, subscription, crowdfunded, trust-funded, patronage, charity, partnerships,[1] retail. But, mostly, advertising-funded.

Because, in the world of journalism, advertising is still king (bringing in roughly two-thirds of income[2]), and it is impossible to look at the future of journalism without looking at how it might be funded. Not just in the world of journalism either – Google, Facebook and techland generally – are all advertising-dependent. Journalism, like search and social, sells attention. Just as the journalism industry has changed, so has advertising – cookies, trackers, native, social and the arrival of ad blocking and ad opt-outs as a challenge to both industries.

This book sets the bar high in encouraging journalists and journalism students to "own" journalism's values and define its future. However, this particular chapter takes a more pragmatic approach in helping the young journalist prepare for a long career in journalism. While not a "how-to" guide (there are plenty of good ones around, some included in the "References and further study" section), I will focus on five possible skills tracks and suggest the student or new journalist develop knowledge in at least one of those areas to enhance their employability.

Instead of an interview, the case study for this chapter is a practical introduction to pro-blogging/vlogging. Not because I'm suggesting everyone can build a decent-paying career from running a blog or YouTube channel, but because the skills involved will teach you how to build an audience for your journalism – and journalism without an audience is an archive. The suggested exercises focus on helping develop creative thinking – following on from Chapter 3, but with emphasis on thinking about the audience or market for content.

A 2014 survey by Poynter (see "References and further study") compared attitudes of editors and professional journalists against journalism teachers, students and freelance journalists on the skills each group thought most important for future journalists to develop.

Not surprisingly perhaps, the editors and professionals rated traditional journalism attributes higher than newer digital skills because, while they live and breathe what is happening in the news industry, their experience is rooted in what is happening around them, right now, rather than what may be on the horizon.

All groups had similar ideas of the most important skills a future journalist would need (accuracy followed by curiosity came top across the board), but varied on the importance they attached to things like ethics and using reliable sources, writing ability, or digital skills. Editors rated (in order) accuracy, curiosity, use correct grammar, handle stress well and select information based on reliability as their top five skills, while freelancers put accuracy, curiosity, write in a fluent style, be acquainted with journalism ethics and use correct grammar top. Educators, students and freelancers rated being able to handle and interpret data around the 70–79 percent mark in terms of importance – editors and professional journalists rated those skills in the 55–62 percent range. Similarly, while educators and students rated multimedia skills highly, working journalists didn't (although their editors were a bit keener).

The new journalist entering the industry will need to show that they have both the traditional skills and attributes managers are looking for, and that they can bring something new – something that will fill a current skills gap or potential future gap in that organisation. Basically, you need one foot in journalism's past and one in its future. As Tom Huang of the Dallas Morning News, quoted in the survey report (page 3), said:

> [W]hile I recognize the importance of digital skills, if I had to choose, I'd first choose journalists with "traditional" skills and then train them on digital skills, rather than the other way around. I think the point of the survey, though, is that we shouldn't have to choose. New journalists should come equipped with a whole host of skills, both traditional and digital.

Here then are my five suggested skills routes for young journalists:

1. Embrace "portfolio" working.

I've called this portfolio rather than working freelance because the reality for many journalists today is a portfolio of work which mixes freelance, contract and salaried work to varying amounts over time.

For example, a colleague of mine delivered training courses in crisis PR as a self-employed contractor, while teaching journalism skills to students as a part-time employee and delivering occasional news shifts as a freelance journalist. Another delivers teaching for around three months of the year as a part-time employee, while working on books as a commissioned and self-employed writer, and producing three or four articles a month as a freelancer for regular mainstream press clients. For many years, I taught on a part-time contract myself, while working as a self-employed business consultant, running my own tech start-up as an unpaid director, and topping up salary by renting out a holiday home.

Portfolio working is a legitimate and, for many journalists, a desirable way of working. While it can be a response to a lack of security in the jobs market, it can also be a much more creative and fulfilling way of working and a better fit for anyone trying to juggle home responsibilities, launch a business, or write that book. Having one full-time job is easier, particularly if time-management isn't your strong point, but it can also be less interesting.

Attributes you'll need to develop are:

Be flexible. A willingness to try something outside your immediate experience. That doesn't just mean trying something new, but allocating time to research and developing new areas of your portfolio, including teaching yourself new skills if necessary.

Be pushy. You're going to need to get used to picking up the phone and asking editors whether they've read your pitch, or chasing accountants to pay your bill. Set realistic deadlines for when you expect a response and chase when it's late.

Be creative. You're the one who'll be coming up with the ideas so a creative mindset is essential. Allocate time to thinking and developing ideas, because the value of what you offer will depend on your ability to come up with attractive ideas for stories, posts, courses, products, etc.

Be organised. From hitting deadlines, to making sure you're prepped for meetings, training, etc., to getting your tax return in – you'll have to do it all yourself. But at least you'll know it's been done. Successful freelancers tend towards over-prep.

Be well-read. You need to be looking for opportunities all the time – whether articles you might pitch; training you might offer; or newsrooms that might be short-staffed. Read everything – ideas need sparks. Part of what you offer, your USP ("unique selling point"), is that you will know more about your specialism than the people offering you work – it's what they're paying you for. Show that by being able to reference sources they don't know.

Be entrepreneurial. Sort of follows on from all the other things, but you need to think of yourself as a brand (note item 2, discussed next). Who are you, and what do you offer that's different? Have a specialism, but also don't be defined by that – you need to look to expand into related areas or "channels" in the same way that a company would.

2. Become good at social journalism, not just social media.

One reason I'd chosen to interview Jim Waterson (Chapter 3 case study) was because of his very active use of Twitter. He said he sees his personal Twitter feed as part of his journalistic output – adding press releases, small items, or comments that aren't worth writing up as a story but are worth sharing. Something re-tweeted 100 times, he said, means it's seen by around 5,000 people who "got some new information from me, and therefore think that they were reading a BuzzFeed report on it".

"It's just trivia, Twitter basically," he told me. "I know which buttons to press. It's quite easy to work out what will fly the moment you phrase something in a certain way. I try to avoid doing the really obvious, cliché sort of thing: 'Here's an empty chamber while MPs are discussing the homeless' because otherwise, you're not reporting, you're just putting bad polemics out online."

Social journalism is that – seeing Twitter and Facebook as an extension of your output, but it's also knowing how to use the material that's on social media. Working out who is worth following, not just forever but perhaps in relation to particular stories or sectors that you're reporting on. Knowing how to check and verify information that other people post or share (see Chapter 6) and using it to find stories and to cultivate sources and witnesses for stories.

Research each platform – Twitter, Facebook, Instagram, Snapchat, Facebook Live, Periscope, etc., and focus on what each platform offers in terms of a particular audience demographic and what type of content works best (the case studies in this book will help). You need to fully understand what each platform can do for you in order to make a decision on whether you should use it to promote yourself or your journalism (don't use everything or you'll never have time to write anything!). Doing the research will help you stay a step ahead of your potential employers so when one of them asks you whether they should have a Periscope stream, you'll know exactly what to say.

Jim Waterson again:

> One outcome could be, you sort of have Twitter as the sort of rolling news face for news journalism, Facebook as the place replacing your news at 10 broadcast, populist, I only check in for two minutes a day, tell me what's going on. News websites somewhere in the middle in trying to pick up a bit of traffic from both segments because to be honest, the number of people who click articles on Twitter is so amazingly low.

Be very aware of how you use social media in terms of your own "brand". Facebook may be more personal, but lock it down in terms of who can see what you post; Twitter should be a more professional (and witty) reflection of who you are as a journalist or would-be journalist; Snapchat and WhatsApp can be more personal if you're using closed friendship groups, but otherwise keep it mostly professional, mostly fun. And cut down on the selfie count, particularly on Instagram; there's a limited number of people in the world who want to see lots of pictures of you, and most of them are your relatives.

The basic brand you're going for in social media – particularly public spaces such as Twitter – is "decent wo/man, knows what s/he's talking about". Reflect who you are right now (including, if you must, what you're eating) but also who you aspire to be. If you're a journalism student, over half your tweets should be about media issues and reflect your interest in news and good journalism. Because if you're not shouting about the importance of journalism in the world, who should be?

3. Learn to love (or not to avoid) data.

I haven't specifically dealt with data journalism in this book – not least because there are already plenty of excellent books and resources around on the subject (some included in "References and further study"), but that doesn't mean that I don't believe in it as an important part of journalism with a range of skillsets, any of which should be developed.

The case studies in Chapters 7 and 8 will give you an idea of how data, as in parts of stories or sets of facts, is changing how content is constructed and delivered. The case study in Chapter 6 (and in section five, below) shows how tools used by data journalists can also be used to help verify information and reports. But neither of those are data journalism.

Learning to love data may be about knowing where to look for and gather data – for example open access datasets provided by governments and public bodies (e.g. www.data.gov in the US or data.gov.uk in Britain); it may be about knowing how to do basic data scrapes (collecting) and work with data in Excel files; it may be about knowing how to map data into programmes such as Google Fusion Tables or Google Maps to create a narrative; it may be knowing how to create simple visualisations or infographics from data using tools such as Tableau or Raw, or it may be about developing the skills to an expert level and becoming the data wizard in the newsroom.

What's important is that you don't start by assuming you won't "get" data. Start by looking at what it can deliver as journalistic form in its own right,[3] and then sign up to an online course, or step your way through the data exercise in the suggested assignments, at the end of this chapter.

Learning to like data is also about better understanding your audience and what they do with the journalism you produce. Chapter 4's case study looked at how important it is for the journalist to understand story analytics and the metrics used to measure audience response. At heart, understanding that analytics narrative is about taking responsibility for selling your story, and that isn't about clickbait, it's about understanding the necessity of engaging your audience.

Aron Pilhofer, when I interviewed him at the Guardian, was about to leave to become an associate professor of journalism at Temple University. For him, it's crucial that young journalists learn about that relationship with their audience.

"You need to start from a different mindset. It is thinking about the user," he told me. "It is thinking about product. It is thinking about how to be distinctive. It is thinking about value. I will encourage my students [at Temple] to look at the person next to them who might be majoring in advertising and marketing, and if you intend to go into journalism, you better understand what marketing professionals do, and what people do on the ad side."

4. Become more creative.

Write better. Produce better. Mix things up. Knock those write-by-numbers robots out of the ballpark.

I've shown you a gazillion stunningly different examples of "new" journalism in this book – particularly in Chapter 5 – but there were many more that I couldn't fit in. More importantly, hundreds more great examples are being produced every year – look out for them.

Becoming more creative begins with being inspired by what other creatives are producing. Sites such as NiemanLab, Poynter and journalism-co.uk should be on your watchlist. Be inspired both by other journalists, but also by producers in other media – YouTubers, game makers, filmmakers, for example. It also means challenging yourself to learn new technology and software; to be comfortable using a camera, a recorder app, putting a graphic together or working with charts.

5. Become the queen or king of verification.

At the top of the list of most important skills for journalists in the survey I mentioned earlier was accuracy. Editors, journalists, students and educators all listed accuracy as the most important attribute a future journalist needs.

Maguire (2015) wrote about the role of the journalist in pursuing authoritative facts through a three-part system of observing, analysing documents and interviewing people. Most journalism training tends to focus on the first and third of these – reporting what we observe at the scene or an event and interviewing people. Much of newspaper journalism became focused on these two, and often squashed the two together – so a story carried enough authority if it only had quotes from someone who was there. Effectively, we are giving over our authority on the facts of the story to the person we're quoting.

Guardian editor Katharine Viner (2016), in an article about how web technology has disrupted truth in reporting (see "References and further study"), tells how a story about former UK Prime Minister David Cameron (so-called "Piggate"), based on a biography co-written by a Daily Mail journalist, and reported by both the Mail and other media, was – knowingly – based on unverified information, i.e. gossip. Viner writes:

> Pressed to provide evidence for the sensational claim, Oakeshott [Isabel Oakshott, the journalist biographer] admitted she had none. "We couldn't get to the bottom of that source's allegations," she said on Channel 4 News. "So we merely reported the account that the source gave us. . . . We don't say whether we believe it to be true."

Oakeshott went further, saying: "It's up to other people to decide whether they give it any credibility or not." She had not only given up her responsibility as a journalist to provide verifiable facts, but absolved herself of that responsibility by giving authority over truth to the reader.

Online, the ability to link to source material (including original documents, the second of Maguire's three-part system) makes it more likely that we will use documents in verifying a story, although that can sometimes be at the expense of getting original quotes. It can seem easier to put a story together from linking to lots of other stories about the same thing.

Accuracy, verification – these are the basics of real journalism (as opposed to reporting possible truths). Chapter 6 looks at deeper skills of verification, particularly through social media, but there's also a growing number of organisations and newsrooms teams focused on fact-checking as a distinct form of journalism.

Poynter has produced a code of principles for fact-checkers,[4] endorsed by Facebook, with signatories to the code working with Facebook to minimise "fake" news by identifying and flagging disputed stories.

Verification isn't just about checking or proving individual facts or stories, but filtering information in order to identify what's most important or relevant. Solid verification methods are also crucial to find the gaps in a story – the "what have you not been told?"

CASE STUDY: HOW TO BLOG OR VLOG LIKE A PRO

You may have been thinking about starting your own blog or a YouTube channel for some time. You may already have one. Or you may be one of those people who thinks blogging is for amateurs and YouTube is for teenagers.

To a degree, you're right: YouTube's audience is predominantly aged 18–24, and tens of thousands of blogs are launched every day – it's unlikely they're all amazing. But in one essential way, you'd be wrong. Because successful blogging/vlogging is a great way to learn how to write for or speak to an audience. The skills that you'll pick up will help you to understand that, as a journalist, nothing that you write or say will matter unless people read or hear it.

It's also more than that. Chapter 6 mentioned some of the bloggers who built their site into important parts of the journalism multiverse, including Andrew Sullivan of the Dish. In one of his last blog posts, Sullivan tells us that blogging "requires letting go". It is closer to performance than writing in that bloggers need to be willing to make mistakes, even to hurt feelings.

> I have said some things I should never have said, as well as things that gain extra force because they were true in the very moment that they happened. . . . [B]logging comes as close to simply living, with all its errors and joys, misunderstandings and emotions, as writing ever will.[5]

Because that's the other big thing you'll get from running a blog/vlog you care about – the chance to play with your writing and experiment with your ideas. Blogging is about your audience but it's also about you and what you want to achieve through it – creative space, attention, fame, a better job, an income?

So, how do you get started as a "pro" blogger? Here are my seven tips.

1. Only blog or vlog about a subject you really care about.

It's your passion for the thing you're talking about – whether that's politics, fashion or football – that will bring in your audience. You have to want to tell the world how great this thing is and why they should care about it.

And focusing on one, clear subject (at least to start with) will make it easier for you to find your audience. So focusing on, say, PC games or indie games, rather than trying to write about all types of videogames, or one team rather than track the whole NFL, will help you to reach an audience of people who are interested in that same thing.

If you're a fan of something, you probably already have a good idea of where other fans of that subject are gathering to talk about it – forums, Facebook groups, your friends and their friends: that's where you start in building your audience.

2. Only blog or vlog about something you know about.

You don't need to be the world's top expert in, say, astronomy, but you have to be an astronomy geek. Your audience has to feel they will be informed by you and that you are talking to them on their level about something you're both interested in.

It's OK for your blog to be a journey of discovery – maybe you're trying to understand Middle East politics and want to blog about your research and your perspective on what you find out. So, starting from zero knowledge and taking your audience with you on your personal journey to learn something new – that's OK; that's still informing them.

You need to be honest about who you are in relation to your level of expertise on the subject.

People have taken time out of their life to read something you've written or watch something you've made and your job is to entertain and inform them. If all you want to do is have a moan about things that annoy you – do it on Facebook or keep a diary. The best bloggers and vloggers give their audience something to think about, or to smile about, or help them to make decisions in their own life (that counts even if the decision is shopping-related).

Blogging and vlogging is a one-to-one engagement with your audience – they need to trust you and like you; they need to feel that, at heart, you're just like them in your passion for the subject.

3. Don't copy what's already out there – put your own twist on it.

If you're writing about Manchester United, there's no point in just reporting what the national press or the club itself is saying – tell us what you think, as a die-hard fan. Or focus on other things such as the u-21s team, or the best players from the past. Have a look at what the big sites are doing and think of the things you could do instead.

Your twist could be creative – adding funny videos, cartoons or graphics – or informative – perhaps adding extra detail or depth to an issue with graphs, or charts, or links to pages and information your readers may not know about.

That twist might come from your own personality – particularly if you're YouTubing. I said earlier that your audience needs to like you, and that's especially important on screen. No-one gives up time to regularly listen to someone they don't like. In a crowded market (there are 300 million blogs on Tumblr alone, according to Statista), people will choose the blogger/ vlogger they feel they have most in common with.

4. Think about your blog/vlog's future and pick a great name.

On YouTube (as I write this) you don't get to choose a name for your channel until it hits 500+ subscribers; however your username is fixed when you sign up. On a blog, the first thing you're asked to do when you sign up to software such as Wordpress or Blogger, is to give your blog a name. It will look something like: //myblog.wordpress.com, and you can't change that name unless you buy your own name (domain) at that point, or later.

There's a good chance that you may decide to buy a domain sooner rather than later to use on your blog or YouTube channel, so thinking of a name that will still work for you in four or five years' time is a sensible thing to do. It's also the first step in thinking about brand and image – part of thinking like an entrepreneur.

One of the most important things you can do is to come up with a name that sounds like something your target audience might search for.

A few years ago, I started a blog called "Wreck of the Week". It was initially intended as test site for some of the things I teach around SEO and blogging. I picked the name because it was a phrase that was used by a couple of national newspapers at the time for a small but popular section on property pages about dream houses to renovate. I reasoned therefore it was a phrase that people who were interested in properties to renovate or remodel would search on.

I bought the domain, started the blog and posted a handful of pieces about properties to renovate. Within a few weeks, the blog was top of page one of Google not only for "wreck of the week" but for a bunch of other property-related terms. It's never lost that No. 1 position. The blog has now had close to four million views and has a life of its own. I have fabulous, involved readers and dozens of emails from them every week, and the blog is an enjoyable side line to my "real" job (and earns me a small salary top-up).

SEO can be a complicated process but at its core is thinking about what words and phrases your readers or viewers are most likely to search on (see Chapter 4) and then trying to get those words high up in the HTML code on your online site, page or video. The name of a website comes pretty much at the top of the site's code so picking a name that reflects what your readers might search for will boost your blog's results.

On YouTube, the name of the channel is less important for search (although it helps your viewers to find you) but the titles you give your videos are really important, so get your keywords in there.

5. Get to know the software and what you can do with it.

The more you understand about the software you're using to blog or vlog, the better the end result will look. You don't have to be a techie – the software is built to be simple to use – but you are going to have to put time into teaching yourself not only how the publishing software works (i.e. how you upload a video to YouTube, or publish a post to your blog), but all the other technical and creative skills that will help you to make better-looking videos or create a more professional-looking website.

YouTube's Creator Academy[6] is great and its videos will help you learn how to build an audience. There are plenty of videos on YouTube itself to help you work out how to do things such as create good-looking thumbnails or light your videos. If you're going into blogging, pick software that most other bloggers use (such as wordpress.com or Blogger) because it will be easier for you to find how-to guides and get help on user forums.

Wordpress.com is the one most of my students use. It's the most popular blogging software, not least because it's possible to use it at a very basic level and then gradually build up to using more complex design, tools or plug-ins, or move across to the "pro" version – wordpress.org. However, although the basic wordpress.com system is free, you currently have to pay for upgrades and extras such as domain mapping (adding your own website name) or more complex templates. And wordpress.org is complicated for anyone starting out in blogging, not least because there are several stages to go through before you can get going, beginning with signing up to a web hosting service.

I created Wreck of the Week on Blogger, partly because I wanted to test it on the most basic software my students might use, but also because I wanted to be able to add adverts. Blogger is owned by Google and has Google's AdSense system on tap so you can start earning money as soon as your views climb (same goes for YouTube, also owned by Google).

6. Find your audience and help them find your content.

There are two parts to building your audience – the first is helping them to find your blog/post/page/channel/video for the first time; the second is getting them to come back again.

I mentioned that Blogger and YouTube, because they're owned by Google, help you to make money either through the AdSense gadget (on Blogger) or through YouTube's Partner programme. However, you need to be attracting 50,000+ views every month to make around £50 a month, and both programmes will only start paying out once you reach a minimum threshold. But, every penny you earn – like every positive comment you get on your blog or vlog – will encourage you to do more to grow your audience.

Getting those first 1,000 views on a blog post or a video is the start – and it's a tough start. Putting something on the web doesn't mean anyone will find it. The web is just too big and Google can take around three months to even find your site the first time around. You have to tell people it's there.

Start with the people you know – friends, colleagues, family and your own social media accounts. Join in conversations on forums and sites where your post is relevant and worth mentioning (Eliot Higgins – case study in Chapter 6 – started out as regular commentator on the Guardian's Middle East news section). Basically, look for the people who might be interested in what your blog or vlog is about, go online and find them, and tell them – politely – that you've written or videoed something they might like.

And then do it again and again and again.

If you already have a blog, you'll know that writing a post and putting the link to it on Facebook doesn't mean thousands of people will read that post. Research has shown that the majority of links that are shared on Facebook are never clicked on.[7] Your Facebook Friends may Like or share the message about your blog post, but most won't click the link to read it.

Posting an excerpt of your post, or a shorter clip of your video, can work in encouraging people to click the link to get the rest, and if you use the share tools on your blog or on YouTube to share the link with your Twitter, Facebook or Instagram account, they often work by posting a thumbnail or excerpt to encourage people to click to see more.

Keywords are incredibly important – added as tags or keywords on videos or posts and included within post headlines or video titles. Keywords are the sorting hats of the internet – grouping content to make it easier for both search engines and people to know what that content is mainly about.

Don't scatter them like ground bait; think about the most relevant and effective keywords to your post or video, and aim to use somewhere between three and seven each time.

7. Be the boss of your online world.

Blogging and vlogging is a responsibility. I started by saying it's a great way to understand how to reach an audience as a journalist. But you also need to know that this site or channel is wholly your responsibility – you're the editor; you're in charge. So, don't take risks with things like picture copyright, or music rights, and research things like Fair Use[8] and Creative Commons.[9]

Always reply to and thank genuine readers/viewers who make valid points, or who tell you that they like what you do, or say positive things on Twitter or Facebook about your work. Recognising that they've taken the time to do that and thanking them for it is about more than being polite – it will encourage them to come back and to stay involved; they'll feel part of what you're trying to build. Seeing that you respond positively will also encourage others to comment or support you.

On the other side of the coin, don't get into online arguments with trolls and idiots. If you're blogging, make sure your site's discussion and comment settings are enabled so that nothing is published on your blog until you've seen it and decided whether to allow it – it's called moderating. That doesn't mean block everything you disagree with, but it does mean you can stop anything being published that is racist or offensive, to you or your readers.

YouTube doesn't give you the same level of control but you can block certain words and you can report or block abusive viewers.

I talked about site names and domains at point four, but one thing I haven't mentioned is who you are when you register (sign-up) to YouTube or Blogger or any other social software. You should be yourself online but you don't have to use your real name, if that's an issue for you. There is a strong tradition of using pseudonyms in literature, particularly for women, and you may be someone who prefers – or needs – to keep your real-world identity separate to your online persona.

But remember that a big part of blogging and vlogging is the relationship between you and your audience. They need to trust you as well as like you, and pretending to be someone else might undermine that relationship. For most bloggers and vloggers (including myself) the encouragement they get from their audience enriches and enhances their life, and the odd negative comment is normally only that – the odd blip in a sea of support.

Suggested assignments

Student assignment

You need to come up with an idea for a product that you will research and pitch to a panel. You will devise either a) a new content-led product, b) a new news-tech product or c) an idea for improving an existing news business. Your idea should be feasible but you do not have to build it, simply make a strong case for it. Your idea must have a clear target audience/users, supported by market and competition research that shows your target group will want this.

> Tips for delivering your pitch:
>
> The objective of the first ten or 15 seconds is to make the panel want to listen intently to rest.
> You need a "story" that illustrates why your idea is important – what is the problem . . .
> . . . And how your idea will solve it.
> How exactly will it work? (Simply put, it will. . . .)
> Who will it benefit? (target audience/users)
> Why do they need/want this – and how do you know? (market research; scale/potential)
> How is it different to what's out there? (competition research)
> Be memorable! In the product name, slides/graphics, show your enthusiasm!
> Your pitch should be two minutes and maximum five slides (if using slides).

Analysis and research

An increasing number of journalists and bloggers are going direct to their audience for support for their work, through crowdfunding sites such as Kickstarter or Patreon. Many are in entertainment journalism (particularly games journalism), but there are also investigative journalists and organisations such as Bellingcat (see Chapter 6). Research crowdfunding sites and identify the ones that include journalism as a category for support. From these, pick two or three "live" projects to research as case studies, including tracking whether they meet their funding goal, what happens afterwards, whether the journalism project is completed, whether it changes. Include interviews with the journalists involved.

Group exercise

Pick one out of the six individuals (target audience) listed here and come up with a blog or vlog or app (your "product") that you think that target demographic would want. What sort of content and/or services would you provide for that audience, and why would they want it? You need to be able to say what they would expect you to provide for free and what they might be willing to pay for as extras.

A. The lifetime (sport) club fan
B. The student fashionista
C. The migrant missing home
D. The would-be journalist
E. The eSports watcher

Notes

1. There's an excellent 2014 report by Pew focused on case studies of legacy media organisations working in partnership to produce more expensive journalism, suggesting: "This is a time when journalists need to huddle together for warmth." 'Journalism partnerships A new era of interest', Rick Edmonds and Amy Mitchell, December 4, 2014.
2. 'The revenue picture for American journalism and how it is changing', Jesse Holcomb and Amy Mitchell, March 26, 2014. Pew Research Center: www.journalism.org/2014/03/26/the-revenue-picture-for-american-journalism-and-how-it-is-changing/.
3. I suggest having a look at Datassist's online portfolio (http://idatassist.com/portfolios) or the data features produced at FiveThirtyEight (for example 'Gun deaths in America'), or Nathan Yau's pick of the best data visualisation projects each year on his blog, Flowing Data (which also offers courses in working with data).
4. 'International Fact-Checking Network fact-checkers' code of principles', developed by the International Fact-checking Network at Poynter. "We believe nonpartisan and transparent fact-checking can be a powerful instrument of accountability journalism; conversely, unsourced or biased fact-checking can increase distrust in the media and experts while polluting public understanding."
5. 'The years of writing dangerously', Andrew Sullivan, February 6, 2015, Dish.
6. YouTube Creator Academy was set up to help YouTubers produce better work and attract more viewers and subscribers. You can choose to watch individual videos or follow it as a "course", with a certificate at the end.
7. '6 in 10 of you will share this link without reading it, a new, depressing study says', Caitlin Dewey, June 16, 2016, The Washington Post.
8. YouTube explains Fair Use and the platform's own rules here: www.youtube.com/yt/copyright/en-GB/fair-use.html.
9. Creative Commons is a licensing system designed to say what original work is available to be reused on the internet, and how it can be used.

References and further study

Further study on data journalism: Data tutorials on Flowing Data blog, at: http://flowingdata.com/category/tutorials/ and on Google News Lab, at: https://newslab.withgoogle.com/course/data-journalism. Also see Bradshaw, P. (2017) *'Scraping for Journalists'*, e-book, at: https://leanpub.com/scrapingforjournalists for more tutorials.

Finberg, H. and Klinger, L. (2014) *Core skills for the future of journalism*, Poynter Institute for Media Studies, St. Petersburg, FL.

Maguire, M. (2015) *Advanced reporting: Essential skills for 21st century journalism*, Routledge, New York.

Viner, K. (2016) 'How technology disrupted the truth', *Guardian*, 12 July 2016.

10
MY TURN

For the past seven years, I've delivered an annual lecture on where journalism might be going. The details and the predictions change, as you'd expect, but there are three common strands: identity – who is a journalist and how that may that change; relevance – how and why journalism continues to matter to society; change – in the technology and behaviour that will affect how we gather, deliver and consume journalism.

This book has broadly focused on those three areas – starting with changes in technology and behaviours (Chapters 1 through 4), moving on to look at who – or what – can be a journalist (Chapters 6 and 7), and at new formats for journalism (Chapters 5 and 8), with that thread on the place of journalism and why it matters in societies running, hopefully, throughout the book.

In this final chapter, I'm going to do the prediction bit but within that context of why journalism matters.

My introduction to the importance of journalism began as a ten-year-old, the first day my dad handed over his newspaper to me after he'd finished reading it. He bought the UK national daily the Daily Mirror in the morning, on his way to work emptying ships berthed at the dockyards that then lined the Humber side of Hull's Hedon Road. He bought the local daily, the Hull Daily Mail, on his way home from work. When the BBC news came on TV, we had to be quiet so he could listen (difficult for five young children).

His reverence for news didn't extend to believing everything he read or heard. He would question it and argue back, particularly on stories about Palestine and Korea, where he'd fought in two wars. But he started from a position that the journalists brought the story to him and if he disagreed with the line they took, that was based on his own experience and his own reading around the issue, not on some angry gut response that all journalists lied.

By the time I was 16, I was only skimming through the newspapers he still handed to me. I was a punk, I dressed in chains and ripped jeans and spent my money on music. I was more interested in the words on album covers than in newspapers. Local news had no relationship to me as a teenager growing up in an expanding Northern city on the largest council estate in Europe.

Some stories broke through: international stories mostly and political stories about marches against the government and nuclear power: the rising anti-establishment of music and youth. My world then, as it is for younger people now, was international and national. Local only gets interesting when you put down roots and become part of a neighbourhood.

But like the youthful audience of BuzzFeed (Chapter 3) and Vice (Chapter 5), just because I didn't buy many newspapers didn't mean I wasn't interested in the news. I was – massively – just not the news the traditional media was offering.

As Chapter 5 outlines, you build an audience by reporting on the stories that audience is interested in. Trouble is, how do you know what they might be interested in, and who decides what they should be interested in?

The journalist's job isn't about getting to the end of your article and thinking: "Frack me, that was good!", the job is about helping the world to a more evolved state, and humanity a step forward of where we left it. You up for that?

Journalism earns its relevance to the world. Journalists are not owed attention. Just because we've been here for a couple of hundred years reporting what's going on to our (mostly) impartial best doesn't mean each successive generation has to listen to us. We have always earned our place as the Fourth Estate.[1] But that job got tougher this century, so we have to toughen up too. Because we're needed more than ever.

I started writing this book in January 2016 and finished it in January 2017. It's been a struggle to write about the future of journalism and not to be influenced by the events of those twelve months. When I started writing, the UK hadn't made its mind up on Europe and Donald Trump was one of 12 candidates for the US presidency (at odds of 6:1 to win).

By the time I stopped writing, Brexit had happened and Trump had been inaugurated as the 45th President, and – well, the rest will be in the history books.

I watched as traditional media struggled to reflect, never mind engage with, the 21st century complexity of a mass audience talking to each other across continents. A tangled mess of weakening influence of the rational news media; the rapid rise of irrational media and fake news, powered by social media algorithms which reward (any) attention; and people in power urging people without power to distrust experts, professionals, journalists and anyone who might offer a less comfortable truth.

And throughout the year I worried about the profession of journalism itself and the role of journalists and the media itself in undermining journalism's value. We take ourselves too seriously and the importance of the work we do not seriously enough.

With that in mind, here are my five predictions. Or perhaps they're hopes.

1. The fight for journalism will have to start with redefining journalism.

We're really not all journalists now. Not even most of us who call ourselves journalists. We need to find ways to divide up and describe this profession and its many and varied jobs that does not give equal status to partisan opinion peddlers and heroic investigators.

Similarly, the editor, page designer, listings writer, on-screen presenter, radio news reader, review writer, teacher of journalism, producer, columnist and dozens and dozens of other job titles within the news matrix play an important role but not that of a journalist.

I would also argue that the job of a reporter is not the same as that of a journalist. Reporting on a news event is important. Reporting truthfully, adding facts and information – these are important, even more so today. But it is not the same as the investigative, "holding power to account" journalism that, as Chapter 1 showed, journalists themselves think of as journalism.

So, here's my first future journalism prediction: the news industry has lost the trust of much of its audience, and unless we can rebuild that trust, we'll lose more of our audience. The starting point for recovering that trust will be to define journalism so that our audience will be able to recognise and value it. We have to come up with clear descriptions of what journalism actually is, and the standards that journalists have to meet to earn the title.

At 5.43pm, on January 19, 2017, Tom Robins (@tommy_robbins) tweeted:

> On the drive to the hospital where he breathed his last, Wayne Barrett was still doing interviews for a big, tough story on Donald Trump.
> *(Source: Weinstein, 2017)*

Wayne Barrett was a political journalist. Tom Robbins was his journalist partner on many of his investigations – including 30 years of writing about Trump and publishing the first and probably best investigative biography of the businessman.

Barrett produced columns for the Village Voice (see Chapter 3) and this quote, from his final column,[2] is a good starting point for a new definition of the role of a journalist:

> [T]he joy of our profession is discovery, not dissertation. There is also no other job where you get paid to tell the truth. Other professionals do sometimes tell the truth, but it's ancillary to what they do, not the purpose of their job.

Barrett wrote about being asked to give a talk at his son's elementary school about what a reporter did. He turned up in a trench coat "with the collar up and a notebook in my pocket, baring it to announce that 'we are detectives for the people'."

Wayne Barrett died the day before Trump's inauguration. He missed White House Press Secretary Sean Spicer delivering obvious falsehoods from the White

House podium,[3] and Trump spokeswoman Kellyanne Conway justifying them as "alternative facts".

Washington Post columnist Margaret Sullivan wrote a rallying call for a different, tougher journalism the day after Spicer and Conway's TV performances. Press briefings were "access journalism", spoon-fed reporting taken at face value. Spicer's statement represented the death of that access journalism. Journalists "recalling at all times that their mission is truth-telling and holding public officials accountable" should "dig in" and focus on what Trump and his team do, rather than "sensational tweets or briefing-room lies – while still being willing to call out falsehoods clearly when they happen" (2017). (See "References and further study".)

"We are detectives for the people", said Barrett. Journalists are not press conference note takers, press release rewriters, establishment mouthpieces or even opinion leaders. Journalists discover what's happening and they report on what they find. They might interpret what's happening to make it a little more interesting or a little easier to understand, but journalists are not analysts, commentators or news producers.

As Chapter 1 outlined, our understanding of what journalism is is largely based on what journalists themselves think it is – an occupational ideology that defines "real" journalists and "real" journalism, as a set of ideals shared among journalists to self-legitimise their position in society (Deuze, 2005; see Chapter 1 references). Those ideals had coalesced around values of public service, objectivity/balance, autonomy, immediacy and ethics. So, the definition of a good journalist – according to journalists themselves – is not someone who works for a legitimate news publisher or producer, but someone objectively and ethically delivering a public service.

If we define journalists by who employs them, rather than by what they produce, we undermine journalism's importance. Content is not journalism. By defining what a journalist must do, we define journalism and its place in society. By coming up with a definition that the public can see value in, and hold us to, we reclaim our relevance in their lives.

So, here's my suggestion as a starting point for further discussion: a journalist must be someone who is paid to discover and tell the truth about news events and issues that impact on local, national or global society. Who delivers that truth to engage and inform their audience. Who is ethically committed to delivering verified news and information. Who challenges falsehoods with provable truth and facts. Who serves the broader public by representing their best interests through investigating and holding the powerful to account.

2. Truth is more important than we realised; journalism needs to be ready for a fake news backlash.

Wayne Barrett may have sought the truth but he wasn't without bias – none of us are. He had a liberal-leaning perspective that informed whom he chose to do his detective work on. Personal bias is something we need to recognise and deal with but it shouldn't prevent truthful journalism, and it cannot be allowed to lead to partisan, fake or truth-ish news.

Among all the reporting of the rise of "fake" news[4] during the period I worked on this book, analysis by BuzzFeed suggested fake news sites were less of an issue in the UK because British newspapers were already so partisan in their reporting:

> [T]he most popular dubious stories on British politics were almost always the work of long-established news outlets and relied at most on exaggeration rather than fakery. The evidence suggests that rather than reading complete lies, British audiences appear to prefer stories that contain at least a kernel of truth, even if the facts are polluted or distorted.[5]

Exaggeration, falsehoods, truth-like rather than truthful, wilful distortion and attention-chasing partisanship. None of that is journalism. As I hope I made clear earlier, you are not a journalist if what you are producing is wilfully distorted content designed to influence public opinion rather than deliver facts. If journalists don't – or won't – distinguish between truth-led journalism, fact-based event reporting and attention-chasing or space-filling content, then why should the public?

Outlets that don't produce decent journalism will fail, not least because there are a lot of bottom-feeding competitors in that ocean of content our audience is swimming through. I'm going to quote you something, from an editor's end-of-year message to staff.

> The internet next year [2015] is going to be unbelievably stupid and condescending, confusing and deafeningly loud, red-hot with misplaced outrage, unable to calibrate its reactions. "News" is going to be increasingly served by companies whose only real mission is to create shareable units of distracting content. . . . Already ankle-deep in smarmy bullshit and fake "viral" garbage, we are now standing at the edge of a gurgling swamp of it.

The writer was Max Read, then editor-in-chief of Gawker. Six months or so after writing that message,[6] promising his readers a fast, sophisticated, sharp, funny, fearless, surprising and "most importantly, honest" Gawker, Read had resigned. A year or so later, Gawker itself had folded.

Begun in 2003 as a media gossip blog, by 2014 Gawker had mushroomed to become a network of seven websites with strong and distinct online identities – Life Hacker, Gizmodo, Kotaku, Jezebel, Deadspin, Jalopnik. Gawker Media was rich, growing and seemed to reach effortlessly across generations and interests (games, cars, tech, sports) with its youthful, renegade, gossipy content style.

But in 2016, the company had declared bankruptcy following a bruising court battle over privacy and the company sold at a knock-down price to Univision. Gawker itself was shut down and the group's other sites remain and continue (currently) to be profitable.

Read's 2016 post on "Who killed Gawker" (see "References and further study") is a good read on the possible reasons for the site's demise, but it also shows the editorial tightrope that sites which set out to reach a younger, anti-establishment audience walk. It's OK to criticise and make fun of the rich or powerful – until your site itself becomes rich and powerful. It's OK to hold a mirror up to establishment hypocrisy, but not to attack another media boss for having a gay fling, or allow a writer to vent about the girlfriend who dumped him,[7] or post a video of a drunken woman having sex in a bathroom. There is no point in being a journalistic bottom-feeder in a world where anyone can – and does – post any gossip, rumour or outright lie, and where subhuman packs can newsfeed live videos of bullying, torture or rape.[8]

Craig Silverman tells the story[9] of how, in 2015, two teenage boys in Canada set up a news website and posted a completely false story about how Prime Minister Trudeau planned to open cannabis stores in every city. The story made them thousands of dollars in AdSense earnings and their site, hotglobalnews.com expanded, earning them thousands of dollars a month for their made-up stories about Trudeau and celebrities.

The teenagers – Daré Adebanjo and Yaman Abuibaid – told Silverman that the secret to creating a viral hoax is to tell people things they want to hear: real news stories tend to be too boring and filled with facts. "Anytime we write we always try to start off with a lot of facts, but then we make it really interesting," Adebanjo said.

One such "interesting" fake story had an ISIS member enter Canada as a refugee at a time of growing anti-refugee, anti-Muslim sentiment. The story was "not biased", Abuibaid, himself a Muslim, told Silverman. People "think that we hate liberals and we're conservative fans, but the truth is we're not anything."

Pablo Reyes, the mid-20s owner of fake news site Cartel Press, was making similar amounts off the back of made-up scare stories. He told Vice reporter Elle Reeve[10] he posted fake stories because "news lies a lot" anyway. "Cartel Press gives people the opportunity to write their own bullshit, instead of going to CNN or Fox and reading their bullshit."

Reyes isn't the only person to think that news is mostly lies – regardless of whether that's a valid reason to post more lies. As Chapter 4 shows, we tend to believe what most of our friends believe (or rather most of the people whose opinions we trust). Lerman et al. (2016) identified the "majority illusion" – behaviours and attitudes spread through a population as individuals copy the actions of people in their own network. A minority thus may influence the majority because we come to believe that the behaviours and attitudes we see in our small, local networks reflect what's happening everywhere. If most of our friends mistrust the news, we believe most people think the same and, therefore, that the news can't be trusted.

That's particularly true of the younger, Millennial audience that, as Chapter 5 argues, has largely rejected traditional media. Whether because, like Reyes, they don't trust it, or because it doesn't reflect their world, or from laziness – when news arrives via Facebook's out-of-town content hyperstore, why visit half-a-dozen artisan shops to fill your basket?

But legacy news media which choose to only reflect the protectionist, nationalist views of older people are fighting over a generation which will die out. Newer media such as BuzzFeed and Vice, trying to reach that younger generation by reporting news that matters to them, will have to win the battle to reach that follow-on audience for news before it entirely loses faith in journalism.

Journalism got lazy too. Too dependent on PR to fill the acres of space new media created; too settled in our vox pops, our personality politics, our he said/she said substitute for balance. A re-assessment of journalism as being fundamentally about discovering and reporting truth, with a commitment to avoid bias, will make it easier for an audience tired of "news lies" to find real journalism. As former Guardian editor Peter Preston put it:

> [T]oday's prevailing mood music is harshly unforgiving. It wants enlightenment, not obfuscation. It needs to know what you think, what you conclude, assume and believe.... But truth ... is more than an anxious assemblage of facts. It is a fundamental public service as the mood music stops.[11]

3. Worries over "fake" news will morph into concerns over news "have-nots", and "want-nots".

Public opinion is formed by what we see and read in the mass media; we rely on it to tell us what's happening and, generally, to interpret for us why something is happening. The press "may not be successful much of the time in telling people what to think, but it is stunningly successful in telling its readers what to think about" (Cohen, 1963: 13). If the public shows it cares about an issue, our governments are more likely to care too. If the media didn't have influence over public opinion, governments would not try to control what is reported.

If the role of the press is to speak truth to power, power rests with the public – as voters and as consumers – to create change, and it's the public that journalists need to speak truth to.

But if, as I suggested, sections of that public have rejected news as mostly fake, or lies, and if other sections experience news largely through a skewed prism of filter bubbles and majority illusion, and if other sections avoid news, seeing it as irrelevant to their experience of the world, or too challenging, or just boring, then fake news becomes only a contributory factor to a society with reduced exposure to journalism.

We end up with a broader public that does not know what it cares about, and government that does not need to be influenced by them.

We can argue that there have always been news "want-nots" and, from the early 20th century, a majority public swayed by the bias of majority media. But the issue now is twofold: a majority media that has become more biased, more skewed towards directing rather than informing public opinion and publics spending more of their time within filtered news bubbles. The challenge for journalism will become less about filtering out fake news and more about how to reach people with real news.

In Chapter 1, I asked, what would it take to make journalism the asset sold, rather than the attention journalism attracts? Some news providers have begun to do that – by encouraging readers to subscribe to publications, newsletters or channels, or to simply pay to support the journalism.

The Chapter 2 case study on the Guardian mentioned its membership drive, urging its readers to "join" the Guardian and to safeguard its mission. For other media outlets – online video news pioneers the Young Turks for example – subscription payments pretty much fund the operation, while the spontaneous Twitter #PressOn and #RealJournalism campaigns in support of quality journalism delivered subscription spikes for news organisations from the New York Times to ProPublica. When journalism has value, it becomes the asset people will pay for.

In many ways, that represents a positive change towards a direct relationship between journalism and audience. We'll see that develop more frequently into a direct relationship between a journalist and their audience through crowdfunding sites such as Patreon, but perhaps also through future micropayment systems to reward the journalist or the story (see next section).

However, in the rush to paid-for journalism models, the news industry must not build gated communities. The danger is that good journalism attracting direct funding creates a wider gulf between journalism haves and have-nots. If "real" journalism becomes disproportionally supported by membership, members and news organisations together may create gated communities of news haves. Subscription-funded journalism could encourage further separation between knowledge and ignorance. If the "free"[12] media is largely weak, partisan or unsatisfactory, people will drift further from the journalism they should see.

The problem with leaving the majority news to companies focused on selling attention is that we end up with the superficial in information, yet overly dramatic in narrative "popular news" (Gans, 1979) of TV. But while Gans felt there was nothing wrong with the exaggerated drama of TV news (at least nothing that had been satisfactorily proven by 1979), others have been more critical. Langer's "lament" for news accused the dominant tabloid-style television news of systematically undermining the crucial arrangement between a democracy and its citizens (1998: 2).

In an interview with CNNMoney's Tom Kludt in May 2016, Wayne Barrett was scathing about the quality of TV journalism around the Trump campaign:

> If the media continues to do the job as it has done it, and I am really talking about broadcast media, then he has a chance to win. If they report the campaign truthfully, I believe he has no chance to win.

Forty-percent of Trump voters named Fox News as their main source of information during the 2016 presidential campaign – against 7 percent getting most of their campaign news from Facebook.[13] Among all voters, only 19 percent had Fox as their main source (CNN was second with 13 percent). The issue is what journalism citizens get to see, not where they see it.

4. Journalism will need its AI helpers.

When I picture journalism's technological future, two images from fiction come into my head. The first is from Philip Pullman's *His Dark Materials* trilogy, and our introduction to Lyra's dæmon, Pantalaimon. Each dæmon is friend, family and the external manifestation of the soul of Lyra and her people. I see dæmons when I ponder the future of AI.

The second picture in my head is from the *Transmetropolitan*[14] comic series by Warren Ellis and Darick Robertson. I'm a bit of a comic book fan (if you've read this whole book, you'll have spotted that I'm a geek), and the "I'm a journalist!" frame of Spider Jerusalem kicking his way into a story often makes its way onto my lecture slides.

But, future-wise, it's Transmet's "feedsite listeners" that pop into my head. Not journalists, not reporters, but a separation of event reporting into reporters and listeners-in on events, live streaming – pushing – whatever's interesting back to the newsfeed sites. I said earlier that we need to separate out journalist from other news matrix jobs; a future job may be something like the event "listener" and that job may not be done by humans.

But let's get back to our AI dæmons.

Google, Amazon and Facebook are already in a battle of the superpowers to bring ubiquitous AI to consumers. Google, particularly, has been focused on a move to AI and conversational computing: "We have this vision of a shift from mobile-first to an AI-first world over many years," CEO Pichai told Forbes (see "References and further study"). Remember that bit in Chapter 2 where I talked – probably for too long – about the "big truck of change" and Google and that 2004 TED talk by Larry Page and Sergey Brin? Towards the end of that talk, Page used a picture of Hal 9000, the over-familiar AI antagonist[15] to illustrate their goal of the ultimate "smart" search engine.

Pichai has ramped up that focus: "Personally, there is a renewed sense of focus on our mission and on transforming the company using machine learning and artificial intelligence," he said.

Journalists are never first to new technology; what we do is find a way to use technology that has become, or is on the way to becoming, dominant in order to better tell stories or deliver news. Mobile phones became a tool of the trade as well as an extension of the personal. Similarly, when in future personal AIs become mobile (away from stay-at-home devices such as Amazon's Echo) and more developed (as opposed to the still clunky Siri, Cortana and Google Assistant) they'll become personalised assistants we not only use but become emotionally attached to, like our mobile phones. Or dæmons.

Journalists will be using personal AI to help them research and deliver stories. But more importantly than that, AIs could do the heavy lifting in grading and delivering news. Rather than stop the signal by imposing legal responsibilities on news carriers such as Google and Facebook, use the processing opportunity of AI to grade it.

In January 2017, the Knight Foundation launched a new fund to advance the ethics of AI: "AI in the public interest"[16] with an initial pot of $27 million:

> Even algorithms have parents, and those parents are computer programmers, with their values and assumptions. Those values – who gets to determine what they are and who controls their application – will help define the digital age.

Journalism needs to be around the table as AI is developed, to become part of who determines and controls the values that will be built into AI as it becomes the next big shift in communication technology.

In Chapter 8, I wrote about the experimental work being done in deconstructing news stories to make news more "elastic", less linear. But most of that work has been done by human editors. The processing power afforded by AI technology could – if applied to linking people to knowledge rather than advertiser – deliver a future in which new stories travel around the web, gathering credentials, linked information, background and updates to deliver a deeper news that better reflects the world.

That deconstructed news of atomised units mirrors the internet itself, with its ocean of "packages" – tiny parts of information – transferred across its networks and reassembled at destination.

I believe that the web, as we experience it today, will die before print does. Final destination websites and pages will fade away to be replaced by personalised servers tapping into data pipelines delivering individual news feeds and story threads. We may tap into news producers as a brand, or an individual journalist that we trust, or into a story thread that our AI gathers from multiple sources according to what it knows about our preferences and values.

The challenge then for the funding of journalism will be whether we are able to create locked, encrypted news packages that can travel along those data pipelines without being adversely reassembled or stolen (particularly if the future becomes about paying for feeds or stories we want).

But, as Chapter 7 argued, AIs won't replace journalists. At least not journalists as I redefined them in this chapter. But combining machine learning and human "spider sense" would deliver a promising future for quality journalism. Rather than continuing to write in ways that mean that an AI could write the story, using AI to fast-search acres of data, or to mark up stories so they can be deconstructed and reassembled, or to verify and by extension "grade" stories – yes, AIs could deliver that for journalism.

Dave Cohn (interviewed for Chapter 8) put it this way: "I used to tell people: 'Hey, right now I would put my team up against any AI to do this [news] work any day of the week.' I would still say that. Eventually the writing will get better, but you will still need humans there to really guide it".

Kris Hammond (Chapter 7 case study) told me: "We're going [in AI development] to start swinging back to a side where there is a need for people who actually understand what it means to tell stories, and what editorial judgement means. I think that we are going to see a flourishing, and it's not going to be tomorrow, but a flourishing of the world of journalism, because journalism, the notion of news, will expand beyond the big events, and be brought back down to the level of the day-to-day of human activity.

"We will need people with the appropriate editorial judgement to help craft that world. Those will be the skills that the machine doesn't have."

5. Google and Facebook will have to take their role as news publishers more seriously.

In some ways, this is kind of a given. Even back in 2004, at that TED talk, Page and Brin talked about Google's responsibility to provide the "right" information: "We view ourselves like a newspaper or a magazine – that we should provide very objective information." While, Facebook's Mark Zuckerberg has said[17] his company is not just a technology company, but also a media company – but not a traditional one:

> Facebook is a new kind of platform. It's not a traditional technology company. It's not a traditional media company. You know, we build technology and we feel responsible for how it's used. We don't write the news that people read on the platform. But at the same time, we also know that we do a lot more than just distribute news, and we're an important part of the public discourse.

David Cohn again: "I think everybody is kind of waiting to see what Facebook does. There is a weird relationship that still needs to smooth itself out between traditional news publishers and digital news publishers [like Facebook and Google]. In a weird way, I think the two will eventually become indistinguishable."

I argue that accepting that role as news publishers means accepting the responsibility for news's role in democratic societies. That means delivering journalism rather than content krill. To do that, as Cohn and Hammond suggested, you need human as well as algorithmic editors. Human and algorithm accountability.

The data pipelines I suggested future news stories might travel through are likely to be delivered by Google and Facebook, supported by ad share or direct funding from those internet leviathans, but there could also be new pipeline providers (similar to Netflix coming into the subscription TV market).

The internet in itself is not the disruptive technology – it is the companies that use the web to do something different that are disruptive – Google, Facebook, YouTube, etc. It is who controls the web and whose content dominates the web that creates the dilemma for legacy media businesses.

The web is being corralled by big tech companies, while news businesses compete with each other for the public's attention. For journalism to deliver on its higher democratic purpose it needs to be seen outside of the business of news as non-competitive: a product necessary to a society advancing, rather than just functioning. Those big tech companies need to do more than take their role as news publishers seriously – they need to take responsibility for helping journalism step up to that higher purpose.

Notes

1 In 1841, Thomas Carlyle wrote in 'On Heroes, Hero-Worship, and The Heroic in History: "[Edmund] Burke said there were Three Estates in Parliament; but, in the Reporters' Gallery yonder, there sat a Fourth Estate more important far than they all." Carlyle saw the press as a check on government, essential to democracy.
2 'Wayne Barrett: Time for something new', January 4, 2011, Village Voice.

168 My turn

3 'Spicer rips media's Trump coverage (Full remarks)', CNN (and others), January 21, 2017, when Spicer notoriously claimed Trump had the "largest audience to witness an inauguration ever. Period," despite previous evidence to the contrary. White House Counselor Conway gave an equally notorious interview the following day to Chuck Todd on NBC's "Meet the Press".
4 So-called "fake news" moved from something seen as ridiculous to being seen as a threat to democracy over the year. Facebook responded with the Facebook Journalism Project to create stronger ties between Facebook and the news industry and collaborate on new journalism products and models. That wasn't enough for some – at the end of 2016, the German government threatened to fine companies such as Facebook and Google that allowed fake news to spread on their platform, while the UK government announced an inquiry into the issue.
5 'Fake news sites can't compete with Britain's partisan newspapers', Jim Waterson, January 24, 2017, BuzzFeed. As an aside, this quote is 57 words long. The reason I point that out is because, throughout the book, I've had to chop, rewrite or paraphrase quotes taken from online sources because my publisher is one of those insisting that 50 words is the maximum permissible under Fair Use rules, unless permission is given to use more (Jim said "yes" to 57 words). It's an arbitrary word limit and the more it's used by publishers as a "test" of Fair Use (for example: http://fair.org/home/for-nyt-fair-use-depends-on-whos-doing-the-using) the more likely it is, I feel, to become an accepted test – and the more chilling the effect on critical writing and journalism.
6 On the company's blog, posted December 19, 2014.
7 In a 10,000-word post, Kotaku writer Eron Gjoni falsely accused his ex-girlfriend, indie game developer Zoe Quinn, of sleeping with videogame critics in exchange for favorable coverage, sparking the #Gamergate fire.
8 'Chicago torture: Facebook Live video leads to 4 arrests', January 5, 2017, CNN.
9 'These two teenagers keep fooling the internet with Justin Trudeau hoaxes', Craig Silverman, August 9, 2016, BuzzFeed. Silverman also investigated into how teenagers in Macedonia used similar tactics to influence voters: 'How teens in the Balkans are duping Trump supporters with fake news', Silverman, November 4, 2016, BuzzFeed.
10 'We spoke to the guy behind all those Pokémon Go internet hoaxes', Reeve, July 12, 2016, Vice.
11 'BBC is going to find middle way hard to follow', Peter Preston, 22 January 2017 Guardian.
12 Clearly not "free" but advertising supported and therefore, I argue, focused on attracting attention.
13 Research by Pew Research Center: 'Trump, Clinton voters divided in their main source for election news', January 18, 2017.
14 First published in 1997, the series centred on a dystopian future of rampant populism and reckless experimentation, navigated by dark, violent and disillusioned journalist Spider Jerusalem.
15 From Stanley Kubrick's 1968 movie *2001: A Space Odyssey*.
16 www.knightfoundation.org/articles/ethics-and-governance-of-artificial-intelligence-fund
17 In a one-on-one video conference with Chief Operating Officer Sheryl Sandberg, filmed for Zuckerberg's page on Facebook in December 21, 2016.

References and further study

Barrett, W. (2016) *Trump: The greatest show on earth: The deals, the downfall, and the reinvention*, Regan Arts, New York.
Cohen, B. (1963) *The press and foreign policy*, University of California, Berkeley.
Gans, H.J. (1979) *Deciding what's news: A study of CBS Evening News, NBC Nightly News, Newsweek, and Time*, Northwestern University Press, Evanston, IL.

Helft, M. (2016) 'Google's bold move to reinvent every device on the planet', *Forbes*, 29 June.

Kludt, T. (2016) 'Donald Trump's first nemesis enjoys resurgence of 1991 book', 16 May, CNN.

Langer, J. (1998) *Tabloid television: Popular journalism and the 'other' news*, Routledge, London and New York.

Lerman, K., Xiaoran, Y., and Xin-Zeng, W. (2016) 'The "Majority Illusion" in social networks', 17 February, PLOS: https://doi.org/10.1371/journal.pone.0147617

Picard, R.G. (2015) 'Journalists' perceptions of the future of journalistic work', *Reuters Institute for the Study of Journalism*, May.

Read, M. (2016) 'Did I Kill Gawker? Or was it Nick Denton? Hulk Hogan? Peter Thiel? Or the internet?', *NYMag*, 19 August. https://reutersinstitute.politics.ox.ac.uk/sites/default/files/Journalists%27%20Perceptions%20of%20the%20Future%20of%20Journalistic%20Work_0.pdf

Sullivan, M. (2017) 'The traditional way of reporting on a president is dead. And Trump's press secretary killed it,' The Washington Post, 22 January.

Weinstein, A. (2017) 'Wayne Barrett exposed the real Trump: Now there's only one way to honor him', *Mother Jones*, 20 January.

APPENDIX

Suggested essay assignments with related chapters

Chapter 1

Choose one of the following essay assignments to research and write about:

1   The portrayal of journalists in films and on TV has not always been flattering. Watch these three films from different eras and compare the depictions of journalists. In particular, consider the depiction of the journalist/s in relation to ideal values of: public service, objectivity, autonomy, immediacy and ethics. The films are: *His Girl Friday* (1940), *Ace in the Hole* (1951) and *Spotlight* (2015).
2   In chapter five of his book *The Facebook Effect*, David Kirkpatrick outlines how Don Graham, former owner of The Washington Post, almost became the biggest investor in Thefacebook. Imagine the 2005 partnership between The Washington Post and Facebook had gone ahead and suggest how Facebook might have developed as a news and content business.
3   In May 2016, Trinity Mirror closed the New Day newspaper after just nine weeks of publication. A few weeks earlier, on March 26, the last print edition of the Independent was published. Research and discuss the reasons behind both closures.
4   Which one of these traditional publishers do you think is the most forward-thinking in its digital and social news output: the New York Times, the Wall Street Journal, the Telegraph, CNN, National Geographic or Sky News? Your essay should include a brief outline of company history and include recent examples of output to demonstrate its innovation.

Chapter 2

Media analyst Michael Wolff has written extensively about the business of news and the economic challenges of digital journalism. His quote on the falling value of advertising for news publishers is included in Chapter 1 of this book. At one stage he worked for the Guardian, but became a prominent critic of its business model and "open journalism" ideals. Read his criticism[1] (two examples in the footnotes, but you should look for more) and, using your own research, analyse and discuss the validity of the points he makes and whether you agree, providing evidence and examples to support your arguments.

Chapter 4

Find an example of what you consider to be an extremely partisan headline and/or news story – one aimed at either negatively influencing opinion on a particular group of people (e.g. migrant workers, immigrants) or a particular individual (e.g. a politician or candidate for office). Analyse why that story would negatively influence public opinion, making reference to both recent research and to academic texts in relation to the role of the press as conduit of public opinion and to the importance of public trust in the press.

Chapter 5

In April 2005, Rupert Murdoch made a speech to the American Society of Newspaper Editors seen as seminal (Cole and Harcup, 2010; Allan, 2006) in which he told news editors digital was changing their world: "What is happening is, in short, a revolution in the way young people are accessing news. . . . They want their news on demand, when it works for them. They want control over their media, instead of being controlled by it." Is there still a revolution going on? Is it the same revolution or a new or substantially different one?

Chapter 6

Do we define journalism by where the content is published or by who produces it? With reference to academic texts on how definitions of journalism have developed and changed, analyse and discuss the question.

Chapter 7

Discuss the benefits, the disadvantages and the ethics of sending a robot into dangerous situations to gather material and interview people caught up in war and disaster. Research and use examples of work currently going on in robotics which you believe may be relevant to reporting in those environments.

Chapter 8

With reference to academic texts and to case studies, explore how and why the so-called inverted pyramid developed as a structure for news stories and why it has dominated journalism practice for over a century.

Note

1 www.gq-magazine.co.uk/article/guardian-editor-alan-rusbridger-rupert-murdoch and www.usatoday.com/story/money/columnist/wolff/2016/01/31/wolff-guardian-bet-shows-digital-risks/79468896/

INDEX

Abbate, Janet 19, 23
aggregators 79–80
Al Jazeera 82–3, 98; AJ+ 134; *see also* Ruhfus, Juliana
analytics/user metrics 8, 13, 15, 45, 68 (and chapter four case study), 147
Apple News 16, 72
Artificial Intelligence (AI) 165
"attention economy", the 63, 80; and Goldhaber, Michael H. and Davenport, Thomas H. 80

BackFence 45
Barrett, Wayne 159–60, 164
Bellingcat 98, 101, 104–9; *see also* Higgins, Eliot
blogging and vlogging 95–103; The Dish/ Andrew Sullivan 103, 149; FiveThirtyEight/ Nate Silver 96; guide to 149–54; North, Rachel 97–8; Oestreich, Adam 109; Salem Pax/Salam Abdulmunem 103; The Young Turks 96, 164
Buzzfeed 62–3, 71, 72, 81, 98, 161; case study 45–52; Gibson, Janine 34, 46, 47; Millar, Stuart 46–9, 81, 82, 131; Peretti, Jonah 43; Phillips, Tom 135–7; "social lift" 48; story "blocks" 134–5; Waterson, Jim 49–52, 68, 145–6

Cadwalladr, Carole 28, 59
Carey, James W. 65
changing role of journalist 3, 10–11, 68, 119, 143–4, 159–60; at the Guardian 29, 34

Channel 4 49, 82
Circa 4, 80, 134–5, 137–40
clickbait 10, 67, 69, 90
Cohen, Bernard C. 163
Cohn, David 134, 137–41, 166–7; *see also* Circa
Cole, Peter and Harcup, Tony 7–8
CORRECT!V 42
(de)Correspondent, the 42–3, 109
Crawford, Chris 86
Curran, James and Seaton, Jean 5

Daily Mail 5, 8
Deuze, Mark 9, 160
Dosi, Giovanni 22
drones 115–17
Drudge, Matt (and The Drudge Report) 43, 101–3

Elastic Charles 85
Elliott, Philip 9, 10

Facebook: algorithms and "filter bubbles" 48, 59, 61–3, 66, 79, 123, 164 (*see also* Pariser, Eli); business model 7, 143; early history 25–6, 34; impact on news publishers 26–8, 70–1, 119, 137, 162; News Feed 26, 62–4, 66–7; societal impact 24, 52, 57, 78–9, 167; virtual reality (VR) 86, 87
"fake news" 26, 66, 79, 100, 149, 160–3; *see also* Google, and fake news
Fernback, Jan 61

Flanagin, Andrew J., Flanagin, Craig and Flanagin, Jon 23, 95
Fort McMoney 85

Gans, Herbert J. 164
Gawker 103, 161, 169; *see also* Read, Max
Google: AdWords and AdSense 8, 24–5, 151; business model 7, 24–5; early history 19–22; and fake news 27–8, 59; Google News 26, 123; impact on news publishers 8, 27, 71, 137, 167; Orkut 25–6; and SEO 58–60, 71, 63, 151–2; Trueview 38–9; YouTube 32, 38–9, 96, 132, 152; *see also* blogging and vlogging
Guardian, the 42, 46, 48, 63, 87, 99, 164; case study 28–34; Davies, Lizzy 31–3; membership 33, 70–1, 164; Moran, Chris 63, 68–73; Pilhofer, Aaron 33–4, 42, 147; Preston, Peter 183; "responsible reach" 69; Rusbridger, Alan 29, 43; Teather, David 29–31; Viner, Katharine 29, 46, 148

Habermas, Jürgen 65
Haiti Earthquake (game) 85
headline (A-B) testing 13–14, 43, 58, 63–4, 67, 71
Higgins, Eliot 96, 101, 104–9; *see also* Bellingcat
Huffington Post 43–4, 103
Huizinga, Johan 83–4

Jarvis, Jeff 7
journalism: citizen 43–4, 96, 97–100; data 2, 108, 115, 122–4, 144, 147; definitions 9–10, 101, 159–60; entrepreneurial 40–2, 96, 145; hyper-local 43–5, 96, 124; "Long-form" 51, 132–3; loss of trust in 64–5, 100, 148, 162–3; mission 10, 64, 69, 160; *see also* Bellingcat case study

Katz, Elihu and Lazarsfeld, Paul F. 61
Kirkpatrick, David 25–6

Langer, John 164

Maguire, Miles 148
McLuhan, Marshall 23
Miller, Daniel 23
Mindich, David T.Z. 129–30

Narrative Science 115, 117; case study 119–26; Hammond, Kris 166, 167 (and case study); News at Seven 121–2

new news formats: 360-video 16, 86–7; atomised 57, 133–5 (*see also* case study), 166; "automated" and news bots 118–19; games 51, 82–6; "robot" journalism 113–15; VR and AR 16, 33, 84–7, 137
news business model 4–9; advertising 5–6, 8–9, 26, 33, 143 (*see also* Google, impact on news publishers); membership 164 (*see also* the Guardian, membership); philanthropy 41, 43 (*see also* Philadelphia Inquirer; ProPublica); set-up costs 5–6; subscription 119, 164 (*see also* The (de) Correspondent; Texas Tribune)

Paid Social 63
Papacharissi, Zizi 23
Papers Please 85
Pariser, Eli 62
Pavlik, John 9
Peña, Nonny de la 86
Philadelphia Inquirer 1–3, 43
Pirate Fishing 83; *see also* Ruhfus, Juliana
Pitt, Fergus and Owen, Taylor 87
Postman, Neil 23
Project Syria 86; *see also* de la Peña, Nonny
ProPublica 41–2, 98, 164

Quartz 45

Read, Max 161–2
Reported.ly 98
Republica Times 84
Rosenberg, Nathan 5, 23
Ruhfus, Juliana 82–3; *see also* Al Jazeera

Sambrook, Richard 64
San Francisco Chronicle 4
Schechter, Danny 116–17 and "helicopter journalism"
Schudson, M. 9, 130
Silverman, Craig 65, 162
Silverstone, Roger 23
Song, Sonya 63
Steacy, Will 1–3; *see also* Philadelphia Inquirer
Storyful 98, 100

Temple, Michael 95
The Texas Tribune 42, 109

verification (journalism) 32, 64, 98–9, 104 (and Bellingcat case study), 148–9

Vice 41, 57, 81, 92, 135, 162; case study 87–91; Jenny Stevens 81 (and case study)
Village Voice, the 41, 159

Wardle, Clare 98
Washington Post, The 24, 43, 64, 98, 116; and AI 118; case study 11–16; Gilbert, Jeremy 15–16, 118; Grant, Tracy 11–13; Jeff Bezos 12, 16; Kellet, Ryan 57, 68–74; Rich, Eric 13–14; Sullivan, Margaret 96, 160
Webb Young, James 40
Westport Independent 85
Williams, Andy, Harte, David and Turner, Jerome 96
WITNESS 99, 100
Wolff, Michael 6